# POPULAR MUSIC AND HUMAN RIGHTS

*Nations will rise and fall, but equality remains the ideal. The universal aim is to achieve respect for the entire human race, not just for the dominant few.*

Carlos P. Romulo

*Washing one's hands of the conflict between the powerful and the powerless means to side with the powerful, not to be neutral.*

Paulo Freire

# Popular Music and Human Rights
## Volume II: World Music

IAN PEDDIE

ASHGATE

Published by
Ashgate Publishing Limited
Wey Court East
Union Road
Farnham
Surrey, GU9 7PT
England

Ashgate Publishing Company
Suite 420
101 Cherry Street
Burlington
VT 05401-4405
USA

www.ashgate.com

**British Library Cataloguing in Publication Data**
Popular music and human rights.
   Volume 2, World music. -- (Ashgate popular and folk music series)
   1. Popular music--History and criticism. 2. Popular music--Social aspects. 3. World music--History and criticism. 4. World music--Social aspects. 5. Human rights--Songs and music. 6. Political ballads and songs--History and criticism.
   I. Series II. Peddie, Ian.
   306.4'8424-dc22

**Library of Congress Cataloging-in-Publication Data**
Popular music and human rights / [edited by] Ian Peddie.
   p. cm. -- (Ashgate Popular and folk music series)
   Includes index.
   ISBN 978-0-7546-6852-7 (v. 1 : hardcover : alk. paper) -- ISBN 978-0-7546-6853-4 (v. 2 : hardcover : alk. paper) -- ISBN 978-0-7546-9512-7 (v. 1 : ebook) -- ISBN 978-0-7546-9513-4 (v. 2 : ebook) 1. Popular music--Social aspects. 2. Human rights. I. Peddie, Ian.
   ML3918.P67P66 2011
   781.64'1599--dc22

2011004394

ISBN 9780754668534 (hbk)
ISBN 9780754695134 (ebk)

Bach musicological font developed by © Yo Tomita.

Printed and bound in Great Britain by the MPG Books Group, UK

# Contents

# List of Illustrations

# List of Contributors

**Ian Peddie** teaches English and Cultural Studies at Florida Gulf Coast University. His edited collection, *The Resisting Muse: Popular Music and Social Protest* (Ashgate), a finalist in the Association for Recorded Sound Collections book of the year, was published in 2006. He is an avowed humanist, and one of the harmonizing themes in his work is the way in which human interaction is governed by a cohesive inequality. He has published numerous essays on authors such as Irvine Welsh, Langston Hughes, T.S. Eliot, and Thomas McGrath, as well as on topics such as class, poverty, and radicalism. These topics inform his approach to popular music, where he has written on Led Zeppelin, Goldie, and Billy Bragg.

**William Anselmi** earned his Ph.D. in Comparative Literature from the Université de Montréal, and is Associate Professor in the department of Modern Languages and Cultural Studies at the University of Alberta. He has published numerous articles and books ranging in subject from twentieth-century Italian experimental poetry (Gruppo '63), to Italian Canadian culture and literature, to ethnocultural media representations as well as Italian cinema post-World War II. He has researched and presented for TLN-Television a series of analytical segments on *The Sopranos* (2006). His most recent publication is an edited volume on poet, novelist, and playwright Mary Melfi, *Mary Melfi: Essays on Her Work* (Guernica, 2007). Forthcoming is a fictional narrative, *Orvieto* (Guernica, 2008) as well as a critical text, in collaboration with Dr. L. Hogan, *L'immagine della parola: per una critica della nuova oralità* (The Image of the Word: For a Critique of New Orality).

**Aaron Corn** is an Australian Research Council Future Fellow and Associate Professor of Ethnomusicology at the Australian National University, and is Director of the National Recording Project for Indigenous Performance in Australia. He holds long-term collaborations with Indigenous communities in Arnhem Land on research into the application of their traditions to new intercultural contexts, and his recent book *Reflections and Voices* (Sydney University Press, 2009) explores the cultural and political legacy of the celebrated Australian band Yothu Yindi and its influential lead singer Mandawuy Yunupiŋu. He contributes to numerous Indigenous cultural survival initiatives with Indigenous Australian performers from remote communities, records Indigenous oral histories for the National Library of Australia, and lectures extensively on Yolŋu music, law, and culture in consultation with Yolŋu elders such as Neparrŋa Gumbula.

**Paul D. Greene** is Associate Professor of Ethnomusicology and Integrative Arts at Pennsylvania State University, Brandywine Campus. His research examines sound engineering, engineered musical cultures, and wired sound in South Asia, and also music and Buddhism in South and Southeast Asia. He is editor, with Thomas Porcello, of *Wired for Sound: Engineering and Technologies in Sonic Cultures* (Wesleyan University Press, 2005), and also, with Jeremy Wallach and Harris M. Berger, of a forthcoming edited volume on heavy metal and globalization. He has authored numerous articles and book chapters on music, technology, and culture.

**Angela Impey** has a doctorate in Anthropology/Ethnomusicology from Indiana University (Bloomington) and lectures in the Music Department at the School of Oriental and African Studies, University of London. Her research interests include music, memory, land and environmental development, gender and human rights. She has conducted extensive fieldwork in southern Africa and the Horn of Africa. As an authority on African music, she is a frequent contributor to reference volumes. Recent publications include the essays "Pathways of Song: Re-voicing Women's Landscapes in the Maputaland Borderlands," "Sounding Place in the Western Maputaland Borderlands," "Musical Constructions of Place: Linking Music to Environmental Action in the St. Lucia Wetlands," and "Culture, Conservation and Community Reconstruction: Explorations in Participatory Action Research and Advocacy Ethnomusicology in the Dukuduku Forests, Northern KwaZulu Natal."

**Mark LeVine** is Professor of Middle Eastern History at University of California, Irvine and the author or editor of more than half a dozen books, including *Heavy Metal Islam* (Random House/Verso, forthcoming), *Why They Don't Hate Us* (Oneworld, 2005), *Overthrowing Geography: Jaffa, Tel Aviv and the Struggle for Palestine* (University of California Press, 2005), *Contested Hegemonies* (Palgrave, 2005), and *Reapproaching Borders* (Rowman Littlefield, 2007).

**Valdis Muktupāvels** is Professor of Ethnomusicology and Director of Baltic Sea Region Studies at the University of Latvia. His field of expertise is Latvian or, more broadly, Baltic traditional and modern music culture, its historical and social contexts and traditions, as well as Baltic religion and identity issues. Among his publications is a recent article on musical instruments in the Baltic region for *The World of Music*, essays on Latvian music for *The Garland Encyclopedia of World Music*, and on the new Baltic religious movements for the Macmillan *Encyclopaedia of Religion*. Valdis Muktupāvels remains one of the key figures of the modern folklore revival movement in Latvia, especially during the period of Soviet occupation, when Latvian cultural heritage was endangered, and has promoted the preservation and dissemination of its heritage at home and abroad. He is also a composer of choral, instrumental, and film music, and has published albums including his oratorio *Pontifex*. He is the recipient of the fifth class Order of Lithuanian Grand Duke Gediminas and twice winner of the annual National Grand Prize in folklore.

**Rajko Muršič** teaches popular culture at the University of Ljubljana. He has published four monographs on music and popular music and co-edited seven volumes (six in English). His professional interests include anthropology of popular music, theory of culture, methodology of anthropological research, philosophy of music, cultural studies, political anthropology, kinship studies, and social structure. His regional interests comprise Slovenia, Central and South-eastern Europe.

**John M. Schechter** was Professor of Music at the University of California, Santa Cruz. With his research focusing on the music of Latin America, he has authored *The Indispensable Harp: Historical Development, Modern Roles, Configurations, and Performance Practices in Ecuador and Latin America* (Kent State University Press, 1992), edited *Music in Latin American Culture: Regional Traditions* (Schirmer/Wadsworth/Thomson Learning, 1999), and co-edited (with Guillermo Delgado-P.) *Quechua Verbal Artistry: The Inscription of Andean Voices/Arte Expresivo Quechua: La Inscripción de Voces Andinas* (Cengage/Shaker Verlag, 2004)—a volume dedicated to Quechua song text, narrative, poetry, dialogue, myth, and riddle. Schechter founded and for 15 years, 1986-2000, directed the UCSC Latin American Ensembles, which, during that period, performed Jara's songs, "El Aparecido," "Plegaria a un labrador," "El lazo," and "El pimiento."

**Gerry Smyth** is Reader in Cultural History at Liverpool John Moores University. He has published widely on various aspects of Irish culture. Most of his recent research has been in the field of popular music studies. His publications include *Noisy Island: A Short History of Irish Popular Music* (Cork University Press, 2005) and *Listening to the Novel: Music in Contemporary British Fiction* (Palgrave, 2008).

**Andreas Steen** is Assistant Professor of Modern Chinese History and Culture at Aarhus University, Denmark. He studied Sinology, English Philology, and Modern Chinese Literature at the Free University of Berlin and Fudan University, Shanghai. His main fields of research concentrate on modern Chinese history and popular culture, especially pop music, Peking Opera, literature, and film. He also works on German–Chinese relations in the nineteenth and early twentieth century. Among his many publications are *Zwischen Unterhaltung und Revolution: Grammophone, Schallplatten und die Anfänge der Musikindustrie in Shanghai, 1878-1937* (Between Entertainment and Revolution: Gramophones, Music Records and the Beginning of the Music Industry in Shanghai, 1878-1937) (Harrassowitz, 2006) and *Der Lange Marsch des Rock 'n' Roll: Pop und Rockmusik in der Volksrepublik China* (The Long March of Rock 'n' Roll: Pop and Rock Music in the People's Republic of China) (Lit-Verlag, 1996).

**Sergei I. Zhuk**, in addition to teaching Russian and Soviet history at Ball State University in Indiana, lectures on cultural consumption and youth culture in the Soviet bloc during the Cold War. He has published work in English and Russian, most recently an article about pop music consumption under the title "The Modernity of a 'Backward Sect': Evangelicals in Dniepropetrovsk under Khrushchev and Brezhnev." He is currently completing a book titled *The West in the Closed City: Cultural Consumption, Identities and Ideology of Late Socialism in Soviet Ukraine, 1964-1984*. Built around the question of cultural consumption among the youth of the Soviet closed city, the book will be the first study of how various Western ideas, both imaginary and real, influenced post-Soviet Ukrainian national identity.

# Foreword

Dr. Vaira Vike-Freiberga
President of Latvia, 1999-2007

Songs are carried on the same breath as words, with their melody adding greater range and emotional impact and conveying a mood that transcends the barriers of language and culture. Songs may express joy or sadness, exultation or lamentation; they may lull a baby to sleep, soothe a broken heart, cement friendship and kinship ties, or urge one to strife and battle. Better than spoken anger or words of harangue, they may voice resentment, frustration, and rage. Their lyrics, being poetry, suggest without spelling out, imply without stating explicitly. They allow for multiple meanings that resist the pressure of disapproving neighbors or censoring officialdom.

Music is man-made sound that makes inanimate matter sing through the deft touch of the instrument maker and player. It is the hand taking over from the voice and leaving the words behind. Instrumental music stands on its own or may accompany a singer, clothing a tune in richer harmonies or taking off in ornamentation and modulation. It may fill the hours of lonely shepherds, soothe the tired traveler by a campfire, urge troops to battle, or move the whole tribe to dancing with the rhythm of its beat. That beat comes from the heart, and its pulsations impel the body to move: to stomp the feet and swing the arms, to whirl and to twirl, to jump and to gallop, or to sway slowly and gracefully, like reeds bent by the wind or water-plants swayed by a moving current.

Music of some kind accompanies all communal celebrations. Singing and dancing, just like eating and drinking, are part of all merry-making. Feasts are a collective letting loose, especially for people oppressed by hard daily labor. Kings always had music in their halls and priests knew that it was good to make joyful music unto the Lord. Feudal masters handed out free beer to their serfs for seasonal celebrations, for letting off steam prevents boiling resentment from exploding into actions of protest.

Yet too much singing and dancing, too much loudness and letting go are potentially dangerous. In centuries past, the Church worried so much about the unbridled fun at peasant weddings in Latvia and Estonia, that the violin was declared an instrument of the Devil and its playing forbidden by law. The Latvian midsummer celebrations, with their traditional melodies and texts carrying echoes of ancient fertility rites, were denounced by the Church as too pagan and by the Communist Party as too nationalistic. Jazz and rock and roll were at various times declared subversive in the Soviet Union—and for good cause.

Songs can be songs of protest and music can wail out feelings that cannot be expressed in words. Songs can be pure and true, restoring self-respect and self-confidence to the down-trodden, giving hope to the hopeless and voice to collective longings for freedom and independence. They may also be instruments of falsehood or tools of manipulation, brain-washing, and indoctrination. They may sing the praises of tyrants and glorify the deeds of madmen as well as those truly worthy of praise.

Songs and music can be instruments of power in their own right, working either to support the powers in place or to subvert them. Music may open cracks even in Iron Curtains, and songs may maintain social protest under totalitarian tyranny, like live coals under a banked fire. Trumpets broke down the walls of Jericho. Singing revolutions can bring down a nuclear power stretching over 12 time-zones and overthrow it without bloodshed. Where there is music and song, there will always be breath and heartbeat and life.

# General Editor's Preface

The upheaval that occurred in musicology during the last two decades of the twentieth century has created a new urgency for the study of popular music alongside the development of new critical and theoretical models. A relativistic outlook has replaced the universal perspective of modernism (the international ambitions of the 12-note style); the grand narrative of the evolution and dissolution of tonality has been challenged, and emphasis has shifted to cultural context, reception and subject position. Together, these have conspired to eat away at the status of canonical composers and categories of high and low in music. A need has arisen, also, to recognize and address the emergence of crossovers, mixed and new genres, to engage in debates concerning the vexed problem of what constitutes authenticity in music and to offer a critique of musical practice as the product of free, individual expression.

Popular musicology is now a vital and exciting area of scholarship, and the *Ashgate Popular and Folk Music Series* presents some of the best research in the field. Authors are concerned with locating musical practices, values and meanings in cultural context, and draw upon methodologies and theories developed in cultural studies, semiotics, poststructuralism, psychology and sociology. The series focuses on popular musics of the twentieth and twenty-first centuries. It is designed to embrace the world's popular musics from Acid Jazz to Zydeco, whether high tech or low tech, commercial or non-commercial, contemporary or traditional.

Professor Derek B. Scott
Professor of Critical Musicology
University of Leeds

# Acknowledgements

My thanks go to my fellow contributors, each of whom has brought something new to the study of music and human rights. Heidi Bishop, Senior Editor at Ashgate Publishing and Sophie Lumley, Editorial Assistant, have shown much patience and understanding as this two-volume project has come together.

There are countless human rights. Yet arguably it is extremely difficult to conceive of human rights without at one stage or another thinking hierarchically. This point is important if we are to grasp the connections between power and rights, an association which now defines rights discourse. For all the presence of "inalienable rights," "absolute rights of man," "states of freedom," and other expressions of liberty and self-determination fundamental to the discourse of rights, the idea of some form of mutually respectful ensemble of social relations still remains a distant hope. Along with its companion volume, this book examines the many ways in which popular music has responded to the issues of human rights.

# Introduction

While considering the ways in which music reveals the tensions and contradictions at the core of political action inspired by the dream of human rights, this volume questions the view that the internationalization of human rights has effectively worked to naturalize dominant power structures and the exclusionary practices around which they function. Both volumes in this series, in fact, will be sensitive to the dangers of seeing human rights as an arm of imperialism or as a Eurocentric discourse that reinscribes the very norms it ostensibly seeks to overturn. As they confront many of the most important concerns that have dominated questions of human rights during the last three decades, the various chapters reveal how rights function as a vehicle for hope in a world where so many are denied any form of dignity or self-emancipation.

Perhaps the most suitable means of contextualizing the direction of this volume is to return to the immediate postwar period. On December 10, 1948, the United Nations adopted the Universal Declaration of Human Rights (UDHR), a document whose statutes proclaimed "as a common standard" the ideal that "all human beings are born free and equal in dignity and rights" and that "they are endowed with reason and conscience and should act towards one another in a spirit of brotherhood." Though now these phrases appear if not quite quaint then more like exhortations than the directives they were originally meant to be, in their purest form the models of behavior that the statutes imagined were more than a moral legacy rent by the carnage of World War II. After all, in article after article the Declaration reminds us of our humanist obligations, of our inalienable rights as humans, and perhaps more importantly, of the rights and limits of the nation states that have dominated the world in the postwar era.

Writing more than half a century after the Declaration, one is chiefly struck by the idealism of the document. For all of the stirring rhetoric it advances, for every "no one shall be subjected to" and "everyone has the right to," it now seems trite to point out that the Declaration's vision of unilateral equality has remained an elusive if not unachievable goal. At the same time, while it may be true, as the United Nations Association in Canada claims, that "despite a continuing struggle in many regions of the world, significant progress has been made in developing legal, moral and institutional regimes consistent with the principles proclaimed in the UDHR," recourse to contemporary examples of human rights violations in North Korea, the Middle East, Afghanistan, and so on indicate that the opposite might be advanced with equal veracity. For all the Declaration's resonant and abiding principles, many of which remain the benchmarks used by various organizations to hold governments accountable for their policies and actions, it remains our loss that today the Declaration at times seems rather more prescriptive than descriptive.

Underpinning the Declaration was a belief that human rights reflect universally accepted norms of behavior. The premises behind such an assumption were designed to close the gap between the ideal and the real, and the urgency and vigor with which they were expounded in turn encouraged the notion that basic moral rights were attainable. But in a world order increasingly conceived of in terms of hierarchy, the dream of human rights now appears something of a contradiction. Arguably, the contemporary social visions through which we interpret concepts such as human rights have polarized to something approaching parochialism, a vertical drama wearyingly articulated in terms of a struggle between democracy and tyranny. Nowhere have these contradictions been more fully and fearfully elaborated than in the Middle East, where the Manichean vision of the righteousness of causes confronts the conscience of "democracy" not with the sense of appeasement it so dearly desires, but with still more guilt.

As all of these examples serve to imply, it is concepts such as dominance and subordination rather than tolerance and accommodation that frame the issue of human rights today. With politics as an entity seemingly incapable of addressing the failures of its own discourse, the voices of popular music appear especially resonant. Unlike those politicians or statesmen who champion the goals of human rights at the same time as they undermine them, popular music has long understood that human rights, if attainable at all, involve a struggle without end. In order to achieve any credibility, however, such an assumption demanded that popular music go beyond simple antithetical assertions that could be easily dismissed as tantamount to a lyrical storming of the barricades. And so it has. If the cultural expression of human rights can only be written by those artists willing to assume the burden of complexity, it is no surprise to discover that they have been willing to address issues as difficult as the ambiguity inherent in regarding human rights as an emancipatory instrument as well as the questions that surround those who have the power to shape rights in their own image. These and other relevant issues have been addressed from the perspective of the standards from which popular music and human rights draw much of their legitimacy and authority. Thankfully the right to imagine an individual will, the right to some form of self-determination, and the right to self-legislation—however difficult to imagine or enact these sentiments might be—have long been at the forefront of popular music's approach to human rights. Where music has the power to enlighten, to mobilize, and perhaps even to change there remains hope. As the late Nigerian musician Fela Kuti put it, "music is the weapon of the givers of life."

William Anselmi's titular deployment of the phrase "long played revolutions" introduces a term particularly apposite to a discussion of the "canzone d'autore," the "singer-songwriter song" genre in Italy during the 1970s. After acknowledging that much oppositional song in Italy at the time was a response to a myriad of sociopolitical themes, the author points to the prevalent belief in imagination as a tool of change. Framed by the prevalence of utopic narratives, which themselves imply an identity of interests between songs and the plight of those who are the subject and audience of the songs, initiatives such as Movimento '77 in their desire for change echoed the avant-garde movements of the early twentieth century. In addition to the significant influence of American and French protest singers, however, the politically charged atmosphere in Italy reinvigorated cultural responses to the power relations underpinning human rights

Aaron Corn's reflection on Aboriginal culture begins with an examination of how indigenous artists responded to some of the now notorious laws that virtually denied them any right to self-definition. Many of these laws centered upon land sovereignty and identity, two of any number of issues often disingenuously evoked as a means of denying natives rights. Alongside a discussion of numerous laws and treaties, many of which are documents of dispossession, Corn traces the moving struggle for human rights through the work of some of aboriginal music's most powerful voices.

The violation of human rights is also at the forefront of Paul D. Greene's discussion of the relatively little explored subject of Nepalese heavy metal. In his discussion, Greene maintains that rather than functioning as a tool for mobilization, heavy metal in Nepal serves as a discursive practice that forms a mode of resistance against the will to dominance evident in the propaganda of political parties, the palace, and Maoists. To this end, Greene contends that heavy metal provides a means of expressing emotional loss, rage, and anger, all of which are important steps in the progression toward a sense of human rights.

There are few places where the struggle for human rights has been more agonized than in South Africa. Angela Impey's fieldwork among the indigenous women of western Maputaland traces how two song genres, *toyi-toyi* and *ingadla*, became central to the musical critique of apartheid. Using the metaphor of borders, and particularly the melding of ethnicities that occurs at borderlands, Impey draws a parallel between the "in-betweenness" of border identity and the resulting remoteness from the centers of power experienced by border dwellers. Influenced by the women's geographic and political marginalization, the women's songs discussed in this chapter are narratives of human rights memory just as they are affirmations of shared resistance to apartheid.

Mark LeVine's exploration of heavy metal in the Middle East reveals the extent to which the genre is a form through which increasing numbers of young Muslims make sense of their lives. Not surprisingly given the dominant presence of Islam as a way of life in the Middle East, the vibrancy and popularity of heavy metal in the area are often seen as a threat. Hence heavy metal becomes an important touchstone of human rights, where its political and subcultural implications have not gone unnoticed. Levine contends that heavy metal, as an immanent critique of the social and political discourses in the Middle East, offers a way of illuminating some of the more distasteful aspects of society; concerts, in turn, become "performance philosophy" designed, *à la* Adorno, to revivify political and social systems. For metalheads who see themselves as "warriors in a musical jihad," the goal is acceptance of the music and scenes they love as well as social and political amelioration. Given the worldwide popularity of heavy metal—and LeVine makes a strong case for heavy metal as "world music"—the varied and "post-hybrid" heavy metal scene in the Middle East also has much to say about globalization.

Opposition to a very dominant system is also at the heart of Valdis Muktupāvels's chapter on folk music in Soviet-occupied Latvia during the 1980s. In his examination of Latvian folk as a form of resistance to Soviet mandates, the author considers the birth of the neo-folklore movement and its ultimate dominance over Soviet-backed "folkish folk." Concentrating on the evolution of neo-folklore as a form of cultural and political opposition, Muktupāvels reveals that concerts were transformed into communal events, where the distance between performer and audience was reduced, and where singing and dancing—with the performers often teaching the audience the words and dance steps—were a shared event. In many other ways, too, as Muktupāvels indicates, the neo-folklore movement was a catalyst of the singing revolution that, in the Baltic states, played an important role in ending Soviet rule.

While Rajko Muršič's essay on music and rights in the former Yugoslavia attends the legacy of the country's Socialist past, his focus lies with musical expression during and after dissolution. More specifically, Muršič considers the impact war, nationalism, and ethnic rivalry have had on human rights and how music has responded to these difficult problems. After cautioning against simplistic conclusions of music as a transparent mobilizing force, the author pauses to examine the connection between the social effects of music and the climate in which sounds are received. In the case of the former Yugoslavia, with recurrent episodes of violence beginning in1878, this leads to an enlightening discussion of some of the political ideologies of Central/Eastern Europe, the vestiges of which continue to find expression through popular music.

Colombian folk singer Víctor Jara, one of the most celebrated protest singers of the twentieth century, is the subject of John M. Schechter's essay. Through analysis of the compositional techniques used in Jara's songs, Schechter contends that Jara's work is designed to foreground specific messages, many of which attest to his solidarity with Chile's underprivileged. Jara's empathy with the poor and the disadvantaged, his sensitivity to injustice, and his determination to draw attention to inequality ensure that his legacy continues to resonate long after his death in 1973 at the age of 40. With these points in mind, Schechter considers how a select band of artists have made use of the will to rights fundamental to Víctor Jara and his work.

Gerry Smyth's chapter on music, gender, and the state in contemporary Ireland asserts that the 1984 death of a 15-year-old girl who had attempted to deliver her own baby encapsulates the struggle between modernity and tradition. Pursuing the analogy further, the author identifies Christy Moore's "Middle of the Island," ostensibly a response to the girl's death, as synonymous with the ideological struggles central to contemporary Ireland. Smyth asserts that, in challenging the patriarchal church/state and its attempts to define and represent women, Moore's revisionist stance, itself subject to a variety of ideological influences, ultimately reanimates the moral questions on which rights invariably rest.

In its early years, rock music in China, as Andreas Steen indicates, was often promoted as the authentic voice of protest. Yet while Chinese rock continues to be interpreted through notions of revolution, along with all the ideological accoutrements attached to that term, the author suggests that the enormous changes that have occurred in China since 1989 mean that rock's rebellious image is, inevitably, changing. Nonetheless, Chinese rock's struggle with the state is far from over; while it may be that rock musicians in China produce fewer protest songs than they once did, it is worth remembering that a vibrant underground remains—one that, post-Tiananmen, still clings to the revolutionary spirit.

Sergei Zhuk's study of the influence of Western rock on Soviet Ukraine includes insights available only to those who lived through the experience. With reference to the city of Dniepropetrovsk, a place of great strategic importance to the Soviet authorities, and consequently closed to foreigners until the early 1990s, Zhuk argues that the popularity of Western rock music resulted in strenuous efforts at suppressing it. Anti-rock campaigns took many forms in Ukraine, from KGB harassment of musicians and the interrupting of discos to active attempts to censor the work of bands considered anti-Soviet. Even Pink Floyd, who at one stage were considered progressive and anti-capitalist, eventually fell foul of Komsomol ideologists, while 10cc and Iron Maiden were deemed especially dangerous. Embracing Western rock—and a good many did—was, in the eyes of ideologues, tantamount to rejecting a Soviet prescribed identity. As Zhuk makes clear, all this was a step toward the evolution of new self-identities and, with the fall of the Soviet empire, new forms of rights.

Chapter 1

# Long Played Revolutions:
# Utopic Narratives, *Canzoni d'autore*

William Anselmi

No doubt the universe is unfolding as it should.—Desiderata by Max Ehrmann
(1920s)

Vorrei incontrarti fuori i cancelli di una fabbrica,/ vorrei incontrarti lungo le
strade che portano in India.—Alan Sorrenti (1972)

Modernity can be summarized in terms of its particular degree of self-reflection,
something postmodern critics have characterized as self-reflexivity, and by
doing so claimed an age. *Age*, or *period*, it is worth noting, has come to denote
a personalization of time, at least in the Western sphere, where context is hardly
historical; rather, it is an amalgam of personal quips and stories, whose reflection
harks back to the "I": what were grand narratives have dissipated, obscured by
the affirmation of the (true) individual. *Genius seculi*, this general predisposition
toward reality where irony has no home and narcissism thrives on technology
serves many purposes, one of which is the disappearance of a vocabulary that has
marked the sense of history.

Utopia, in its declinations, and as one of those perilous semantic fields, has
sustained a vision that inexorably parallels that of progress. Both as a rhetorical
strategy and as an investment in the future, utopia invests the political discourses
that erupt from the Renaissance onward with a particular tension and/or destination.
The resistance of the term throughout the centuries to indicate a better world against
any form of oppression affirms the validity of an ascent of humanity, capable of
gathering around itself numerous communities that invest in transnational thought
rather than the rigid parameters of a people, a nation, a God. Yet, in its nationalistic
variance, it serves as a cohesive narrative for the affirmation of the nation-states
that dot the European panorama in the nineteenth century.

**Framing an Ambiguity**

The *short* century—*à la* Hobsbawm—in its declination of crumbled empires,
two world wars, and the fall of the Berlin wall, has produced various attempts at
contesting and contrasting the fluid discourse of capitalism, mass consumption,

and reification in the social sphere. Most celebrated and remembered of all the various strategies of resistance to the above process is, without a doubt, France's May '68, a short-lived, yet now iconic period that has come to delineate for some critics the last attempt at a progressive social change in the West, while others have interpreted it as the final affirmation of a new, affluent class: post-World War II bourgeois youth and its ramifications and/or parallelisms as exemplified by the hippies or the New Left. In both readings, inescapably, the following condition is present: a cultural shift, through these groupings, which still influences present sociopolitical conditions.

Interestingly enough, at first, this is not the case for Italy. Though rich with a leftist political tradition, fully legitimized by the *Resistenza*—the armed resistance to Nazi-fascist occupation during World War II—the country lagged behind other European countries such as France in terms of a critical, mass movement, though attempts for the *unholy* alliance between workers and students were made in the late 1960s and onwards. In short, the cultural shift argued above for the European setting materializes in Italy almost a decade later. Although analogous in portent to May '68 it assumes a different value in the guise of Movimento '77. Such a movement that takes its name from the year that it erupted into media-governed society, lasted the brief span of a year and yet brought to the fore a number of political and social issues still unresolved in contemporary Italy, such as the role of youth and the work-space, the role of media, especially television, in forming identity-paradigms, the relevance of a political class closed in itself, and the nullification of progressive, social changes among others. What this valence is will become apparent as this cultural reading unfolds, yet it is important to point out at the outset that an unresolved ambiguity underscores such a movement. This ambiguity is masked during the 1970s by the so-called *armed struggle*, the final expression of the *lead years* which contains within itself the tension of a will-to-revolution paired with the contradictory praxis of the spectacle as indicated by Guy Debord in his works (1967, 1988). As the process of the armed struggle in the 1970s comes to a close, and as the 1980s affirm themselves through the recuperation of the personal sphere—a period best represented by the "look," or the de-politicized, aesthetic subject—the ambiguity erupts onto the cultural scene. For, the switch to the "look," the de-politicization of the self in terms of aesthetics, in other words from proto-revolutionary activities to the embellishment of the social persona, is tantamount to the surrendering of sociopolitical engagement: Is the armed struggle a spectacular ploy in terms of self-representation? Do my Armani jeans match my El Charro belt? The question still remains, the ambiguity unresolved: Were those who embraced with gusto the 1980s reflux of aesthetic participation the very same who invoked with exclamatory verdicts the 1970s coming revolution?

## It's All About History, Then Words

The alternative Italy that appears after the economic boom (1958-63), if it were to be read through the critical history of Western music, would have the following to offer: a narration grounded in the historical discourse and embracing the utopic imaginary as its fundamental source: from Campanella's *La città del sole* (The City of the Sun) (1602), to Gramsci's study of the subaltern power in capitalist society (1926-37), the narrative's syntax would, fundamentally, point to these as some of its constitutive principles. The narration takes the shape of a musical body between the late 1960s and late 1970s which can be contextualized as *a long-playing utopic narrative* in its various public declinations, manifesting itself on the streets as well as in juke-boxes, *radio libere* (independent radio stations), record players, and stereo systems of the times. In this narration the subject at play, the hero of the story, is critical of an alternative to the society around him/her and posits a better future when things will be changed by the will and desire of the people. Key to this discourse is the notion of *desire*, since it best represents this bridging act toward another possible world. Desire both sustains and fuels the dream, while transforming the everyday in a state of preparation for the auspicated future. It is not surprising to detect a messianic element in this transformational agency since both Christianity and Marxism have been drawn near by an urgency of being, of final change, of heaven/equality on earth. In the Italian case, and with relation to this alternative music history, desire is a long-running discourse that is politically charged at its inception with a progressive line running through the centuries. The constitution of Italy as a national state, a unity of peoples and cultures, is sung in the Risorgimento songs of the nineteenth century; the progressive vision continues to affirm its notes throughout World War I into the Resistenza, always affirming itself against oppressive institutions, dominant discourses, and authoritarian figures. Must desire then be actualized by an oppressive, external agent? It seems reductive if not simplistic to affirm this cultural dichotomy, yet what governs the utopic discourse in Italian music can be visualized as a continuous struggle for the betterment of particular individual and social conditions that have a history of non-fulfillment, even after the realization of an Italian geopolitical reality invoked and narrated as far back as Dante in his *Divina Commedia*.

## Toward 1977

On ilDeposito.org, a website dedicated to social and political protest music, the song "Contessa" (1966) by Paolo Pietrangeli (*Mio caro padrone domani ti sparo*, Edizioni del gallo, 1969) is presented as one of the most played during the May '68 period in Italy. Written as a tribute to student Paolo Rossi, killed by fascists during the students' occupation of Rome's La Sapienza university, it is composed in alternating stanzas/voices: one voice represents the ruling class (commenting on workers' demands), with the other voice affirming the parallelism between the workers and students' sociopolitical engagement. The first two stanzas[1] introduce the addressee, a countess, and denounce the bravado of the workers' occupation of a factory; in this sense the colloquial setup allows the song's listeners to eavesdrop into another world, with its specific mores, codes, vision. The voice we are listening to addresses a countess in a friendly tone, a countess whose role is to give this other world the aura of blue-blooded domination, as if things had not changed in Italy for centuries in terms of the dichotomy oppressor/oppressed: aristocracy on top, the rebellious rabble below. The binary is supported by such couplets as "handful of illiterates"/(cultured), "exploited"/(power), "crazy bums"/(stylish normalcy), (dirty)/(clean).

As a working construct it partakes of historical veracity as well as being a literary trope that represented the theme of oppression. This formula had been successfully used in novels and poetry throughout the centuries, and was especially significant in post-World War II Italy. For example, in Pier Paolo Pasolini's poem *Le ceneri di Gramsci* (Gramsci's Ashes, a collection of poems about Italy's postwar reconstruction), dated 1954, published in 1957 in *Nuovi Argomenti*, as the poet addresses Gramsci in his tomb, the dichotomy that will sustain the poem's political strategy and rhetoric is immediately set by the description of the Protestant cemetery where lie the remains, and the surrounding "patrician boredom" in sharp contrast to the working-class description of the Testaccio area around the cemetery. It is even more striking that the aristocracy will be used as a sign of oppression in Pietrangeli's song, since by 1966 Italy had crossed the economic boom, or the economic miracle that saw Italy achieve in the short span of about five years a process of modernization that by 1963 brought it to the forefront of industrialized countries in the West. However, the implicit denunciation that sustains the song, the oppressor as part of the aristocratic class, is announced in terms of a system of power relations, feudal in thought and practice, that belied the apparent economic progress of which Italy had become part and actively supported in terms of governmental socioeconomic strategies. Two beginning stanzas, then, set up the discursive tone of the protest song, delineating in its fundamental binary strategy a utopic vision where the oppressed will throw off their yoke, finally bringing to earth a new way of life more befitting the possible equality inherent in the recently achieved economic success enjoyed by only part of the population. The call to arms, with its identificatory discourse, "comrades," peasants and working-class alike, is a call to agency and change, to use the tools of the trade as tools of change, with an obvious communist icon superimposed: the hammer and sickle. The unity of intent is the strategy of a common practice, a unity that goes beyond separate groups in order to bring about a total change in the system of oppression. As a truly popular song, the utopic discourse is innerved by an internationalist context, as the

---

[1]    For copyright and publishing reasons, the Italian text is not present. I am, however, responsible for any translation from the Italian. The internet is always a successful resource for lyrics. One Italian website that deals with *cantautori* is http://www.bielle.org/.

Vietnam war looms in the distance, with a final call to a situation where "no one" in the world will be exploited anymore. As the two stanzas, spoken from the voice of he/she who is engaged politically, are sung, the rising appeal to become actively involved in society becomes evident as the only possibility for constructing a new world, a world that is the "true" peace as opposed to the false one of the oppressor. The irony of the present times consigns the song to a particular moment in history—the 1960s—for its far-reaching consequences. The common cause that cuts through nationalistic confinement to embrace the whole world anticipates the economic globalization of decades later that will replace utopic discourses with the hustle and bustle of profit and exploitation as neoliberalism marks its triumph. Yet, if anything, the song proclaims a belief in change that can only come from a common cause, so as to live in a world free of that infamous *homo homini lupus* dictum. But liberation of the individual and the masses, supported by a politicized Freudian reading of the times, cannot be achieved without another dominant topos of the 1960s—sexual liberation—this one imported, ironically enough, from the then perceived most advanced industrial-cultural country, the United States. The basic ambiguity is not just present as an element of self-reflection, for the very same country that is the unspoken but ever-present international oppressor is the very same country in which a cultural-sexual revolution is taking place, and which is alluded to in the stanza following the call to arms.

The stanza that renews the interlocution of the speaking voice addressing an unfathomable "countess," and whose silence assumes the meaning of an all-knowing presence, continues in its depiction of the workers as the refuse of society, indulging in sex without moral or social constraints by the code of the times. By bringing into play the idea of "free love," not only are the workers categorized as "riff-raff" but also as parasitic since they are making love during their work time. Pleasure instead of duty, the substitution according to the double-standard morality of the speaker, is culpable on at least two accounts: of not sticking to the role assigned, and of subverting the morality of society proper. The irony of a social practice imported from the most advanced economic system gives those two lines a critical resonance. During the 1970s, leading to and culminating in the brief season of Movimento '77, the idea of making love without moral constraints is putting desire into practice as well as realizing that hoped-for freedom that a new and better society would entail. That the United States, in its most advanced forms, produces social models of conduct is not ironic in itself since the various progressive movements present in its territory were politically interpreted as manifestations of a progressive thought, the better part of America at the time. There is nothing new in this: under the fascist regime in Italy the United States was seen as an inspiration for a democratic reality, a goal to be achieved from a wide political spectrum as far as Italy was concerned. Further to the categorization of the subversive aspect of the workers—which will be mocked in a very successful 1970 song, "Chi non lavora non fa l'amore" (Who Doesn't Work Does Not Make Love) sung at the San Remo Festival by Adriano Celentano with his wife, Claudia Mori, a major mainstream powerhouse—the concept of caste more than class is inherently reaffirmed. "Even the worker wants a doctor son," claims an entitlement that should not be granted and therefore announces the maintenance of a rigid socioeconomic structure while presenting the utopic vision as a moral world turned on its head. If there is a true irony in this picture, it lies in the fact that by the end of the 1960s the Italian university reform which allows entrance for students of all backgrounds is none other than an expediency: a parking area for a potential mass of would-be workers who otherwise would be jobless. In short, Italy's economic system could not deal with a swelling, jobless youth who would be politicized enough in the university setting to create the backbone of Movimento '77.

Though no song can claim to be the initiator of a movement, the importance of "Contessa" is given by its particular *zeitgeist*, to use another word echoing the changing times. Able to indicate not only a context and its developments, but also the necessity of collective action, Pietrangeli's artistic text shows a successful path to follow. About 20 years later, Francesco De Gregori's "Scacchi e tarocchi," which gives the name to the album (*Scacchi e tarocchi* [Chess and Tarots]) (1985), concludes in its reflection the social trajectory discursively set by the call to arms with a stance that looks back to the recent historical period with an ambiguous gaze about the subject at hand.

The initial, descriptive part immediately foregrounds the origins, "They came from afar" echoing the Italian Communist Party narration of itself, and the ambiguous consistency of the members of the armed struggle, given the various, contrasting, numbers of participants presented. The uncertainty of the actual active numbers involved in the armed struggle lends credence to a widespread movement—as represented in the media—and yet reduces it to the few who actually embraced such a militaristic choice. The stark implicit contrast is with the mass of students, young workers, drop-outs, feminists, "cani sciolti" (loose dogs), "diversi" (different, referring to alternative sexual styles), that constituted in the final analysis the tide of Movimento '77. "They were the salt of the earth" continues in presenting some of the members' origins, in this case their Catholic roots. Such a marker is reinforced by the next line's "they were the sign of the cross." As the Red Brigades' twisted *mélange* of Marxist and Catholic roots is presented, "they had stars," their alterity, "They had wigs and glasses," is given as a masking device for their double-life militarized actions, and is also a sign of their spectacle-based participation in the script of social unrest, actions that the song de-masks as revolutionary pretence, rather than constituting a violent, but politically justified attempt to change Italy's socioeconomic reality.

As a term to describe their actions, *scripted* is certainly strong, yet its implication of a perverted form of social management has been argued in a number of critical texts that have appeared in the last decades. What those authors argue is that above and beyond the lead years, social unrest seems to have been dominated by a strange medley of forces, legal and less legal, ranging from deviant parts of the Italian secret service apparatuses to secret organizations like Gladio or Operation Stay Behind, to particular members in the Italian parliament, to the infamous P2 (Masonic Lodge P2), to part of the Mafia and specific representatives of the Vatican state, to agents of foreign secret services. Suffice it to say that the case made is correlated by documents that give credence to the various analyses that, in the end, paint the complex reality of a parallel state that did not hesitate to use terror and violence as its strategy for maintaining final control. Again, De Gregori's song uses a narrating voice that sums up the history of the Red Brigades, and fellow travelers, with a stark recounting of their "ethical" lifeworld.

"They certainly had instigators, and they were many,/ without a face nor a name and without evidence" is a clear reference to how their actions were scripted into being by economic and political forces that the Red Brigades had only an inkling of. What then follows is the depiction of the breakdown of the Red Brigades as a militaristic-political organization. As the phenomenon of the Red Brigades imploded, and with it other copy-cat groups, the results of that period of "emergency" saw special laws that encouraged betrayal with a heavy discount on years in prison. This gives rise to the following position: those who recanted and betrayed, the "pentiti" (repentants); those who recanted their actions and strategy without betraying their former comrades, "dissociati"; and, finally, the hardliners who never recanted "irriducibili." This part of the song addresses the end of the militaristic-political campaign and with it the role of the Red Brigades in the scripted spectacle of terrorism so lucidly denounced by Guy Debord in his *Commentaires sur la société du spectacle* (1988). What remains, then, of that experience is summed up with the ending lines: "Erano giovani e forti, erano giovani vite, dentro una fornace" (They were young and strong, they were young lives, inside a furnace). If these ending lines had no other significance than to posit the factual aspect of the context, young people involved in the armed struggle in something greater than themselves, the song would clearly be a historical piece. Undoubtedly, "They were young and strong" intertextually plays with the beginning of the 1857 patriotic Risorgimento poem by Luigi Mercantini, "La spigolatrice di Sapri." The poem commemorates republican and revolutionary Carlo Pisacane's Sapri expedition, and De Gregori's use gives the song an ambiguous ending. Such an intentional ending steps out of easy moralistic resolutions, leaving open-ended— for the listener—the history of those in the youth movement who were caught and scripted in a spiral of repression and revolutionary activities: "they were young lives, inside a furnace." Finally, it seems that these last few words from De Gregori's song can be easily applied to all who participated in Movimento '77, from its singers to its actors.

The influence of "Contessa" on the generation of *cantautori* who become central to the alternative music scene of the 1970s must then be seen in terms of its dynamic and its collective resonance. A song that truly achieves this sense of the popular (meaning: of the people) is something to be integrated in one's own work given its widespread circulation, a process that was achieved more by word of mouth than any commercial gimmicks such as television appearances or being presented in music contests such as Cantagiro or San Remo. Even its ending stanza, with its strong political sense of identification and us-vs-them binary, does not preclude the shared enjoyment; if anything, it forges each listener/participant into a living community. What the *cantautori* will do, however, is search for musical expressions that move beyond the folk/traditional style and which, in the end, will prove to have a wider mass appeal. Yet, the social messages and quest of the individual for a better society will remain its dominating features, so that, finally, the 1970s can indeed be categorized as far as the Italian music scene is concerned by the various schools of *cantautori* rather than the disco or punk eras. In terms of "school," however limiting the term, it does help to indicate various areas of the geo-musical scenes in Italy, something that some critics have failed to connect with the explosion of the hip-hop movement in Italy in the late 1980s and early 1990s. After all, the term "school" referred to a sense of *Kameradschaft* among artists who lived in the same city or area and influenced one another so as to years later be identified through certain musical expressions and/or particular thematics present in their songs. What the various hip-hop groups do a decade or so later is to consolidate that experience in terms of an anthropological and linguistic reality—through the rediscovery of dialect and anthropological territory—in opposition to the dominance of a lifeless standard Italian language unity and uniformity brought about by television programming.

## Movimento '77, Utopia, and Its Singers

Fabrizio De André, Francesco De Gregori, Antonello Venditti, Roberto Vecchioni, Lucio Dalla, Angelo Branduardi, Francesco Guccini, and Claudio Lolli are some of the most popular singer-songwriters in the Italian alternative music scene of the 1970s. Their popularity is based on their approach to the youth movement, their political stand, their compositional word-quality, and musical strategies. Sharing in the imaginary of the youth movement, the children of the economic boom sang the aspirations, desires, and criticism of a society embedded in the tensions of modernity and missed structural reforms that would characterize that particular period. At the base of such process, the unmistakable sense of "the private is political" gives rise to personalized and collective accounts of the oncoming utopian community. If, in the end, that brief season of change is underscored by the spectacularization of internal terrorism with its left and right variances, nevertheless it is necessary to point out that throughout the period that has in Movimento '77 its epitome, a process was at work which used imagination as desire as a practice and tool of change, something that was last seen circulating during the avant-garde movements in the early part of the twentieth century.

Movimento '77 is indebted then to such historical practices, which were brought back in the early 1960s by representatives of the Italian neo-avant-garde, to the aftereffects of the French May, and to the spirit of a decaying political and social system which had in its youth—workers and students especially—a possibility of renewal denied, antagonized, and basically sterilized by repressive conservative agencies in Italy and outside of it. Parallel to the *cantautori* experience, to the single singer-songwriters—who were formed upon a variety of international resources from American to French singer-songwriters, from Woody Guthrie, Bob Dylan, Phil Ochs, to French artists such as George Brassens, Jacques Brel, Léo Ferré, to Canadian Leonard Cohen—are groups politically engaged and musically experimental such as Area, Banco del Mutuo Soccorso, Premiata Forneria Marconi, and Osanna. What is shared by both *cantautori* and experimental groups alike is the sense of belonging to a revolutionary era, and that the auspicated change was in the air, palpable, livable. The politically charged atmosphere creates a series of texts that are reflective, introspective, and individualistic and that embrace the utopia-in-the-making as a sense of communal purpose and a shared imaginary. Examples abound, since political participation can also be fashionable and lucrative in the era of the spectacle, but songs like Claudio Lolli's "Ho visto anche degli zingari felici" (I Also Saw Happy Gypsies), from his 1976 album by the same name, or "Incubo Numero Zero" (Zero Number Nightmare), from his *Disoccupate le strade dai sogni* album (1977), point to a reflection and an analysis that starkly circumscribes utopia and its shadow. Synthetically the two albums, recorded a year apart, bring to the fore the dreams and the conclusion of those desires.

If "Ho visto anche degli zingari felici" testifies to the "impossibility of coming together" and in so doing leaving space, in the song, only for the gypsies who get drunk on revenge and war ("ubriacarsi di luna, di vendetta e di guerra"), then whatever little political gain can be had, whatever the possibility of social change, the complex economic and political symbiote that is Italy—and is also the world at large—will be sure to rectify, guide, and spectacularize for consumption, as in this 1977 song: "disoccupate le strade dai sogni."

Who knows if Claudio Lolli in the title song for the *Disoccupate le strade dai sogni* album was thinking of Silvio Berlusconi and his hiccup reign of the last 15 years or so in Italy, as the model for the rest of the Western world? What is factual is the clarity with which this *cantautore* saw through the auspicated change, the desire for utopia and how the transformation, the inevitable recuperation is but a spectacle of ironic self-governance. Inescapable, the paradox remains which only the televisual can resolve: a program here, a film there, and the present is but a "senza fine" (endless, without an end) like Gino Paoli sang in his hit many summers ago: the real, transformative achievement of Italy's economic boom: a flirt, by the beach, as music plays in the distance from a sparkling jukebox.

Chapter 2

# Treaty Now: Popular Music and the Indigenous Struggle for Justice in Contemporary Australia

Aaron Corn

I grew up on the Gold Coast in Queensland, Australia's third largest and oldest state, at a most unusual time in my nation's history. In infancy, my mother took me down the road to Miami Beach almost every afternoon before driving north along the strip of local beaches to collect my father from work in Southport. Unbeknown to me and possibly to my parents at that time, forces were afoot that would radically change Australia's sociopolitical terrain and imbue my generation with a vastly different set of cultural assumptions about what it was to be an Australian. Campaigning under the prominent slogan "It's time," December, 1972, saw Gough Whitlam lead the Australian Labor Party back into office for the first time since 1949, and before its controversial dismissal in November, 1975, his government's social reforms were sweeping.

Free tertiary education, free universal health insurance, financial support for single-parent families, the abolition of capital punishment, the lowering of the voting age to 18 years, language support for non-English-speaking residents, equal employment opportunities for women, and an unprecedented platform of self-determination for Indigenous communities were among the many significant reforms introduced under Whitlam's leadership. The White Australia Policy, which had unjustly restricted the entry of non-Europeans to Australia since the federation of the six British Colonies there in 1901, was formally abolished under the Racial Discrimination Act 1975, and the disenfranchised Indigenous peoples of Australia would also find an unprecedented level of protection for their human rights and freedoms under this legislation.

For the earlier part of the twentieth century, governments, missionaries, and pastoralists had systemically subjected these traditional owners of the Australian continent to harsh and degrading treatment and conditions. All but a few entire Indigenous communities were forcibly removed from their homelands into lives of indentured poverty on missions, pastoral stations, and fringe camps, where they were stigmatized and penalized for practicing their own languages and traditions. Children of mixed descent were targets of a brutal policy of assimilation under which they were stolen from their families, and subjected to high incidences of abuse in orphanages and foster homes, and also throughout Australia, Indigenous men in particular were habitually singled out by police for arrest, leading to disproportionately high numbers of Indigenous deaths in custody (McGrath, 1995; Kidd, 1997; Perkins and Langton, 2008).

The overarching aims of these practices had been nothing less than genocidal. They were methodically perpetrated against Indigenous peoples to bring about the complete annihilation of their pre-existing ways of life and their lingering claims of sovereignty over the Australian continent. I entered primary school in the late 1970s, my mother and I made regular trips down the Gold Coast Highway to Burleigh Heads, and each school day we passed right by a traditional Indigenous *bora* "initiation" ring. Although this was the last known ceremony ground of the local Yugambeh people, the Gold Coast's traditional Indigenous owners, to have survived the city's twentieth-century development intact (Bowdler, 1999), it barely registered in my young consciousness. And of the Yugambeh themselves and their rich local heritage (Yugambeh Museum, 2006), I heard nothing but silence from among my circle of adult carers.

**The Turning Tide**

The Whitlam era also saw the creation of the Australia Council for the Arts in 1973 as a national funding and policy body, and one of its first acts was to convene a National Seminar on Aboriginal Arts in the nation's capital, Canberra (Australia Council, 1973). At this time, the work of Indigenous artists was largely seen by government and industry as a folkloric resource to be plundered freely for political and financial gain. Seeking to end this exploitation, prominent Indigenous elders, such as Wandjuk Marika from Yirrkala, spoke out at this forum for a suite of policy reforms. They called for an independent national network of incorporated Indigenous arts cooperatives, copyright protections for works by Indigenous artists, and an end to all trade in unlicensed reproductions of Indigenous art, and they demanded that all Indigenous artists in Australia receive equal pay for equal work (Marika, 1995, pp. 110-26; Johnston, 1996).

It was on these recommendations that the subsequent Liberal government led by Malcolm Fraser established the Aboriginal Artists Agency in 1976 as a national nonprofit body to protect the legal interests of Indigenous artists, and for the first time in history to ensure that they received royalty payments for their works. This Agency undertook many projects to promote traditional Indigenous artists throughout Australia and overseas. But it also took the unprecedented step of representing emerging Indigenous bands such as No Fixed Address from Adelaide, Coloured Stone from Ceduna, and the Warumpi Band from Papunya. Drawing on a range of globalized popular styles including rock, reggae, and country, their best-known original songs celebrated the strength shown by Indigenous Australians in the face of state oppression, and paved the way for reconciliation with non-Indigenous Australians.

In "We Have Survived" and "Genocide" (both 1981), No Fixed Address, led by singer/drummer Bart Willoughby, recounted the long histories of state oppression suffered by Indigenous Australians. No Fixed Address were formed in 1978 alongside Us Mob at the Centre for Aboriginal Studies in Music, and their music featured in the seminal semi-autobiographical film *Wrong Side of the Road* (Isaac and Lander, prod., 1981), which revealed the endemic racial discrimination, social exclusion, and police harassment still faced by Indigenous youths. "Black Boy" by Coloured Stone (1986), led by singer/drummer Buna Lawrie, railed against the racial mores maintained under the White Australia Policy by encouraging Indigenous Australians to be proud of their dark skins. Similarly, "Blackfella, Whitefella" by the Warumpi Band (1987), led by the flamboyant Yolŋu lead singer George Burarrwaŋa from Arnhem Land,[1] called for an end to the social rift between Indigenous and non-Indigenous Australians and soon became a prominent anthem of the burgeoning movement for Aboriginal Reconciliation in Australia.[2]

By the late 1980s, Labor was again in power under Bob Hawke and I was in my teens. The airwaves bristled with songs by non-Indigenous Australian artists, like "Solid Rock, Sacred Ground" by Goanna (1982), "Beds Are Burning" by Midnight Oil (1987), and "Special Treatment" by Paul Kelly (1989), that had been composed in support of these new ideals, and demonstrated a new yearning among Australians to atone for past injustices against Indigenous peoples. And as I grew into adulthood, even more Indigenous artists joined the chorus.

Songs like "Took the Children Away" by Archie Roach (1992) and "Malcolm Smith" by Tiddas (1994) foreshadowed the damning revelations of the National Inquiry into the Separation of Aboriginal and Torres Strait Islander Children from Their Families, and the Royal Commission into Aboriginal Deaths in Custody (Australian Human Rights Commission, 1997; Council for Aboriginal Reconciliation, 1998). Also popular was "From Little Things, Big Things Grow" on *Comedy* by Paul Kelly and the Messengers (1991). Composed by Paul Kelly and the Indigenous folk balladeer Kev Carmody from southeast Queensland, this song became another prominent anthem of the Aboriginal Reconciliation movement. It celebrated Vincent Lingiari's leadership of the pivotal 1966 strike on the Wave Hill cattle station in the Northern Territory. Sparked by appalling wages and conditions for local Indigenous laborers, this action led to the Whitlam government's eventual handing back of exploited pastoral lands to their traditional Gurindji owners in 1975 (Hardy, 1968; Bird Rose, 1991).

In December, 1991, Prime Minister Hawke was deposed by his former Deputy, Paul Keating, who led Australia into a new era of recognition for Indigenous rights. At Redfern Park in inner Sydney in December, 1992, on the eve of the United Nations International Year for the World's Indigenous People, he gave a moving speech before the media and the local Indigenous community that

---

[1]  All spellings of names and words from the Yolŋu languages follow the conventions used today throughout the Yolŋu communities of Arnhem Land (Zorc, 1996).

[2]  See <http://www.reconciliation.org.au>, accessed September 7, 2009.

irrevocably acknowledged how Australia's prosperity had come at the terrible expense of systemic injustices against Indigenous peoples (Keating, 1992). In June that same year, the High Court of Australia had ruled to overturn the doctrine of *terra nullius*, the legal fiction that Australia had been unoccupied at the time of British settlement in 1788, which had excluded Indigenous peoples from asserting any rights or controls over their traditional homelands. Known as the historic Mabo judgment (Australia, 1992), this case concerned the Merriam people and their native title over their islands in the Torres Strait, and it was ultimately won under the Racial Discrimination Act 1975 (Sharp, 1996). Keating's government subsequently enshrined this judgment in the Native Title Act 1993, and as the nation celebrated, Indigenous and non-Indigenous artists from all over Australia collaborated on the commemorative album *Our Home, Our Land* (Yothu Yindi et al., 1995). "Mabo," the album's second song by Yothu Yindi (1995) from Arnhem Land, opens with the triumphant declaration, "*Terra nullius* is dead and gone."

**Written on a Bark**

In another move to mark the United Nations International Year for the World's Indigenous People, Yothu Yindi's engaging lead singer, Mandawuy Yunupiŋu, was named Australian of the Year on Australia Day, January 26, 1993. Mandawuy was a Yolŋu man from the remote Indigenous community of Yirrkala on the northeastern tip of Arnhem Land, which unlike most other Indigenous communities had not been enfranchised into the Commonwealth of Australia until the establishment of a Methodist mission there in 1934. Before embarking on his musical career with Yothu Yindi in 1986, Mandawuy was already recognized as a gifted and influential educator. He was among one of the first Indigenous school teachers from the Northern Territory to earn a bachelors degree in education and be promoted to principal, and for the first time in history his revolutionary ideas about bilingual and bicultural learning made it legitimate for local Indigenous children to be schooled in their own languages as well as English.

In typically Yolŋu fashion, Mandawuy's grand treatise on these ideas came in the form of a song, which he composed while completing his Education degree through Deakin University in 1986. Called "Mainstream" (Yothu Yindi, 1989), it challenged the prevailing assimilationist notion among Australian educators that schools served Indigenous children best by teaching them only in English. It argued that traditional Yolŋu law enshrines a local mainstream of esoteric thought that long predates the transplanted intellectual traditions of Europe, and building on traditional Yolŋu mechanisms for maintaining amicable relations between different clans, it posited a more balanced and equitable way for Indigenous and non-Indigenous Australians to coexist (Corn, 2009, pp. 25-68).

The balance engendered through Mandawuy's ideal of biculturalism was also central to his greater social project for Yothu Yindi (Yunupiŋu, 1994). This kind of balance was constructive. It made space for different views to be exchanged.

It laid foundations for mutual respect among different peoples, and it created new possibilities for different ways of life to coexist. It was also necessary because for the past quarter-century Mandawuy's family had been fighting an entrenched struggle for justice over the unwelcome mining of their traditional homelands around Yirrkala. The state's repeated refusals to recognize Yolŋu sovereignty over this issue is a theme that runs throughout Yothu Yindi's repertoire, and inspired the composition of its most famous song, "Treaty" (1991).

In 1963, the Australian government granted a bauxite lease over the lands surrounding Yirrkala to the mining company Pechiney while ensuring that their Yolŋu owners were locked out of all negotiations. Mandawuy's father, Mangurrawuy Yunupiŋu, was then a senior elder at Yirrkala, and had recently finished collaborating with 15 other elders to paint the "Yirrkala Church Panels" (Marika et al., 1962-63). Spanning two giant bark panels, this extraordinary document was created as a symbol of contemporary Yolŋu solidarity. The panels incorporated the most sacred hereditary designs of nine local Yolŋu clans, and were initially hung on either side of the crucifix inside the Yirrkala Church to demonstrate the equality of the Christian and Yolŋu faiths (Mundine, 1999, pp. 24-5). Mandawuy was a young boy at the time of the panels' production, and Mangurrawuy cut locks of fine hair from his young head to make the delicate paintbrushes required (Corn, 2009, p. 39).

The newfound solidarity of the Yolŋu elders at Yirrkala would soon be tested when the lands to be mined were summarily excised from the Arnhem Land Aboriginal Reserve. They acted swiftly to register an official protest in the form of the "Yirrkala Petition to the House of Representatives" (Marika et al., 1963), which was again spread across two painted bark panels. This second document incorporated a statement in Yolŋu-Matha and English that beseeched the Australian government to spare their lands. Known as the "Yirrkala Bark Petition," it now resides on permanent public display in Parliament House in Canberra, yet did nothing to change the fate of the Yirrkala community.

When the mining company NABALCO obtained Pechiney's lease in 1967, the nearby homeland of Nhulunbuy was instantly bulldozed to make way for a new town to house its miners, and the mine itself went into production in the following year. Heartbroken, the Yirrkala elders issued a writ through the Supreme Court of the Northern Territory in an attempt to halt these developments (Mundine, 1999, p. 22). Their case, *Milirrpum* v. *Nabalco* (Australia, 1968), was heard by Justice Blackburn, who rigorously probed the depths of Yolŋu law and property management provisions among seven resident clans. Mandawuy's father gave evidence for the plaintiffs, while his older brother, Galarrwuy Yunupiŋu, was present throughout the proceedings as a court interpreter, and witnessed their eventual defeat in Canberra in April, 1971, when Blackburn ruled that Yolŋu land ownership had "never formed any part of the law of any part of Australia" (Australia, 1971, pp. 244-5). Mandawuy would later recall his father's disappointment at this loss:

> My father was devastated when we lost that court case, and I saw most of the
> elders, along with my father, saddened. We'll never forget that those aspects of
> our law, our strength and our unity were not seen as part of Australian culture,
> and the Australian way of life in the Yolŋu way. (quoted in Corn, 2009, p. 41)

Further insult to Yolŋu dignity came when Blackburn determined that the plaintiffs
had not proven their descent from the people who had inhabited Yirrkala when
the British First Fleet claimed Australia for the British Crown on January 26,
1788 (Australia, 1971, p. 198). Galarrwuy scathingly satirizes this judgment in
"Luku-Wäŋawuy Manikay 'Sovereignty Song' 1788" (Yothu Yindi, 1989), which
he composed to coincide with Australia's national Bicentennial celebrations in
1988. The song parodies a federal parliament sitting and relates the strange tale of
the Balanda "Anglo-Australians," who claim to have owned the Yolŋu homelands
ever since the British First Fleet landed at Sydney Cove in 1788. That this singular
act of succession took place some 2,500 kilometers away from Yirrkala, and 146
years before the first missionaries arrived there was apparently of no consequence.
The humor of "Luku-Wäŋawuy Manikay 1788" is further underscored by the
offbeat strokes of its acoustic guitar accompaniment, which is reminiscent of the
many Anglo-Australian folk songs that celebrate unbridled pastoral expansion and
colonial conquest (Corn and Gumbula, 2004).

## Writing in the Sand

By 1988, Galarrwuy was in his third term as Chair of the Northern Land Council,
which in response to Blackburn's ruling against the Yirrkala elders in 1971 had
been founded under the new Aboriginal Land Rights Act (Northern Territory)
1976 to represent regional Indigenous interests in land. Australia's Bicentennial
celebrations that year presented a high-profile opportunity for Indigenous peoples
to reaffirm the collective sovereignty, and so on the occasion of Prime Minister
Hawke's visit to the Barunga Festival in June, Galarrwuy and fellow Indigenous
leaders from throughout the Northern Territory presented him with the "Barunga
Statement" (Yunupiŋu et al., 1988). This new document took the form of a single
typescript bordered by traditional Yolŋu and central Australian painted designs, and
it called upon the federal government to enter into a formal treaty with Indigenous
Australians in recognition of their prior ownership, continuing occupation, and
sovereignty over their homelands, and in affirmation of their human rights and
freedoms.

Hawke's initial response to the "Barunga Statement" was surprisingly positive.
Yet his promise that the process of negotiating a treaty would commence within
the lifetime of his parliament would never be fulfilled (Aboriginal and Torres
Strait Islander Commission, 2001). By 1991, Hawke's promise of a treaty had all
but faded from public consciousness when Yothu Yindi's first hit song, "Treaty"
(1991), began receiving airplay. The band had teamed up with Bart Willoughby,

Paul Kelly, and Midnight Oil's lead singer, Peter Garrett, to create a rock song that would recapture the public's imagination for this cause. Its lyrics were incisive and its chorus infectiously demanded, "Treaty yeah, Treaty now."

The first verse of "Treaty" recounts how Hawke's promise of action at the 1988 Barunga Festival was broadcast worldwide, but then disappeared "just like writing in the sand," and the song's music video (Yothu Yindi, 1992) presents corroborating evidence. It shows the completion of the "Barunga Statement" onsite at the festival, news reportage of Hawke's visit there, and the ravages of bauxite mining on the Gove Peninsula.

The song's second verse contrasts Hawke's unfulfilled promise against the permanence of Yolŋu law. It asserts that the Yolŋu never sold or ceded their "priceless" homelands to the British Crown, and echoing "Luku-Wäŋawuy Manikay 1788," it declares that "the planting of the Union Jack never changed our [Yolŋu] law at all." The ideal of balance and equity between Indigenous and non-Indigenous Australians first set forth by Mandawuy in "Mainstream" is also referenced in this second verse through the traditional Yolŋu metaphor of "two rivers" flowing together and becoming as "one" (Neuenfeldt, 1993; Corn, 2009, pp. 35-6).

Typical of the compositional style that Mandawuy had been developing since the early 1980s, "Treaty" also incorporated two complete quotations of a traditional Yolŋu song, making it the first hit song in history to feature lyrics in a true Australian language. The old song he selected was of the *djatpaŋarri* style, which had dominated as a popular music among youths at Yirrkala from the 1930s to the 1970s (Knopoff, 1997, p. 603). It had been composed by Rrikin Burarrwaŋa in the 1950s, and its presence in "Treaty" evokes Mandawuy's nostalgia for his early childhood before Yirrkala was ravaged by mining. The exuberant rhythmic drive of the *djatpaŋarri* style sets the mood and tempo heard throughout "Treaty," and the repeated melodic contour of Rrikin's old song, C♯-B-A-G♯-F♯-f♯— generically known in Yolŋu-Matha as a *dämbu* "head"—is stated at the opening of each English verse (Stubington and Dunbar-Hall, 1994, pp. 252-3; Corn and Gumbula, 2007; Corn, 2009, pp. 69-81).

The legacy of mining at Yirrkala is cited in many other songs by Yothu Yindi. "Our Generation" (1993) opens with the couplet, "Someone in the city gets a piece of paper/ Someone in the bush holds the law in their hands," which interrogates the ontological schism between Crown and Yolŋu laws in Australia that underpinned the defeat of the Yirrkala elders' legal case against the mine. "Baywara" and "Gunitjpirr Man" (both 1993) were composed in memory of Mandawuy's uncle, Dadayŋa Marika, who gave evidence for the plaintiffs. "Homeland Movement" (1989) recounts how after four decades of mission life at Yirrkala, Yolŋu spent the 1970s building outstations on their remote homelands in the aftermath of Blackburn's judgment, and "Lonely Tree" (2000) laments the very last sacred banyan tree left standing in the vicinity of the local bauxite plant. Finally, the fate of the "Yirrkala Bark Petition," displayed behind glass near the "Barunga Statement" in Australia's Parliament House, is remembered in "Written on a

Bark" (1999). Its opening verse evokes contemporary Australia's great failure to recognize the Indigenous rights and freedoms that from 1788 onward, "were taken away in the name of a King," and the grave suffering inflicted upon Yolŋu by the state in recent history.

## Treaty Yeah, Treaty Now

Despite the tragedy of Blackburn's ruling against the Yirrkala elders in April, 1971, some good did come from it in the longer term. Upon coming to power in December, 1972, Whitlam's Labor government established the Royal Commission into Aboriginal Land Rights, which led to the creation of Australia's first piece of native title legislation, the Aboriginal Land Rights (Northern Territory) Act 1976, and the formation of the Northern and Central Land Councils to enforce its protections for Indigenous land interests in the Northern Territory (Northern Land Council, 2002; Central Land Council, 2008).

While Prime Minister Hawke's later promise of a treaty in response to the 1988 "Barunga Statement" similarly failed to bear fruit, it too led to his Labor government's establishment of the Aboriginal and Torres Strait Islander Commission (ATSIC) in 1990 as an elected representative body which enfranchised Indigenous Australians into government funding processes that impacted upon their lives (Aboriginal and Torres Strait Islander Commission, 2005). The Council for Aboriginal Reconciliation followed in 1991 (Council for Aboriginal Reconciliation, 2000), and under Prime Minister Keating's leadership of Labor, so too did the pivotal "Redfern Park Speech" (Keating, 1992) and the Native Title Act 1993.

Yet with the election of the Liberals led by John Howard in March, 1996, Australia entered a renewed era of conservatism not seen since Whitlam had come to power, and the nation's Indigenous affairs policies took a series of retrograde steps. In the aftermath of the National Inquiry into the Separation of Aboriginal and Torres Strait Islander Children from Their Families (Australian Human Rights Commission, 1997), Howard refused to offer a national apology to the many Indigenous Australians who had been stolen from their families by government decree in the twentieth century. Sustained public outrage at this refusal was reflected in the Closing Ceremony of the 2000 Olympic Games in Sydney, at which Yothu Yindi performed "Treaty" (1991) and Midnight Oil appeared on stage to perform "Beds Are Burning" (1987) wearing costumes boldly printed with that most elusive of words, "sorry."

In the aftermath of the *Wik Peoples* v. *Queensland* case in 1996, the Howard government successfully introduced the Native Title Amendment Act 1998, which sparked the lengthiest federal Senate debate in Australian history and greatly curtailed the rights enjoyed by Indigenous claimants under the original Native Title Act 1993. In 2005, his government disbanded the Aboriginal and Torres Strait Islander Commission amid allegations of entrenched internal corruption, and in an effort to garner voters' support ahead of the 2007 federal election, it launched the Northern Territory National Emergency Response, which without warning or consultation introduced sweeping mandatory changes to welfare, law enforcement, and land tenure provisions among Indigenous communities of the Northern Territory. Prompted by spurious claims of organized child sexual abuse within these Indigenous communities, the most controversial aspect of this so-called Intervention has been its blanket suspension by the federal government from the Racial Discrimination Act 1975.

Although the election of a new Labor government led by Kevin Rudd in November, 2007, precipitated a long-anticipated Apology to the Stolen Generations of Indigenous Australians on the first sitting day of Parliament in February, 2008, the Northern Territory Intervention continues unabated despite mounting evidence to suggest that it remains a chronically ill-conceived and ineffective infringement of Indigenous human rights (Australian Human Rights Commission, 2007; Northern Territory Emergency Response Review Board, 2008; Anaya, 2009; Rothwell, 2009). Public concerns over this policy have recently been compounded by federal funding cuts to the many hundreds of homelands that sustain Indigenous laws and ways of life throughout the Northern Territory, and the Northern Territory government's rash withdrawal of support for the bilingual school programs that Mandawuy and his contemporaries worked so hard to establish in the 1980s.

Despite these current challenges, many Indigenous peoples throughout Australia continue to observe their laws, languages, and traditions regardless, and from among them, a new generation of popular musicians has arisen in the guise of bands such as Saltwater from Galiwin'ku, Nabarlek from Manmoyi, and Yilila from Numbulwarr (Saltwater Band, 1998, 2004; Nabarlek Band, 1999, 2001, 2005, 2007; Yilila, 2005, 2006; Yunupiŋu, 2008). Following in Yothu Yindi's stead, many of these artists incorporate into their original songs quotations drawn directly from traditional music and dance repertoires that express the ancestral roots of their respective people's continuing sovereignty over their homelands (Corn, 2002, 2009; Corn with Gumbula, 2003, 2005). As Mandawuy explains:

> We're still practicing our law. We're still doing it regardless of our laws being rejected or being trivialised by mainstream Australian law. We don't care. We keep going because it's important to pass our law on to the next generation. It strengthens our identity as Aboriginal people, the First Nations of this country. (Quoted in Corn, 2009, pp. 29-30)

Yet hope for the future, and for a reconciled Australia still remains. As recently as July, 2008, Prime Minister Rudd and his Cabinet travelled to Yirrkala where Galarrwuy led local elders in presenting him with a new "Yirrkala Bark Petition," which called for renewed national leadership toward the full recognition of Indigenous rights and title in Australia through constitutional reform (Yunupiŋu, 2009). Even though Rudd's Cabinet includes the former lead singer of Midnight Oil, Peter Garrett, as Minister for the Environment, Heritage and the Arts, it remains to be seen whether their government will advance Australia toward this end. In the meantime, at least two generations of Australians remember the haunting words of "Treaty," and as sung in its second verse, are "dreaming of a brighter day when the waters will be one."

Chapter 3

# Intense Emotions and Human Rights in Nepal's Heavy Metal Scene

Paul D. Greene

During the 2000s, young urban Nepalis found themselves in a frustrating, terrifying, and confusing social milieu. Their country underwent a civil war, bombings, and violent clashes between the military, insurgents, and protesters. Thousands of people lost their lives. Nepalis were confronted by conflicting propaganda from three political factions: the Nepali king, the political parties, and a Maoist insurgency. All three struggled to control the people and enlist their support, using both force and propaganda. Some propaganda presented half-truths, some glossed over serious problems, and some included outright lies. This predicament elicited many emotions, including frustration, loss, and rage. This chapter is a study of how a highly emotional music, in a context in which human rights were violated and lost, could function as a means through which citizens could process, feel their way through, and in certain ways resist, discourses of domination to which they were subjected. As urban Nepalis explored and shared emotions of loss and rage through music, they worked from intense emotion toward a sense of human rights. Heavy metal became a way in which they struggled toward realizing what rights and justice meant to them in their uncertain and frightening milieu. And even when a sense of rights was only partially articulated in the music and the scene, the expressing, exploring, and sharing of emotion itself came to function as vehicles for resisting discourses of domination.

I analyze heavy metal as a music that is always already social and political. But I also want to stress that it is an *emotional* discourse, in order to avoid a potential pitfall. In discourse analysis generally there is a tendency to consider discourse dispassionately. Following Jürgen Habermas, for example, scholars often model social and political discourse in the public sphere as taking place in settings of quiet, detached contemplation, like cafés. There is a tendency to focus on discourse participants who are well informed about social circumstances, and whose discourse culminates in well-reasoned social action. In this approach, intense emotion is often considered something that clouds the more significant, dispassionate, verbal modes of discourse. In contrast, what I found in my interviews was Nepali metalheads who *dwelt* on emotions of loss and anger. To be sure, heavy metal songs often drew on a partial control of the facts at hand, and rarely articulated a coherent plan for social action. But rage, instead of clouding social discourse, was a primary means through which these young Nepalis processed their circumstances. In many ways, for these metalheads, it was the intensity of shared emotion that helped to galvanize resistance, much more than well-articulated verbal arguments or formulations of rights. Further, it was anger that led them to say that rights were being violated, not the other way around. In my interviews with over one hundred participants in Kathmandu's thrash metal scene, I found very few individuals who clearly articulated a sense of rights. Instead, as Nepalis shared and discussed with me their emotional and musical responses to hegemonic discourses and frustrating and frightening circumstances, they often *then* began to grope toward propositions about rights and justice. One X-Mantra fan talked about the centrality of emotion:

> Heavy metal will have a good impact on Nepal. We have to be angry. [We] have to make others angry. In the angry person there is more power than in the other [i.e., non-angry] person. This is the time to be angry. We are still sleeping. [We should not always] listen to the love song. This is not the time to love. This is the time to do something for [the] country. Country is in [a] great dilemma. We must wake up. But we are not; we are just listening to music. (Personal interview, Kathmandu, December 31, 2002)

The setting of this chapter is the heavy metal scene of Kathmandu during 2000-2009, a period of civil war followed by uneasy peace, in which urban Nepalis lost and partially regained significant human rights. To understand the nature of the struggle it is necessary to take stock of the country's history, which in many respects is one of human rights struggles. In 1768, King Prithvi Narayan Shah united what is today the country of Nepal through conquest, beginning an absolute monarchy. Under his rule, the dominant religion was Hinduism, and administrative positions were given to the conquering Parbatiya people, high-caste Hindus (Brahmins and Kshatriyas), and the Newars of the Kathmandu Valley. Nepal's numerous Buddhist peoples, such as Tamangs, Sherpas, and Gurungs, received less favorable treatment, and the majority of Nepalis lived below the poverty line. People's movements arose, particularly in the 1940s-50s, and 1980s (*jan andolan*), in which individuals and groups, inspired by Western democratic models, pressed for rights. The concept of human rights in Nepal was in many respects an import from the West, although there were South Asian precedents as well.[1] Protests and resistance eventually led to the drafting of a new constitution in 1990, in which rights, such as freedom of speech and due process, were specified in some detail, and Nepal became a constitutional monarchy.

The 1990s was a period of great freedom for urban Nepalis. Nepal was rapidly opening up to trade goods, ideas, and other cultural influences from the West and India. In addition to state-run media, hundreds of small, privately-owned newspapers flourished, and 19 private radio stations emerged.

---

[1]   A significant and fairly well known South Asian model for human rights is that of the empire of Ashok the Great, of the third century BCE.

There was tremendous social mobility in a new cosmopolitan Nepal. Nepalis, particularly in the growing urban middle class, enjoyed unprecedented employment opportunities, and greater scope to interact, in schools and workplaces, and with people of different caste and ethnic backgrounds.

All of this was jeopardized in the late 1990s and 2000s. In retrospect, one could say that this was partly because the 1990 constitution left much of the hegemonic cultural architecture of royal rule intact. Nepal continued to identify itself as a "Hindu Kingdom" (*Hindustan*) thus symbolically centralizing the monarch in the way the country was conceptualized. Consequently, the King continued to wield considerable power, including the power to dissolve parliament, and to command the army during periods of emergency. Further, the symbolic identification of Nepal as a *Hindustan* facilitated continuance of the patterns of dominance that began with Prithvi Narayan Shah: of Hindus over Buddhists, Parbatiyas and Newars over other groups, and Brahmins over other castes. Hence during 1990-2006, the political parties in many respects continued to exercise power through a hegemonic sociocultural system that marginalized the rural, the poor, and the Buddhists. Moreover, elected governments were unstable, lasting no more than two years at a time. They would be dismissed by the King, or collapse due to internal tensions, necessitating new elections. There was frustration at the more than 40 political parties and the elected politicians, and widespread concern that they spent their time squabbling with each other instead of coming together to solve the country's problems.

Starting in 1996, the Communist Party of Nepal (Maoist) withdrew from the democratic process and began an insurgency, which became particularly violent during the 2000s. The Maoists enlisted rural peoples to their cause, attacked police stations, bombed power stations, and eventually came into direct conflict with the Royal Nepali Army. In time they became the de facto government in many districts. One of their most effective tools was to call a *bandh* (strike) proclaiming that no one in a city be allowed to work for days, or weeks, at a time. *Bandhs* were supported by violence: strikebreakers would face retaliation, in the form of damaged vehicles or property, or bodily harm. Among other things, *bandhs* allowed Maoists to display their influence, command respect, instill fear, and persuade citizens seriously to consider their propaganda. The violence and restrictions of *bandhs* were justified by propaganda that the Maoists were involved in a "People's War" (*jan yudh*), with the aim of improving living conditions for all.

King Gyanendra ascended to the throne following a massacre in June, 2001, in which six members of the royal family were killed. Full details of the incident remain unclear. King Gyanendra took royal rule in new directions. In 2003 he dismissed the Prime Minister and appointed his own Prime Minister. In 2005, citing increasing Maoist violence, he declared a state of emergency, took direct control of the country with the support of the Royal Nepali Army, and began to rule through his own officials. He stationed military officers at newspapers to control the press. During 2005-06 he gave numerous speeches and conducted public ceremonies, including elaborate Hindu rituals, in an attempt to solidify his power. At the same time, the Maoists continued their insurrection and propaganda of the "People's War." Meanwhile, supporters of the political parties took to the streets to call for the reinstatement of an elected government.

The three-way power struggle between the King, the political parties, and the Maoists was transformed in November, 2005, when the Maoists signed a truce with the political parties. Following mass protests coordinated by the parties and Maoists, the King relinquished power, and in 2007 a constituent assembly was elected to draft a new constitution, which excluded the King. The Maoists, organized as a political party, were then elected to power. Violence persists as of 2009, the time of this writing, but all-out civil war has ended, at least for now.

Although heavy metal is largely a form of youth entertainment, it is also notoriously sacrilegious and symbolically transgressive. For example, lyrics of mayhem often transgress cultural limits of decency, and the hallmark distorted guitar timbre indexes transgression beyond the usual limits of music technology. As a symbolically transgressive music, then, Nepali metal was able to function as a vehicle of resistance to the propaganda efforts of all three powerful factions. Thus, when King Gyanendra justified his actions by invoking Hindu Kshatriya ideology—that a king should powerfully crush state enemies, as described in the *Mahabharata*—Nepali metal responded by raging against many of the symbols and tenants upon which this royal discourse was constructed. The band UgraKarma attacked the sacred symbols and rituals of Hinduism, and X-Mantra vented at government policies. Thus, the music and its attendant scene posed challenges for the King's claims to power.

Making and listening to heavy metal music became a way of processing violent and uncertain social realities, and also loaded or deceptive propaganda. Inspired by a powerful sense that something was wrong, Nepali metal raged outward at leaders, politicians, and propaganda statements, galvanizing these urban, middle-class Nepalis in a critical, resisting stance. To be sure, the argument here is not that heavy metal—an entertainment genre primarily for students—was solely responsible for the resistance of the entire urban middle class. Heavy metal was just one sphere in which this class resisted discursive strategies intended to co-opt and dominate it; there were other spheres as well.[2] But metal played a significant role, and the general resisting stance of the urban middle class arguably led to a transformation in the nature of Nepal's conflict. According to recent political analyses, such as those of Saroj Giri (2008) and Winne Gobyn (2009), Maoist leaders attempted repeatedly to draw the urban middle class into their movement. But they realized in 2006 that their efforts would never succeed. The urban middle class, while critical of all three factions, particularly resisted Maoist rhetoric, and

---

[2]    Another place to look would be *gyanmalabhajan*s: populist songs of Buddhist wisdom performed at shrines like Swayambhu. During the turbulent 2000s, these songs not only disseminated Buddhist wisdom but also raised social concerns, in indirect ways, among the urban middle class. This was likely a significant and effective mode of resistance, worthy of further study.

gravitated toward the political parties. Unable to enlist their support, the Maoists changed tactics and began to cooperate with the political parties.

The fact that the songs presented only a partial articulation of human rights reflected the nature of urban Nepalis' struggles. While a war was being waged, a cultural struggle was also taking place to win their allegiance. Heavy metal was a way in which Nepalis participated in this cultural struggle, processing the propaganda they received, and raging back at it. In some ways some metalheads may have been unclear about precisely who or what they were raging against, but they nevertheless became all the more convinced that there were real problems, injustices, and violence to be angry about.

This cultural struggle is well modeled by the concept of hegemony, as developed by Antonio Gramsci. Hegemony is an active cultural process through which dominant groups gain consent and support for their leadership by adopting certain cultural symbols and then connecting these to their own ideologies and political agendas. Hegemonic domination involves management of various oppositional— or potentially oppositional—beliefs or philosophies, which are redefined in relation to a particular agenda. Subjected to such cultural discourse or propaganda, dominated groups often have difficulty articulating the nature of social injustices they suffer, or identifying practical courses of action. Nepal's urban middle class, although in many respects a privileged group, struggled greatly during 1996-2006 under hegemonic discourses from the three forces that sought to co-opt them. In this context of hegemonic domination, struggling simply to apprehend and rage about rights was itself a significant mode of resistance.

Nepali heavy metal was not always so deeply engaged in politics. It emerged within Nepali pop, a genre and scene that formed in 1990, primarily in Kathmandu, among young, middle-class Nepalis, mostly students. These students came from ethnic groups and caste communities from throughout the country, and were steeped in Western culture and technology. They were largely pre-professional and oriented themselves toward careers in the rapidly modernizing cities. The first Nepali heavy metal band was Cobweb, who first incorporated the hallmark sound of heavy metal—the overdriven electric guitar—though they also, in many respects, retained the generally polished aesthetic of Nepali pop. Nepali metal started to shift in the direction of thrash metal in 1999 with Dristhy, Iman, Sharad, and others. With UgraKarma, Stash, and X-Mantra, a full thrash metal scene emerged.

Whereas heavy metal started in the United Kingdom and United States as a working-class music, in Nepal it was primarily a middle-class phenomenon. One reason that the urban middle class was the key prize in the three-way power struggle was that within this class could be found critical discursive spheres that cross-cut the social divisions endemic to hegemony. Heavy metal was one such sphere, shared by young people from Nepal's many ethnic and caste groups. It drew together individuals from many of the groups that had been kept separate and treated differently as part of the cultural work of hegemonic domination over centuries.

In the early 2000s Nepali bands such as X-Mantra, Arachnids, Taamishra, 72 Hours, Rubicon, Ugaa, and Jhumi began to write songs that dealt with human rights and politics. Among these, X-Mantra and 72 Hours were the most prolific. Generally, it seems that metal musicians, unlike the newspapers, escaped governmental monitoring and punishment. This was likely because the music was considered "entertainment," and also because people outside the scene found it difficult to understand the words, which were delivered in typical thrash metal growled fashion. Still, an UgraKarma band member told me he wrote a song titled "War," but ultimately agreed not to release it.

A recurring theme in my interviews in Kathmandu's metal scene was criticism of Hinduism. Anti-Hindu symbolism in Nepali metal was reminiscent of the anti-Christian imagery and lyrics of some Western metal. For example, UgraKarma's band logo included a trident—a symbol of divinity in Hinduism— in an inverted position, much as Western metal bands sometimes use an upside-down cross to denote Satanism (Greene, forthcoming, 2012). This anti-Hindu stance was relevant to the political struggle because the King was attempting to use the discourse and symbolism of Hinduism to enlist the support of the masses. Hindu symbols and beliefs have, since King Prithvi Narayan Shah, functioned as powerful vehicles of cultural hegemony in Nepal. Ali Riaz and Subho Basu argue:

> Since its emergence in the late 18th century the Nepali state has remained an extractive patrimonial state representing a small segment of the society, and therefore disconnected from the society it rules ... Despite this disconnect, the state has succeeded in maintaining its hold over the population through a constructed Hindu identity and a complex connection between this identity and the cultural legitimacy of the social order. (2007, p. 124)

Nepal is a remarkably culturally diverse country, composed of a number of ethnic groups, each with its own language. Many peoples, such as the Tamangs, Sherpas, and Rais, are culturally connected to Tibetans and traditionally Buddhist. The "small segment" of the Nepali population that Riaz and Basu identify as the dominating bloc is the Parbatiyas together with Brahmin priests and the Newars of the Kathmandu Valley (Gellner 1997, p. 8; Dahal 2008, p. 7).

Despite the fact that Nepali metalheads shared a fascination with imagery of gore with metalheads everywhere, they were quite critical of Hindu animal sacrifice rituals: "You should not hurt the animal so badly. The animal is still alive; you cut the throat so the blood spills on various things. But the object you make the offering to is not a living thing. It doesn't need the blood. You do it on a Honda vehicle, to make it safe from accidents. We must eliminate such bad things" (Greene, 2002). This position is relevant because, since unification, Nepali kings have performed public sacrifice rituals to the Hindu goddess Gorkhakali, who was widely believed to be a particular source of the royal family's ruling power. Kings also worshipped and made public sacrifices at the temples to many other goddesses and gods throughout the country. Hindu blood sacrifices were widely believed to renew a ruler's power (*shakti*). Accordingly, in the 2000s, King Gyanendra conducted many public Hindu rituals of animal sacrifice, likely with the intention of convincing the people that, despite protests and the growing Maoist insurrection, his power to rule was being renewed. Such public rituals have been much less common among politicians; however, there has been one tradition, at the time of the installation of a new Prime Minister, of sacrificing a goat before entering his or her quarters. In interviews with over one hundred Nepali metalheads, I never heard a musician or fan voice frustration at Buddhism.

To be sure, Nepali metalheads were largely focused on how their personal freedoms were being restricted by Hindu ritual obligations. So much of their rage at Hinduism was personal, not broadly political. Still, heavy metal was a rare cultural space within which Nepalis challenged Hindu symbolism and discipline. And since discourses of domination have for so long rested on tenets and rituals of Hinduism, metal music opened up new possibilities for political critique.

**Expressive Strategies and Styles**

Nepal's political heavy metal employed many of the same expressive strategies used in heavy metal worldwide. A common approach was to use symbolism of violence and death to draw out emotions concerning loss of human rights. For example, X-Mantra's song "Sinoo" (Corpse) described the democracy movement of the 1980s as a corpse. This tied in to the sense of loss that had been triggered by the fact that rights enjoyed during the 1990s, particularly by urban Nepalis, were now dead. This approach was also evident in the cover of X-Mantra's album *Crying for Peace* (Figure 3.1). The cover presents a familiar Nepali symbol: the all-seeing eyes of Lord Buddha, which have been painted, in this style, on the pinnacles of the Bodhnath and Swayambhu Stupas, and elsewhere. The image was distinctively Nepali, and also functioned as an emblem of Nepal itself. But in this case, the eyes were crying tears of blood. This was not an anti-Buddhist statement; instead, violence to a beloved image triggered a powerful sense of loss. This general strategy was also used in metal songs about love lost: for example, UgraKarma's first album grappled with the emotions of a heartbreak, and its cover depicted a man whose heart had been extracted from his chest. A focus on gore and mayhem was not so much intended to celebrate violence as to heighten the emotional impact of the music, and to represent and trigger powerful emotions through metaphors of bodily harm or death.

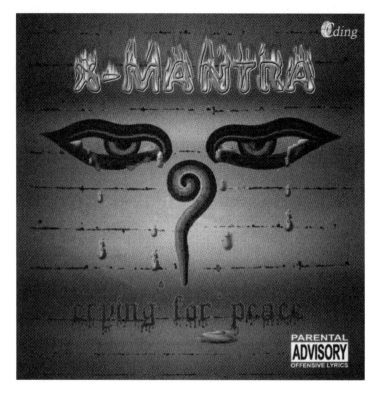

Figure 3.1    Cover of the X-Mantra album *Crying for Peace*, by Rojesh Shrestha

A second expressive strategy was to scold. X-Mantra's "Chidiyaghar" (Zoo) likened Nepalis to animals. The leaders, like lizards, changed their spots—positions—according to shifting circumstances, and the people, like sheep, followed mindlessly. "Shaheed," also by X-Mantra, scolded politicians for invoking the rhetoric of freedom movements to facilitate their election, but then not following through on their promises. "Shaheed" accused politicians of "playing a game" on the corpse of a freedom fighter (another instance of death imagery representing the loss of rights previously won). As a heavy metal concertgoer put it: "We want to scold the family, scold the politicians ... We have deep feelings. If you feel this way how you can do it [sing] in a soft voice? Such emotion should be loud. In loud voice we want to lose control, just say anything and not have a fear" (Greene, 2002).

A few songs, like X-Mantra's "Ek" (One), urged Nepalis to band together. "Ek" proclaimed that one plus one is not two, but 11 (1+1=11). Inasmuch as this was a call to action, it was somewhat exceptional among Nepali metal songs. It was also somewhat unspecific: it did not specify what kind of social action was required.

A third approach was to dwell on specific lines or forms of propaganda, take them to extremes, and rage at them. "Jaya Bandh" (Hail to the Strike), by the band

72 Hours, was an example. Having declared, "Thanks to the person who calls the strike," the song lists some of the results of the action: rising unemployment, holidays from business, and the opportunity to improve one's ability to throw stones. 72 Hours expressed being "proud" of the country's recent history, in which the political leaders did no work, reached no agreements, and allowed donations to the country to go to waste.

Thus the song employed irony in order to rage at the Maoists' rationale for calling *bandhs*. The Maoist movement justified the disruptive and violent events by invoking the concept of the "People's War": because their efforts would culminate in greater freedoms for all, it was acceptable temporarily to restrict productive activity and to engage in violence. But *bandhs* were experienced by urban Nepalis as much more than mere inconveniences:

> Normally we youngsters don't care about what the political scenario is going on in the country. We never cared or kept in mind who is becoming Prime Minister of Nepal or who is becoming the other ministers. But nowadays we are bound to care about it. I mean, even if you are not a politically motivated person you have to face the impact caused by the political movements. For instance, I told you that, in order to reach here, I had to go round and round the back way, because there was a traffic jam because of the political movement. So even if you are not part of it you have to face the problems caused by it. (Greene, personal interview, 2009)

*Bandhs* were crippling, restrictive, and violent, and they stunted Nepal's economic growth during the 2000s. Hence, the song's allusions to progress and development expressed the heightened exasperation that people were feeling, for the strikes stymied much-needed development work for which Nepal was receiving foreign aid. The contradiction in the strike action, therefore, was that strikes aimed to make progress by stopping it, and to empower people by denying them their rights to work and trade. However, the focus of "Jaya Bandh" was actually not so much on deconstructing this contradictory propaganda as dwelling on and heightening the rage one experienced when subjected to it.

The song ended with the declaration that there was "no need" to call a strike to eradicate poverty; "no need" to call a strike to end unemployment; and in the final line, "no need" to call a strike "to end the strike." This final line brought exasperation to a head. Throughout, the song developed the idea that strikes were very real social problems, like poverty and unemployment. Thus the song suggested that the Maoists would approach *this* problem in the same way they approached so many problems: by calling a strike. The song aimed through its expression, therefore, to take the Maoists' logic to an extreme in order more powerfully to lead the listener to rage. Moreover it critiqued other political leaders, whether elected or royal, as ineffectual in overcoming strikes. In so doing, however, it provided no solution of its own.

A related expressive approach was taken in "Kunni Ke" (Undefined), also by 72 Hours. The song explored, among other things, what "peace" meant in a context in which leaders called for protests to be made against other protests, as violence continued unabated. In such a context, "peace"—whatever it was—was "cruel." When asked to tell one's children what peace was, the answer was: "no one knows what it is." The song also explored what law and order meant in a country where the leaders were "vandals," merely "making money," and culprits gave speeches declaring themselves to be "right and good." Written in 2008, "Kunni Ke" grappled with the discourse of domination expounded by Nepal's newly elected government, which the Maoists, organized as a political party, came to lead. It exposed how in the leaders' discourse very real and concrete problems became vague and undefined. They "just talk, and never think of work," and in such a situation, "whom should we complain against?" Further, "a person who tries to do something good is pushed back by others." Moreover, it was very unclear how to seek justice; there was "crisis in everything"; and "no one gets his or her basic needs" met.

"Kunni Ke" declares, "It is said that no one should be concerned about 'minor issues'." This is a reference to a specific incident that took place at the Hotel Woodlands in Kathmandu, where a hotel worker violently attacked his superior, leaving him maimed and deformed. The worker was part of a union affiliated with the Maoists. The government took no action, and Prime Minister Prachandra urged Nepalis not to focus on the incident, calling it a "minor issue." In doing so, Prachandra invoked the Maoist notion that violence must sometimes be accepted as part of a process through which a new, better society could be forged. However, 72 Hours asked, in "Kunni Ke," if such an act of violence were merely a "minor issue," then what would constitute a "major issue"? The song could be said to expose the contradiction of tolerating violence perpetrated on the people in order to achieve liberation for the people. But again, the focus of the song was more on emotion than propaganda deconstruction: how frustrating and frightening it was to have a government that, instead of maintaining social order, tolerated certain acts of violence. One of the aims of bringing the Maoists into the government was to create peace, which the Maoists, despite their history of violence, said they supported. Yet violence continued during the new era of "peace." "Peace" therefore became something that could not be defined; a state of affairs that, according to the song, was patent even to children. Hence use of the word "peace" here invoked, for many Nepalis, a sense of false promise, and therewith anger.

Many Nepalis clearly felt bedeviled in their attempts just to articulate problems, rights violations, and injustices to their new government. To them, goals such as "peace" broke down in a context where "peace" was the governing responsibility of a Maoist leadership with a history of violence. "Major problems" and "minor" ones were undefined and undifferentiated. It was not clear whom to complain about, because responsibilities were poorly defined. In the rhetoric of the Prachandra administration, as it was presented in this song, the terms of discourse about rights and social justice became meaningless, violations continued, and problems festered in the real world. The song dwelt on the exasperation of seeking justice in a context where the very terms used to talk about it broke down.

"Jaya Bandh," "Kunni Ke," and other songs like them are evidence of a sphere of political discourse in which Nepalis groped feelingly toward a sense of rights that they knew were being violated. As the songs built on, triggered, responded to, and amplified their rage, they may also have led to consideration of the rights whose violation was (evidently) indexed by the rage they were feeling. Yet Nepali metal rarely offered specific plans for social action to reinstate human rights. Thus this Nepali case suggests that heavy metal may function more effectively as a mode of resistance to hegemonic propaganda than as a tool for mobilizing a proactive political movement.

By exposing contradictions in hegemonic discourse, and by inspiring strong feelings around issues of human rights, discursive practices such as those examined here helped to galvanize Nepal's urban middle class to resist the dominating moves of the palace, political parties, and Maoists. And at least for now, this resistance has forced the Maoists to cooperate with the political parties, resulting in an end to open war, a return to elected government, and hopeful prospects for a more stable and peaceful Nepal.

## Chapter 4

# Songs of the In-Between: Remembering in the Land that Memory Forgot

### Angela Impey

"Haibo! These *izitweletwele!*"[1] exclaims MaKhumalo, exchanging a large one for one of a more familiar size, "Ha! This one is better! We used to come together like this and play when we were young!" We are sitting in the yard of the Ngwenya homestead. I have just started a research project on mouth-bow practices in western Maputaland and have brought with me a box of Austrian jews harps in a range of different sizes. It has been three decades or more since these instruments were sold in the local trading stores, and as long since the women have played them.

"Hey! This instrument reminds me of my sister!" responds MaFambile, one of the older women in the group. "We used to walk across the flood plains at Banzi Pan to visit our relatives in Mozambique. All the way we would play *isitweletwele!*" "It reminds me of those days when I was young before I accepted Ngwenya [husband]." MaMkhize offers, "Hey! Wearing *amafaskama* [colored hair combs]! Once there was a man from the Mlambo family. He called to me, 'Hey Mnakeni, where is that *wiggie* that you came with when you came to this place?' Ha! It was destroyed by the pot. It was still those days when we used to fetch water from the Usuthu River with *ukhamba!*"[2]

While the women reminisce enthusiastically about music-making during their youth, MaGumede quietly focuses her attention on the instruments. She tests each one, listening attentively to its upper harmonics and its deeper resonances; she experiments with short, stop-start phrases. Finally she settles on one instrument and its liquid tone appears to draw her into a particular song. As her melody takes shape, the other women quieten down, lured, so it seems, by the intensity of the sounds and the memories it invokes:

> Naliveni bakithi naliveni! (There is the van, my people!)
> Naliveni bafana naliveni! (There is the van, boys!)
> Balekani bafana naliveni! (Run boys, there is the van!)
> Lizonibopha! (They will arrest you! They will tie you up!)
> (Personal Interview with Eziphosheni women, August 31, 2003)

---

[1]   *Isitweletwele*: jews harps (sing.).

[2]   *Ukhamba*: clay pot used by women to transport water on the head.

Nowhere, it could be argued, has the force of music to communicate and persuade been played out more vigorously than in apartheid South Africa. During its final and most rigorous years, when most forms of oppositional oratory appeared to have been all but silenced by a brutal and assiduous government intelligence apparatus, the public found expression in the bare bones of a rhythm, seemingly stripped and innocuous, yet intoxicating in its appeal. This rhythm, known as *toyi-toyi*,[3] dug deep into the energy of resistance politics, raising fists of defiance and mobilizing millions into collective action. Characterized by regular beats produced by a stationary but vigorous dance, and punctuated by a simple pattern of off-beats articulated by political watchwords, *toyi-toyi* throbbed at the heart of public dissent and delivered an insistent chorus for human rights and equal justice.

Yet while *toyi-toyi* may have carried the force of resistance in the cities and townships across South Africa in the 1980s and early 1990s, there were many who were too remote from the urban centers to feel part of the action. They, like most black South Africans, had been forcibly removed from their ancestral lands; they had suffered the consequences of familial fragmentation brought about by labor migrancy and grinding poverty, and had been undermined at every level by a government that vehemently refused to consent to their civil liberties, or indeed their humanity. One of the consequences of extreme marginalization, particularly for those who inhabited the interstitial spaces on state boundaries, was that their protestations fell off the edges of the collective movement, their exclusion compounded by their characteristically fluid cultural identities, by livelihood practices that depended on high levels of mobility, and by their apparent indeterminate citizenship. This proscription was the consequence also of a generalized assumption that borderland people were exempt from the racial oppression and political authoritarianism experienced at the center; their physical locality enabled them to retreat to the relative protection of neighboring independent states when conditions in South Africa became untenable.

**Protesting at the Margins**

In southern Africa, borderlands are distinguished by major rivers, deserts, and mountain ranges, which offer themselves up as natural partitions for the marking of territories and the distant making of maps. While stark and unyielding in their geographic form, they are in reality spaces where ethnicities bleed liberally

---

[3]     *Toyi-toyi* is believed to be a siNdebele word meaning "to move forward while remaining in one place." While its exact derivation is debatable, it is generally believed to have been used by guerilla fighters in the Zimbabwean War of Liberation to accompany training exercises. It was subsequently adopted by South Africans exiled in Zimbabwe who introduced it to political rallies in South Africa at the end of the 1970s. By the 1990s, *toyi-toyi* had become synonymous with mass political protest throughout South Africa. See Maluleke (1993); Olwage (2008b).

into one another, and where the contemporary flow of languages and cultural practices reflect centuries of economic and political fissure and fusion (Harries, 1994; Kloppers, 2006). Within the context of contemporary national constitution, borderland people are simultaneously part of and excluded from multiple centers. The cultural theorist Homi Bhabha has pointed out that it is precisely in this state of "in-betweenness" that borderlands "provide the terrain for elaborating strategies of selfhood—singular or communal—that initiate new signs of identity, and innovative sites of collaboration, and contestation, in the act of defining the idea of society itself" (1994, p. 4). However, while cultural values in the borderlands may be negotiated through the interplay between or among groups, at the center they are generally considered to lack identity.

The history of apartheid has been appreciably influenced by the mass media and by a burgeoning heritage sector, which have distilled the past into a master narrative that many argue has been constructed to validate the new political order (Baines, 1998; Guy, 1998; Nuttall and Coetzee, 1998). Protest songs, such as *toyi-toyi*, have been likewise packaged as a coherent repertoire, sutured into national memory as "show pieces or slogans" (Masekela, 1993, cited in Gilbert, 2008, p. 177) during the height of the anti-apartheid movement by official cultural ambassadors for the ANC in exile (such as the Amandla Cultural Ensemble) and popularized within the country at mass rallies, funerals, and celebrations (Ansell, 2004; Gilbert, 2008, p. 157). In contrast, this chapter aims to explore the notion of protest at the margins as resounded in songs made popular at the local level. I argue that these songs provide an equally dense ethnographic register of human rights violations in apartheid South Africa as did those that were rallied to by thousands on the city streets. Yet while no less compelling in their appeal for economic, social, and political rights, their remoteness from organized opposition politics has rendered them barely audible in the post-apartheid "struggle memory." This chapter therefore seeks a place in a growing body of particularist histories in South Africa that privilege the multiplicity, diversity, and quotidian nature of histories and identities in the practice of social and political reconstruction.[4] Further, the focus on "popular music" departs from its more commonplace designation in the academy as that which is founded on the mechanics of production and technological mediation, and by its constitution in mass culture and industrial capital (Frith, 2004). Rather, the songs with which I am concerned are conceptualized as popular because they carry meaning through shared expression in everyday contexts, providing a discursive reflection on the lived experiences of political repression and economic rupture, and offering consolation, however fleeting, through the collective performance of noncooperation. Drawing on Vansina (2006), Vaughan (1987), Perks and Thomson (2006), and Finnegan (2003, 2007), who similarly recognize the value of songs as situated sites of oral history, the focus here is

---

[4]   A number of influential studies have been conducted on popular music and resistance during apartheid; however, their focus has been almost exclusively urban. See, for example, Ballantine (1993), Allen (2003), Erlmann (1991), and Olwage (2008a).

on a body of expressive activities that elaborate social and political meanings as both audible and corporeal, and that have remained embedded in cultural practices across time and space. These songs are rooted in orality, improvisation and collective invention, and while not linked to organized political action, their role as instruments of mobilization at the individual and community level warrants their recognition within a broader constellation of "struggle" discourses in South Africa.

## Mapping the Place In-between

In the far northeast of South Africa, where the province of KwaZulu Natal borders Mozambique and the small mountain kingdom of Swaziland, the landscape is marked by a vast network of coastal sand forests and shallow flood plains. The area is rich in endemic fauna and flora species, and is highly valued as a transitional zone between southern and east African ecosystems (Bruton and Cooper, 1980).

From afar, the landscape is distinguished by forests of lime green acacia trees that proliferate in the savannah marshlands. The people who live here call the tree *umkhanyakude*: that which shines brightly from a distance. It is believed that by bathing in water boiled with its bark one will assume its luminous quality, a particularly useful attribute when competing for a job or attempting to attract the attention of a potential lover. On the other hand, to the European hunters and traders who crossed into the area from Mozambique in the mid-1800s, the tree became known as the *fever tree*, a visual icon of malaria and sleeping sickness; diseases to which many succumbed, and which ultimately prevented widespread white settlement in the area. This tree, with its oppositional good luck/bad luck allusions, symbolizes a landscape that has been and continues to be highly contested. For the people of western Maputaland, who are of mixed Zulu, Swazi, and Thembe-Thonga ethnicity, it signifies a cautiously adapted livelihood based on shifting agriculture and cattle, a life at once rooted to land, yet dependent also upon the establishment of extended kinship networks across the region which were used to support a system of in and out migration during times of environmental stress, disease, or warfare.[5]

For the white South African government of the early 1900s, however, the tree signaled an environment that required re-landscaping.[6] Ironically, they sought to control the environment by keeping it wild. Instead of removing the mosquitoes,

---

[5]   Harries suggests that people of western Maputaland have historically identified themselves as "being from the land" of the clan dominating a particular chiefdom, rather than by ethnicity or affiliation to the nation state (1994, p. 6).

[6]   The southern border of Mozambique was drawn up under an antislavery treaty in 1817, recognizing Portugal's suzerainty from Cape Delagoa to Delagoa Bay. Border disputes flared up intermittently and the issue was finally submitted for adjudication to President MacMahon of France in 1872. An Anglo-Portuguese treaty defined the border in

they removed the people, creating a buffer that functioned as both a militarized zone to control border crossings and a compensatory wilderness constructed for the rapidly urbanizing white population. Formally demarcated a protected area in 1924, Ndumo Game Reserve, as it was later designated, was gradually cleared of all inhabitants, and by the 1970s it had been duly refashioned as a pristine, timeless space in nature; a space outside history.[7] The "timelessness" installed in the image of the game reserve has, however, become memorialized as a critical moment of loss for the local people, who were made to settle on the perimeter of the reserve, and for whom conservation has remained associated with a profound sense of dispossession.

Today, western Maputaland is interlaced with fences that encapsulate the floodplains and mountains with borders and boundaries: state fences, game fences, veterinarian fences, fences of commercial properties. Some function as symbolic spatial demarcations only; others comprise electrified cabling and stand 14-strands high. These fences cut across histories of everyday movements, trade routes and the age-old seasonal migrations that were established to maximize adaptation to environmental stresses on food production and disease (Harries, 1994). Significantly, the spatial rupture caused by fences affected a new pattern of mobilities and immobilities that cut across gender, forcing men into the migrant labor system in the gold mines in Johannesburg or on sugar farms in southern KwaZulu Natal, and confining women to ever-decreasing fixed tracts of land upon which the survival of their families became increasingly dependent.

**Women's Songs as Markers of Memory**

The notion of borders or boundaries brings together two related concepts in this chapter. The first pertains to the geopolitical demarcation of the modern nation state, which determines citizenship and political rights.[8] The second is embedded in cultural practice and relates more specifically to the notion of "genre" as bounded by mutually understood form, performance context, and meaning. The denotations of boundary in both context and practice are given meaning in this study through their transgressive relationship to states of fixity and closure. Both geopolitical and musical borders are divergent, overlapping, and exist in a state of "in-between." While the political ambivalence of borderlands has already been discussed in relation to its political constitution and to constructions of identity, the following section will focus on two genres of women's songs, and examine the ways in which these song and dance forms, normally associated with frivolity

---

1891; four years later "British Amatongaland" was proclaimed a Protectorate and in 1897 it was incorporated into Zululand (Harries, 1994).

[7]    For further discussion on nature and temporality in the making of game reserves in KwaZulu Natal, see Brooks (2000) and Beinhart (2008).

[8]    For a more detailed review of borderlands, see Alvarez (1995).

and youthful pastimes, became the sites for the collective expression of women's protest against the state during the 1950s and 1960s, a period which marked a particularly oppressive moment in apartheid history.

This section draws on research conducted with two groups of elderly women in western Maputaland whose families had been removed from the Ndumo Game Reserve in the 1940s and 1950s. I argue that women's songs provide a more consistent, visceral historical narrative of the politics of locality than do men's musical practices, as men were often absent from the area for years at a time. Memories of these songs provide insight into the history of women's experiences, and reveal the essence of their agency which was mobilized through narratives of social critique (Scott, 1990; Friedman, 1998). As suggested by McEwan (2003, p. 739), women's experiences have been significantly marginalized from dominant accounts in South African history, and have been largely denied agency in the construction of collective memory. This research focuses on women's narrative poetics of geopolitical identities in particular, stimulated by the recollection of two genres of walking songs that were last performed some 30-40 years ago. The demise of these songs is attributed to both cultural change (and in particular, the introduction of radios and cassette players brought back from the cities by husbands and boyfriends) and the loss of the spatial context that had provided their social and poetic mooring.[9]

The first set of songs is associated with walking great distances across state lines to buy cloth and sugar from the trading stores in Swaziland or to visit family in Mozambique. Referred to as "*amaculo naniwasebenzisa manihamba*" (songs that are used when we walk), they were performed to the accompaniment of two mouth-bows (*umqangala* and *isizenze*) and the jews harp (*isitweletwele*). Lyrics were implied in the melodies played on the mouth instruments whose pitch contours are shaped by tonal inflections of the three languages spoken in the region. Sometimes the songs were performed in a call-response format; the instrumental melody providing the "solo" to which a group of friends walking with the player would respond with a sung chorus. These songs were comprised of short, cyclical melodies, their simple, repetitive, driving phrases providing rhythmic impetus to sustain long-distance walking.

The second set includes songs that were sung at carefully designated localities conceptualized as "far away." These songs/dances, known as *ingadla*, were associated with youthful *isigcawu* gatherings that would take place on moonlit nights or on special occasions such as the annual return of young men from work in the mines of Johannesburg. People would walk great distances to attend these events, which took place within proximity of a trading store or a similar such communal place-marker. *Ingadla* songs were performed in a circle, and young women would take turns to dance into the center, either individually or in pairs, showing off their talent and dramatizing humorous events, while their friends sang, ululated, and cajoled from the outer circle, and the men observed from a distance.

---

[9]    For more details on these genres, see Impey (2006, 2008).

*Ingadla* songs were more rhythmically, melodically, and lyrically complex than mouth-bow songs, but were linked to the former, whose principal performance context was the bush paths that wove across the landscape and connected fields and homesteads to *isicgawini*:[10]

> When we went there, we would take *isitweletwele* and these bows. It just depended on what you liked. We would take the instruments and put them in our mouths and walk through the bush. We would go straight to Ndumo or to *isicgawini*. It helped to cover the long distances when we played these instruments along the way. When we got there, we would dance *ingadla*. When we were tired, we would make a fire and the boys would cook birds and we would eat honey. Then we would take up our instruments and play until we were ready to dance again. (Personal interview, Makete Nkomonde, Usuthu, April 24, 2004)

The songs collected during the research period encompass a performance history of some 100 years. Their thematic content varies from simple greetings and proposals of love (often associated with the songs that were inherited from mothers and older sisters, otherwise expressed as "those that were before"), to "corrective" or "regulatory" songs that were sung as a mechanism of reestablishing the social order. Songs in the latter category provide evidence of an embedded symbolic regulatory system that, while by no means unique to these communities, is in this context a relevant indicator of a culturally sanctioned system of social critique, a poetic strategy that linked music to different forms of social action. The following song, for instance, is typical of those that were performed to publicly shame indolent women. It is a shrewdly constructed piece in which the solo-chorus format is effectively inverted: the soloist is assigned the lyrics in which various invitations are made to join the work party, and which in reality would be proffered by a group. In turn, the excuses made by the culpable individual are delivered by a chorus. This inversion is used as a poetic strategy to detract from direct criticism and relies rather on coercion by consensus, its potency effectively carried by culturally understood structures and inferences:

| | |
|---|---|
| Solo: | Asambe siye'masimini (Let's go to the fields) |
| Chorus: | Ngiyazigulela mina (I am sick) |
| Solo: | Asambe siy'ezinkunini (Let's go and fetch firewood) |
| Chorus: | Ngiyazigulela mina (I am sick) |
| Solo: | Asambe siy'otshwaleni (Let's go and drink alcohol) |
| Chorus: | Ngizakutotobela khona (I will try to follow you) |

(Personal interview with women in Usuthu Gorge, August 27, 2003)

The performance of such corrective songs was explained thus:

---

[10]    *Isigcawini* refers to the places designated for *isicgawu* gatherings.

Siphiwe: When we were young and a person was doing something wrong, we would challenge them with a song. If you wanted to show them something, they would be the ones to feel ashamed for what they did. Then you would be happy and they would be sad. That way your heart would be opened.

Fambile: If that person comes and finds you singing about the thing that she is doing, she might think that this is about her. If a girl has many men—she has one here and there and there—that is a song! She might stop doing this when she hears it. It was like that! So in those days, these songs were our newspapers. It was our thing because there was no education at that time. (Personal interview with Siphiwe Cele and Fambile Khumalo, Eziphosheni, August 31, 2003)

On the surface, both mouth-bow and *ingadla* songs appear to support everyday, youthful concerns and activities. However, closer examination of the lyrics across the combined repertoire reveals an astonishingly high number that describe quite the opposite. Far from portraying a pastoral existence that was exempt from institutionalized racial oppression, these songs describe a life under intense surveillance, under which people were forced to conceal their possessions, disguise their livelihood activities, and live as fugitives from their homes. The common thread that weaves through these musical scenarios is one of the police, the visible instruments of the state. Some songs provide warnings to other women of their impending arrival, some report specific incidences involving them, and others still express outward defiance toward them. The essence of flight expressed in these songs speaks strongly to the fragmentation of the community and the family that resulted from increasing state control of the borderlands in the late 1950s. In reality, therefore, while always appearing to be on the run in their songs, the escape routes available to women were becoming increasingly obstructed by fences and by a mounting body of apartheid laws.[11] While on one hand these songs clearly reveal the underlying disposition of guilt or civil disobedience that shaped the social and political consciousness of all black South Africans under apartheid—the dominance of which in such a remote borderland locality provides testimony to the omnipotence of the apartheid hegemony—on the other they were strategically deceptive. By inhabiting the same melodies and performance spaces as those genres that focused on relatively innocuous girlish pursuits, the protest element in the songs was effectively camouflaged from the police. It may also have been that these fugitive songs were so commonplace and embedded in everyday experience that they didn't warrant a separate musical space, as herein lay their agency.

One of the most poignant in the combined repertoire of songs is the song that makes direct reference to the removal of the communities from what is now Ndumo Game Reserve. This song lies at the core of the dispossession trope in the

---

[11]   A series of draconian laws were passed during the two decades following the installation of the Nationalist government in 1948, enshrining apartheid in legislation and marking this as the period of "high apartheid."

repertoire as it represents the actual moment of forced displacement from the park, and remains powerfully associated with a more generalized experience of loss. It is a necessarily over-simplified song, the lyrics so unspecific that we were only able to understand their context and significance through the explanatory narratives that were later provided. Yet its use of repetition and short, cyclical phrases vividly portrays the panic and intensity of that final encounter, as well as the powerlessness of the people to protect themselves against the violence of the state:

> Balekani nonke! (Run away everyone!)
> Kukhona okuzayo! (Something is coming!)
> Gijimani nonke! (Run away everyone!)
> Kukhona okuzayo! (Something is coming!)

MaFambile explains:

> We were running away from the white man from *KwaNyamazane* called *Umthanathana*.[12] We were not removed at once. My father had two homesteads. They started by moving the cattle to this side. Then we moved to another homestead. Others were left on that side. They were later arrested and forced out. They were arrested if they were found with an antelope. If they were found fishing in the river, they would arrest you. You couldn't eat your fish freely. They chased everyone then; they said they didn't need them there. They chased us from our land. We're now suffering from hunger. We don't eat anything and we don't have any water. Our cabbages are getting dry. We were drinking from the big river they called Banzi. Today, that's where they built a hotel for the tourists.[13]

---

[12]  *KwaNyamazane* means "the place of the antelope" and refers to the Parks Authority or Ndumo Game Reserve. *Umthanathana*, translated as "the one who speaks contemptuously and we shut our ears," was the name given to the Parks official responsible for the removal of the communities from the game reserve.

[13]  An online brochure advertising the Ndumo Wilderness Camp aptly reflects the way in which the tourism industry has rendered invisible from the landscape any memory of its human inhabitants: "Proclaimed in the 1920s, Ndumo Game Reserve, (formerly known as Ndumu), is one of South Africa's oldest and most scenic parks. It is situated in northern Natal and just south of the Moçambique border. The Nyamithi and Banzi Pans, which are surrounded by beautiful yellow Fever Trees, are the focal points in the reserve. These pans are on the Pongola and Usutu floodplains and attract wildlife in large numbers. The Ndumo Reserve is not well known, even to many South Africans, as accommodation has previously been limited. Now, Ndumo Wilderness Camp has been built on the edge of Banzi Pan. The view from the camp's deck over the Banzi Pan is one of the most extraordinarily scenic of any camp in Southern Africa" (http://www.eyesonafrica.net/south-african-safari/ndumo.htm, accessed November 10, 2008). The Ndumo Wilderness Camp has since been closed and discussions are in process to integrate the formerly displaced communities into its management under public-private partnerships.

Angela: Did anyone try to resist the game reserve authorities?

Fambile: No, they just took their belongings and ran. Even today we miss that place! There we were free to go to Mozambique to visit our relatives. We remember the places where we lived and used to meet to dance. Now we can't do that. If we go back, we are arrested. We have graves there but we have no access to them to talk to our ancestors. Our grandmothers' and grandfathers' graves are on that side. We were never even given the chance to do *umlahlankosi*.[14] (Personal interview with Fambile Khumalo, Eziphosheni, September 1, 2003)

Once removed from Banzi Pan in the Ndumo Game Reserve, people were made to settle on land on the periphery of the park, where they pledged allegiance to local leaders, built new houses, and prepared new fields. In some instances a mere 14-strand game fence separated women from their old fields, their proximity serving as a constant reminder of the humiliation of removal over the ensuing years. The displacement of the communities marked the onset of a much more pervasive and insidious policing of the borderlands, however, endorsed by the institutionalization of apartheid legislation in the 1950s that sought to control the actions and movements of all black South Africans at all times. The 1952 Pass Laws Act, for instance, made it compulsory for all black South Africans over the age of 16 years to carry a "pass book" (locally referred to as *dompas*). The document operated as an internal passport, containing vital details of the bearer such as fingerprints, address, and employment status. Despite their remoteness, their songs prove that the women of western Maputaland were as vulnerable to the controls enforced via the *dompas* as were their fellow citizens in the cities:

Naliveni bakithi naliveni! (There is the van, my people!)
Naliveni bafana naliveni! (There is the van, boys!)
Balekani bafana naliveni! (Run boys, there is the van!)
Lizonibopha! (They will arrest you! They will tie you up!)
(Personal interview with women in Eziphosheni, August 31, 2003)

MaFambile explains:

From Ndlaleni's house we walked all the way from Makanyisa, playing *isitweletwele* (jews harp). That's what we were doing when we were going to eat sugar (to buy goods at the trading store). And we were singing "*iveni*" because the police cars were giving us problems. They wanted us to pay for "*dompas*." We remember that song well! That is why we still sing it. (Personal interview with Fambile Khumalo, Eziphosheni, September 1, 2003)

---

[14]    *Umlahlankosi* refers to the ritual delivery of the spirit of the dead from the exact location of death to the homestead of the family. The ritual is mediated through the branch of the *Ziziphus mucronata* (Buffalo Thorn) which is believed to have ancestral power.

The increasing economic and social challenges brought about by forced displacement were often embedded in simple songs of farewell to fathers and husbands who had departed for the cities. Despite the use of the characteristic upbeat "walking/jogging pace" of mouth-bow songs, the lyrics grieve their separation from their loved ones, and vividly express the powerlessness of women to alter their circumstances against the forces of the developing apartheid industrial economy. The following song is likely to have been played while walking alone to the river to fetch water or from the homestead to the fields. Using the same repetitive melodic format and performance context as that of other mouth-bow songs, its solemn sentiment is disguised by the sweetness of the melody: *Sala kahle ntaka baba* (Goodbye, child of my father [husband]). It was played for me by MaNonyi Ndabeni, who claimed it as a song belonging to her mother who had performed it many years previously:

> My mother was saying farewell to her man, my father, when he went to *Ezilungwini*.[15] He used to work in Empangeni. I don't know when this was. I know that he left when I was young and when he came back he was sick and died and the children were all grown up. I don't know exactly where my father worked, but it was somewhere in town. He used to send us money. I don't know the years because I am not educated in numbers. (Personal interview with MaNonyi Ndabeni, Usuthu, November 18, 2003)

With the loss of land and resources, so the local economy became increasingly unstable. Male unemployment in the cities and faltering remittance payments forced women to take on supplementary cash-based work in their home areas. Many were forced into illegal activities such as the brewing of alcohol. This increased their vulnerability to police harassment and stimulated the composition of a range of songs about work, shifting their focus from criticisms that had as their objective the regulation of an internal socioeconomic status quo to a collective statement of noncompliance with the external forces of the state. Again, the lyrics implied by the melodies are minimal, delivered as sharp cautionary phrases and embedded within a mutually understood performative context. There are a large number of songs in the repertoire that have at their core phrases such as "Iveni liyalandela!" (The van is coming to fetch us!), that were played to communicate the panic experienced by women when the police invaded their homes: "This song says that I'm running away from the police van. The van is inspecting the homesteads to find out whether the women are making alcohol from sugarcane" (Personal interview with Siphiwe Mzila, Eziphosheni, August 31, 2003.)

The penalties for illegal beer-brewing were often severe, and the following key phrase of a mouth-bow song refers indirectly to the consequence of arrest: "Emsebenzini kukhala ingolovane" (The bell/siren [of the train] is calling us to

---

15    *Ezilungwini* : "the place of the white people."

work). The song refers to the train that would take the men to the gold mines in Johannesburg. However, as the men would first be transported long distances by bus to the train stations in Siteki in Swaziland or the town of Pongola in the south, it was unlikely that women would have seen or heard them, and the composer explains her song in the following way: "Once I saw a train when I was coming from Pongola where I had been in prison. I was arrested for brewing alcohol and sent to jail for three months. I was quite young then and strong, not like now. Singing it made me think of my husband and helped to soothe my heart" (Personal interview with Makete Nkomonde, Usuthu, November 18, 2003).

Many of the songs recount actual incidents involving the police. While their precise meanings may have been lost in time, the songs have remained in the collective memory, their appeal located in the expression of defiance or reckoning that they communicate. Although my research collaborators were unable to explain the meaning of the following song, it was a well-remembered piece in the *ingadla* repertoire:

| | |
|---|---|
| Solo: | Mabopha' ubopha abanye (The one who arrests others; |
| | You are arresting the others) |
| Chorus: | Uyeheni mayebabo shii! (Statement of shock) |
| Solo: | Uzwile ulayikile (You got a taste of your medicine: I told you so) |
| Chorus: | Uyeheni mayebabo shii! (Statement of shock) |
| Solo: | Isandla sengwenya (The hand of the crocodile) |
| Chorus: | Uzwile ulayikile (You got a taste of your own medicine) |

(Personal interview with women in Usuthu, August 28, 2003)

A similar such *ingadla* song refers to the death of a policeman which appears to have occurred when he attempted to procure a bribe from a member of the community. This song demonstrates that some encounters with the police were confrontational:

Uyadela Babo! (You are happy!)
Babulal'iphoyisa (They killed a policeman)
Ngoba imali bayifaka ebhokisini (They put the money in the box)
Babulala iphoyisa (Killed a policeman)
Imali bayefaka ebhokisini (Put the money in a box)
(Personal interview with women in Usuthu, August 27, 2003)

The final song that I wish to look at was not composed as a mouth-bow melody or *ingadla* dance-song. It was sung by women after the first nonracial democratic elections in 1994 as a response to the establishment of a National Land Claims

Commission.[16] Interestingly, the lyrics of this song are far more reliant than the songs previously discussed on deeply encoded natural metaphors—reminiscent of Zulu *izibongo* praises—that were used as a culturally sanctioned medium of political mobilization.[17]

> Baleka mfana lashona ilanga (Run boy, the sun is setting)
> Gijima mfana (Run boy)
> Awekho amanzi (There is no water)
> Awekho amanzi (There is no water)
> Asemfuleni (It is in the river)
> (Personal interview with women in Eziphosheni, September 3, 2003)

The song urges men to take up the opportunities provided by the new government to reclaim the resources that they had been deprived of under the apartheid system. It is an explicitly political song intended to advocate collective action around social, economic, and political rights, and stands in contrast to the mouth-bow and *ingadla* songs, whose expressions of noncooperation were shrouded in musical and contextual ambiguity. Where the performance of this song is a response to political possibility, and imagined as running *toward* the state, women's walking songs recount a moment in history where life in the borderlands was experienced in a perpetual state of strategic avoidance of the state.

**Conclusions**

This chapter has explored the creative mechanisms by which two seemingly frivolous musical genres were redistributed by women in western Maputaland during the height of the apartheid era to accommodate a "shared critique of domination." These songs provide valuable insight into the everyday responses by women to the strictures of the state, and are particularly relevant in a context where the "in-betweenness" of borderland identities and the physical and political remoteness from the centers of power have rendered their experiences little understood. Like *toyi-toyi*, these songs were propelled by driving rhythms that sustained movement and found their expressive potency in performances that drew on the collective. Unlike *toyi-toyi*, however, their embeddedness in everyday expressive activities meant that they were not profiled as "showpieces and slogans" as were the protest songs used by the organized political opposition, and have thus remained largely overlooked as valued oral evidence in the construction

---

[16]   The derivation of the song is not certain, although it is claimed as a collective composition by the community.

[17]   *Izibongo* praises are an ancient genre of isiZulu oral poetry that are generally associated with a chiefly clan or with royalty. They are a powerful, metaphorical, and highly refined rhetorical practice. Their delivery is rapid, and often defiant and authoritative.

of a more pluralistic post-apartheid "struggle memory." While these songs may relate to key moments of political activity during the apartheid era, they operated more significantly as visceral narratives that gave voice to women's experiences and agency, and continue to function as a powerful mnemonic of the struggles fought for human rights and justice in the borderlands and margins of apartheid South Africa

Chapter 5

# How a Music about Death Affirms Life: Middle Eastern Metal and the Return of Music's Aura

Mark LeVine

Rock 'n' roll has long been considered a quintessentially Western, even American art form. The social practices associated with it—or with its caricature—such as youth rebellion, hedonism, and unregulated sexuality, alcohol, and drug use—seemingly violate too many of the most basic values of, for example, Confucian or Muslim societies to imagine that the music would take root in China, Egypt, or Iran, among more than a tiny subculture of members of these societies who are associated with the intellectual or cultural elite. The reality, however, is not merely that rock music long ago became rooted in non-Western societies, although it is clear that politically and culturally, as well as aesthetically, rock music's impact has been global. In fact, rock wouldn't exist without the formative impact of the musical cultures of the Muslim world and Africa on the shape and sound of music in Europe and the Americas. From the oud-inspired surf-guitar sound of guitar legend Dick Dale (the "godfather" of heavy metal, née Richard Mansour of Lebanese parents) to the "discovery" of the Master Musicians of Joujouka by late Rolling Stones guitarist Brian Jones and the unquestionable Middle Eastern influence on groups such as Led Zeppelin, rock music has long been inspired and influenced by the music of the Middle East and North Africa (see LeVine, 2008, introduction).

This chapter explores the birth, development, and aesthetic embedding of various subgenres of heavy metal across the Middle East and North Africa. It examines how the aesthetic embeddedness of the music within larger social and political struggles mirrors that of many other styles of "world music," a genre in whose company heavy metal is rarely, but should more often be, placed. The metal scenes of the Muslim world boast a myriad of styles from Morocco to Pakistan, and then again in Southeast Asia (Malaysia and Indonesia), from meticulously faithful recreations of the classic "death metal" sound to hybrids that combine various subgenres of metal with indigenous styles—sacred as well as secular—tonalities, rhythms, and instruments.

Together, the varied expressions of hard rock and related forms in the Muslim world, as well as the circuits of their production and distribution, have much to teach us about the nature of globalization today. Although it is rarely expressed openly, these scenes have a strong political component and often achieve a level of cultural and political subversiveness that have put them in the crosshairs of both authoritarian governments and conservative religious officials and movements who see the music as a threat to the established political and social order.

The vibrancy of the music and the political persecution and social ostracism suffered by its practitioners and fans point to the need to assert more vigorously the universal nature of the freedom of musical expression as a fundamental human right. This is already occurring in the Muslim world, where heavy metal is gradually being accepted by mainstream religious forces as a non-threatening, if still strange-sounding, form of cultural expression for young people. This process is enabling an era of renewed, and in some cases unprecedented freedom for the musicians—as long as they don't cross certain religious and political red lines. Perhaps more surprising than the music's political salience, and its slow push toward mainstream toleration (but certainly not commercial success), is the philosophical implications of the metal scene's social and political position within the region. Specifically, the dynamics of subcultural performance encountered in these scenes point to a reversal of the process of commodification of art described by Walter Benjamin and Theodor Adorno in the first half of the twentieth century, and the attendant loss of authenticity and power it is supposed to have caused. Instead, it is precisely the "aura" and "ritualistic" nature of the scenes, their music, and performances that makes them simultaneously threatening to the established order and potentially liberating for the often marginalized young people who participate in them.

### "Music is the Weapon of the Future"

These words are the title of the last album of the great Nigerian Afrobeat pioneer Fela Kuti, who was himself no stranger to censorship and political repression, having used his music and the fame it accorded him to challenge the Nigerian government at every turn. For his courage, he was jailed, his house burned down, and his mother thrown out of a window to her death by police.

Although rare, artists have been physically attacked and even killed in the Muslim world. Among the most well-known cases are the murders of Algerian Rai artists Cheb Hasni and Rachid Baba Ahmed by militant Islamists during the country's decade long civil war, and the murder of Afghan singer Qhurban Nazar and six musicians by militants in 2005. Iraqi and Somali musicians have also been murdered, while Pakistani artists and CD shop owners have faced constant harassment from ultra-conservatives and militants.[1] To date, no Arab/Muslim metal musicians have been killed, but many have faced beatings, arrest, prison and rigged trials, police and government harassment, and social marginalization. Why have heavy metal musicians faced such attacks? Because the music, although usually

---

[1]    See the website of Freemuse.org for a complete list of attacks.

not articulated openly, offers a powerful critique of the corruption, violence, and stifling oppression of the status quo. And in so doing, metal in the Muslim world is carrying on a tradition that lies at the heart of heavy metal's emergence as a musical genre in the late 1960s.

The political grounding of heavy metal in the Muslim world is not without historical precedent in the genre. In the early 1970s metal pioneers Black Sabbath produced a series of albums that defined the new genre, with a combination of relatively slow tempos, heavily distorted guitar riffs in various minor modes, half-tone and even tri-tone modulations (known since the Renaissance as the *diabolus in musica* because of the immoral, even lustful feelings it was felt to encourage), and morbid, death-inspired lyrics that spoke to disaffected American and European youth. The sound also reflected both the dreariness of life in working-class cities like Birmingham, where Sabbath was founded, and the anger such an environment produced (see Kahn-Harris, 2007, pp. 97-120).

By 1975 a new style of metal had emerged, dubbed "the New Wave of British Heavy Metal." Led by bands like Judas Priest, Motörhead, Venom, and Iron Maiden, the genre was distinguished both by the increased speed and musical complexity of the songs and also by a working-class image that fitted the painful process of deindustrialization and economic adjustment (which would later be known as "neoliberalism") experienced by working-class communities in Britain and the United States beginning in the 1970s and intensifying in the 1980s. Some of the bands, particularly Def Leppard, played up their sexuality and conspicuous consumption in their image and music videos—a trend that was followed by many rappers as well—starting a trend that would become central to the popularity of 1980s glam or hair metal, much to the chagrin of parents and religious conservatives around the globe.

The emerging neoliberal order in which metal developed weakened the power of workers, as manufacturing jobs moved, first, out of urban centers, and then to less expensive Third World countries. With the decline of the working class came a fraying of the postwar welfare state more broadly, which increased the saliency of powerful and angry styles of music such as heavy metal, punk, or gangsta rap. The same phenomenon would be repeated in the Middle East and North Africa in the 1980s—where the working class was in a much weaker position to begin with— at the very moment heavy metal arrived in the region, in the guise of structural adjustment programs that countries across the region were forced to adopt in order to receive loans or development assistance from the International Monetary Fund and World Bank.

At the same time as we recognize its political context, it is important to consider that heavy metal is very much a global phenomenon, far more so, in fact, than the political or economic integration normally focused on by policy-makers and commentators. Indeed, it was among the first "globalized" art forms, spreading from the United States and Western Europe across the then Soviet Bloc and Third World during the 1980s and 1990s as a harbinger of the defining role culture, and especially cross-cultural communication and integration would assume, in the dynamics of postCold War globalization (see LeVine, 2005, pp. 81-210). It is indeed, across the Global South and particularly in the Muslim world that heavy metal retains its greatest social and political relevance, and, in good measure because of this, has its most precarious existence.

It is in this context, as a response to economic distress and political oppression, that heavy metal became so popular globally, particularly outside the West. Like rap music, it became a symbol—or better, sound—of resistance to political and cultural systems from which the music's fans feel estranged or marginalized. As Timothy Ryback explained in his seminal 1990 exploration of the phenomenon, *Rock around the Bloc*, hard rock, metal, and punk became popular among young people behind the Iron Curtain soon after their emergence in the West. In the absence of other outlets for expressing discontent, many young people in socialist countries used the music to articulate otherwise inexpressible, intense emotions related to life under these systems (Ryback, 1990).

Hence it is not surprising that across the Middle East and North Africa the most popular forms of metal have been its more extreme genres: death, black, goth, doom, grind, grind-core, progressive, and nu metal, a hybrid subgenre of metal that combines elements of funk, hip-hop, hardcore, and more traditional metal. Uniting all these genres is the military style discipline necessary to play them correctly at super fast tempos, and the violent, war-laden themes that dominate their lyrics (Kahn-Harris, 2007). As one Israeli black metal artist described how musicians approach playing black metal, "You play it like you're a warrior" (quoted in Kahn-Harris, 2007, p. 38) Many bands, most notably Iron Maiden, designed their album covers and stage shows around the warrior image, although their warriors looked more like orcs from *The Lord of the Rings*, in order to emphasize the essentially corrupt and evil nature of warfare, regardless of the presumed justice of each side's claims. Indeed, with the exception of Satanic metal and some styles of Scandinavian extreme metal more broadly, most of the violence in heavy metal has been depicted as part of a critique of the violence of society at large, especially its warlike propensities. If one listens to the classic early metal albums by Black Sabbath and other bands, their songs could be quite political, as epitomized by Black Sabbath songs like "Lord of This World" and "War Pigs," which offered one of the most trenchant critiques of the Vietnam-era military industrial complex ever recorded.

## "It's Like Walking without Legs": The Aesthetic Dialectic of Heavy Metal in the Muslim World

It is easy to become over enthusiastic about the power of music to change society on its own. A more accurate description of music's role in struggles for social change is that music, and especially underground genres of popular music, are avatars of change or struggles for greater social and political openness. They point out cracks in the façade of conformity that is crucial to keeping authoritarian or hierarchical and inegalitarian political systems in power. That is certainly the role that heavy metal, punk, and hardcore rap played in their early days, before their increasing mainstream success led to their increasing corporatization and depoliticization.

Some forms of music, such as the great American folk tradition epitomized by singers like Pete Seeger, Joan Baez, and Bob Dylan, are specifically geared toward protest, even when the lyrics are not overtly political. For their part, early metal classics like Sabbath's "War Pigs," Iron Maiden's "Run to the Hills," punk classics like the Sex Pistols' "God Save the Queen" and The Clash's *Sandinista!* album, or early hip-hop and later gangsta rap classics such as "The Message," "F**k da Police," and "Cop Killer" all carried political messages or allusions, although some were diluted by the focus on sex, drugs, and alcohol that characterized the emerging mainstream metal and rap scenes

The hyper-hedonistic forms of heavy metal and hip-hop never became as popular in the Muslim world as they did in the United States. This is no doubt in good measure because such a sensibility is so at odds with normative morality and practice in Islamic countries. But equally important, from the standpoint of the artists involved in those genres, is, in the words of one artist, that "guns and bitches and hos don't mean anything to us. It's not part of our environment" (author interview with rapper, name withheld upon his request, Tehran, 2007). Rather, it was the intensity and ominous musical aesthetic of extreme metal and gangsta rap, and political inflections of many of the most important exemplars of both genres, that seemed relevant to their own experiences. Bands like Metallica, Slayer, Deicide, Cannibal Corpse, Possessed, Angel, Machine Head, Lamb of God, Kreator, Testament, and other extreme metal groups captured the ears and imaginations of young people in the region precisely because they offered a cathartic response to, and even critique of, the corruption-plagued, authoritarian regimes under which they lived. But these experiences have never been uniform, and remain very diverse—musically no less than religiously and politically.

Like other forms of popular music, heavy metal exists in very divergent forms in the countries of the Middle East and North Africa. Yet whatever the sonic and political differences most scenes emerged in the latter half of the 1980s and early 1990s as products of the spread of satellite television, the increasing ease of international travel, and the circulation of underground records and tapes. The music also arrived at the moment that the so-called "youth bulge"—the explosion in the number of young people as a percentage of the population of most Muslim countries—became noticeable across the region, presenting new challenges to political and religious leaders, and to the patriarchal structures of the societies more broadly. So it is not surprising that from the start, metal faced attacks from governments, often spurred on by conservative religious forces. It was not merely the harshness and distortion of the music; equally offensive were the harsh, often "brutal" vocal styles, and lyrics that scoffed at accepted authority, often including religion. At the same time, the music provided an alternative to both the dominant "traditional" forms of Arab music and the hyper-commercialized form of Arab pop music that still dominates the region's radio and video channels (Kahn-Harris, 2008; LeVine, 2008).

The youth bulge, in which people under 18 years of age make up 60 percent of most societies, has produced a disproportionately large generation of young people who are facing economic conditions even worse than those endured by their counterparts in the United States or Britain a generation or two ago. Their inability to integrate quickly into adult norms—work, early marriage, and children—leads to improper socialization into what their elders consider properly Islamic values. This makes them particularly amenable (critics would say "vulnerable") to global influences beyond the control of state, society, and religion. The frustrations this situation produces are compounded by the authoritarian regimes under which they live, and by the continued perception of Western/American power over their societies. Together these factors have encouraged, on the one hand, the closed, hostile, and sometimes violent identities characterizing extreme religious movements in the region (LeVine, 2005), and on, the other, the much more positive, if equally angry, array of identities among metalheads. Precisely because of their potential to be "competition" for radical movements for the attention and allegiance of young people (Salman Ahmad, personal interview, Los Angeles, August, 2007), metal's global reputation for being associated with sex, drugs, and even Satanism inevitably led it to be seen as a threat to the already fragile connection of young people in the region to their religion and patriarchal cultures.

And so, beginning in 1997 and continuing through to the present day, this dynamic led governments, first in Egypt and continuing to Lebanon, Iran, and Morocco, to arrest, try, and jail members of their respective country's metal scenes (14 were arrested and convicted in Morocco, well over 100 in Egypt) on charges of Satanism and harming Islam (for details, see LeVine, 2008). The response of the scenes—from being crushed in Egypt to fighting back, organizing protests, and forcing the government to overturn their convictions in Morocco—reveals much about the relative balance of power between governments and potential opposition forces in their countries.

The growing number of female metalheads, many of whom see no contradiction in headbanging next to their male peers at metal shows wearing headscarves and even joining bands, are particularly threatening because they offer a clear alternative, and even an antidote to, the "traditional" roles assigned to women in Arab/Muslim societies. More broadly, young metalheads of both genders are a reminder of the threat of losing an entire generation to Western-dominated globalization, and the supposed social deviance and perversion it brings with it (personal interview with al-Zubaidi, Beirut, 2006).

Despite setbacks and repression, however, in the last two decades heavy metal has become increasingly popular in the Muslim world. One reason for the resilience of the metal scenes is that in many ways they mirror the kinds of practices and "rituals" of the scenes' primary antagonists (at least on paper)—conservatively religious young people who inhabit what is ostensibly the opposite cultural poles in their societies. As one young Shi'i cleric from Baghdad explained to me:

"I don't like heavy metal. Not because it's irreligious or against Islam; but because I prefer other styles of music. But you know what? When we get together and pray loudly, with the drums beating fiercely, chanting and pumping our arms in their air, we're doing heavy metal too" (interview with author, Messina, Sicily, June, 2005). It is precisely because heavy metal addresses similar psychological and even political needs as supposedly "extreme" religion that it attracts the attention of governments, whose responses have ranged from repression to co-optation—with the former dominating official policies until the last few years, when a more liberal version of "repressive tolerance" began to take hold (Freemuse, 2005). One of the main strategies has been to keep the artists divided from religious forces by playing each side off the other. This has worked well in the past, as the "Satanic metal affairs" of the 1990s and early 2000s demonstrated across the region. But then it was the metalheads who were sacrificed at the altar of religion, while today many governments are showing more lenience toward metal scenes while cracking down harder on Islamist and other more overtly political movements.

However powerful, censorship has not succeeded in stifling musical production or circulation. In particular, with the arrival of mass production and distribution technologies such as CDs, and more recently the internet, it has become impossible to stop the dissemination of music, regardless of its content. Indeed, in a 2005 conference sponsored by Freemuse on music censorship in the Arab/Muslim world, artists generally described official government censorship as meaningless in practical terms, other than helping raise their profile or street *caché* (much as has occurred with the "explicit lyrics" sticker in the United States). Even religious forces were felt to be less of a threat in the majority of countries (excluding Iran, Pakistan, and Afghanistan) than they had been in the past. What was most feared, however, was the burgeoning private Arab media sphere, which is dominated by companies such as the conglomerate Rotana, the largest entertainment company in the Arab world, owned by a senior Saudi prince. What makes them so frightening is their ability to control the recording and distribution of music, giving them a more effective ability to limit the commercial circulation of music, or even censor it, than most governments (Freemuse, 2005; LeVine, 2008).

Arab digital music gateway Rotana might present a problem for pop singers and commercial groups, but for the underground metal scenes, its power is largely irrelevant as metal and rock more broadly don't sell enough to be on Rotana's radar and they have their own, autonomous internet-based circulation/distribution networks. But there is a big difference between having the ability to produce and circulate recorded music, either privately or through the internet and gray markets, and having the ability to perform that music publicly and exist as an underground or subculture of artists and fans in the public arena. In fact, for most artists I've encountered, it is the difficulties of performing live that have been the hardest to cope with as artists. Being a band that can't play live is "like trying to walk without legs" is how one Iranian musician described it, a sentiment shared by his peers in most every country I've studied.

Indeed, however hard their image and sound, in Iran the government has gone after metal artists and fans for being "velvet revolutionaries." The evocation of the Czech Velvet Revolution is especially apt since many of the key forces behind it came out of the country's rock scene—most recently as part of a massive crackdown in response to unprecedented protests against the allegedly fraudulent re-election of Mahmoud Ahmadinejad in June, 2009. The government clearly knows well how threatening a culturally grounded rebellion against the political status quo can be; the central role of musicians and artists more broadly in the "Reformasi" movement that toppled the Suharto dictatorship in Indonesia demonstrates this all too well. To the extent that bands or fans continue to support the metal scenes despite suffering political oppression and/or social ostracism demonstrates both the perseverance of the musicians and fans and the ability of governments and others to co-opt and depoliticize them. With these dynamics in mind, the experience of heavy metal in the Muslim world provides important clues to understanding the dynamics of repression, resistance, democratization, and negotiation between governments and young people in these regions today. In particular, it helps uncover how governments practice, and young people resist, policies of "repressive tolerance"—as the twentieth-century German philosopher Herbert Marcuse described it—through which governments and corporations attempt to maintain political or cultural-economic control over young people across the region.

## Subculture, Counterculture, or Something More?

However subterranean, the political implications of the metal scenes in the Middle East and North Africa raise the question of how best to describe them sociologically. We might be tempted to consider them the latest iteration in a long line of youth subcultures that first emerged in the post-World War II era, most famously in the UK and the United States, and that have been defined by their opposition to the cultural and behavioral norms of their larger societies. But the metal scenes in the countries I have studied are quite different from most classic subcultures in several important ways.

First, while the metal scenes emerged in response to changes in global capitalism and the rise of neoliberalism, they differ from earlier, Euro-American scenes in that they are not centered around, nor do they arise from, attempts (even subconsciously) to resolve some inherent contradiction(s) within the capitalist culture of the "parent" society. In the largely working-class subcultures of 1950s-70s (bikers, "surfies," mods, teds, punks), this was accomplished primarily through leisure-based, commodified consumption (Hebdidge, 1979; Gelder and Thornton, 1997). Such a focus made sense in postwar democracies undergoing a profound shift toward a consumer society, but they aren't the first order of business in the metal scenes located in *fin de millénaire* authoritarian societies of the Muslim world, precisely because they continue to exist largely outside the circuits of commodified cultural production and circulation.

Another characteristic of many of the first generation of largely white postwar subcultures has been the tendency to appropriate the cultural markers or practices of postcolonial minority groups (e.g., Jamaicans in the UK), often while excluding members of those groups from the subculture. Quite the opposite is the case in the metal scenes, as the cultural markers at the heart of their music are identifiably Western, while they remain open to anyone who respects the music.

Third, while most subcultures seek to articulate unique identities through differentiating themselves from the dominant society (visually through their look, fashion or movement, aurally through the sound of their music or unique vocabulary and grammar), most members of metal scenes in the Muslim world I have encountered do not seek to be recognized as essentially "different" from their larger society, even as their looks, dress, and music ostensibly mark them so. Instead, they consider themselves—or would like to be considered—as "good" Moroccans, Egyptians, or more broadly, Muslims; their hope is for greater acceptance, or at least tolerance, from their compatriots. (Perhaps the one case where metalheads articulate an identity specifically opposed to conservative Islam is in officially secular Turkey [Hecker, 2011].)

While in some countries, such as Morocco, Egypt, Lebanon, and Turkey, one sees growing acceptance, or at least a *laissez-faire* attitude for the time being, toward metalheads, that level of mainstream acceptance has not reached the point of commodification of defining elements of their aesthetic production or style; this is due to both the still strong normative cultural barriers against the music and, as important, the little chance of local or international capital making a profit from commodifying their style or sonic markers. Unlike the hippie, hip-hop, or punk looks and sounds, which were commodified, adopted by society at large, and in the process politically defanged almost as soon as they were created, the lack of circulation within a commodity field has helped prevent the co-optation or domestication of the Middle Eastern scenes through their transformation into safe, if exotic spectacles or objects of consumption or other forms of depoliticized mimicry.

A final difference between the classic subcultural scenes and those under discussion here is that while classic subcultures such as punks, mods, or more recently hip-hoppers have been characterized by their attempts to carve out public spaces where they could gather and perform their culture, the struggles over public space, and the public sphere more broadly, have been far more intense and consequential in the largely authoritarian societies of the Middle East and North Africa. To wit, if punks or hip-hoppers have used "spectacular" or outrageous dress, hairstyles, or behavior to call attention to themselves, and in so doing challenge or even provoke the more conservative members of their society, most Middle Eastern metalheads have faced significant harassment and even violence merely for walking down the street with long hair or wearing rock T-shirts.

For the majority of members of these scenes, the primary goal is to be left alone while moving through the streets and other public spaces.

At the same time, however, the prohibitions on live performance in most countries (at least until the last few years when some but not all countries have begun to allow them in certain circumstances) have made the creation of autonomous public spaces—that is, the conversion of space into "place"—among the single most important and politically charged goals of these groups (LeVine, 2008). Most metalheads may not want to provoke other members of their societies, but they are willing to fight to secure some public space to perform, and thus feel whole as musicians, fans, and human beings.

Clearly the metal scenes in the Muslim world are more than mere subcultures. But do they rise to the level of countercultures? That is, do their values not merely oppose those of the dominant group but directly challenge the political and economic structure and strive toward a social revolution—a cultural equivalent to more purely political opposition movements (see Roszak, 1995; Frank, 1998; Heath and Potter, 2004)? This cannot be answered in one way, as there is a great variety in the political impact of the scenes across the Muslim world. To be sure, most scenes are too small and too weak to imagine bringing about such a social or political transformation on their own. Rather autonomy is the goal; to be left alone.

On the other hand, in Morocco and Indonesia metal scenes have had a much more directly political impact. In the former country, the protests organized by the scene that led to the overturning of convictions of 14 musicians and fans led to much greater social and governmental acceptance of the scene (even the country's main religious opposition movement, the Justice and Spirituality Association, has adopted a live and let live attitude toward the scene), many of whose members are actively involved in human rights and other forms of activism. As previously mentioned, in Indonesia, metal and rock musicians followed a path even closer to that of the original Velvet Revolutionaries, participating in large numbers in the democracy protests that ultimately toppled the Suharto regime and brought democracy to their country.

In some ways, then, the more activist metal scenes described above fit the typology of countercultural movements. Another important similarity has to do with the concept of "authenticity." In an age where "reality TV," "virtual reality," and hyper-commodified consumption has blurred the line between substance and ephemera, "authenticity"—being "real"—has become the new counterculture. Even in the 1960s there was a strong awareness by those most deeply embedded in the counterculture that its aura was being siphoned off and commodified by corporations, and then sold to mainstream America as an "inauthentic" approximation of the true hippie ethic and aesthetic (Frank, 1998). Perhaps because of that seminal experience, studies of subcultures have tended to focus primarily on their early period of aesthetic (visual, aural, fashion) development as the only authentic iterations—not surprisingly since in most cases, as the subcultures spread they became diluted and went mainstream, losing their subcultural character.

Indeed, the metalheads I have encountered seem less like the hippies, who were in good measure co-opted from the start by their corporate cousins, and more like the era's often religiously grounded New Left activists, who hoped to "recover a sense of personal wholeness by healing the wounds of society" (Rossinow, 1998, p. 113), and for whom a passion for authenticity led them to have greater compassion for and solidarity with others and even to work toward creating more humane social institutions in their countries (Rossinow, 1998). Perhaps it is not surprising that many of the most devoted metalheads are quite religious. As one Egyptian metalhead, the son of long-jailed presidential candidate Ayman Nour, put it to me, "Friday is my favorite day of the week because I spend three hours at the mosque for juma' prayers and then go play black metal for four hours" (interview, Cairo, December, 2006).

## Heavy Metal: World Music's Most Immanent Art Form?

Heavy metal in the Middle East and North Africa can be viewed as offering a potentially profound immanent critique of the dominant (and often at least partially hegemonic) social and political discourses in the societies in which its fans and artists live. The critique reflected in the music of artists across the region, as well as in the larger style and behavior in the scenes exposes the way the realities of life in their societies conflict not merely with the supposedly "transcendent," ahistorical, and universal rationality that many Islamist and leftist critics in the region argue is being imposed by the West, but rather with their own stated norms and ideologies surrounding how to achieve a healthy and just society where, according to Islamic law, the good can be "enjoined" and evil "prohibited" (Salvatore and LeVine, 2005).

Hegel points out that such a journey of discovery is in fact a "pathway of doubt, or more precisely as the way of despair" ([1807] 1977, section 78); not surprisingly, this is precisely the feel of the road charted by the forms of extreme metal preferred by most metalheads in the Muslim world. Moreover, such a negative sentiment arises, as Adorno and Horkheimer argue, with the realization that "mankind, instead of entering into a truly human condition, is sinking into a new kind of barbarism" (2002, p. xi). This sentiment is shared by most metalheads, who see the actions of the dominant political, economic, and religious/cultural forces in their societies as inevitably producing a "suffocating hatred" that chokes anything positive out of society and culture (founder of Egyptian death metal group Hate Suffocation, explaining the origin of the name, author interview, Cairo, December, 2006).

Like many other cultural critics, including Adorno, the metalheads at the forefront of the scenes I have explored are "not happy with civilization"; and that is reflected in the music and their larger attitudes toward life. They see their countries as "schizo," or hopelessly confused in terms of which identities to choose, and they see themselves as having mental problems brought on by the knowledge of just how screwed up their world is. As the Egyptian band Beyond East sings in its "Beyond the East" song: "I threw a glance in the haze, beyond the east/ Where dead men would walk and live beyond oblivion ... These are molested days ... Denial what keeps the breath/ Blindness ... Remedy of reason/ Madness ... murder of pain."

Instead, when one listens to the music—particularly when it "has legs"—that is, is performed live in front of welcoming fans—it becomes clear that the metal scenes in the Muslim world, like the early punk, hardcore, and rap scenes before them, are not just musical performances, or more critically, "performance art," but equally "performance philosophy." If Adorno argues in his seminal *Negative Dialectics* that the task of immanent critique is to "reliquify" "congealed" ideological thought, "its validity traced, in repetition" (1983b, p. 97), one can feel the best extreme metal songs attempting by force of the blast beats, guitar armies, and brutal screams to uncongeal, or at least shake up, their seemingly frozen political and social systems (and here the similarity in both affect and impact between metal and ancient but still existing *zar* ceremony, a type of cathartic or exorcistic ceremony that exists in most Middle Eastern and North African cultures, is striking).

It might be difficult to imagine Theodor Adorno strategizing about the best way to critique globalized consumer society and the repressive tolerance that governs it with a long-haired, Cannibal Corpse T-shirt-wearing Egyptian metalhead. After all, in his view any style of music outside the European classical tradition and the most sophisticated representatives of its (then) contemporary avant-garde was parasitically incorporated into the culture industry and little more than a "capitulat[ion to] barbarism" (Adorno, 1983a, p. 127). But whether he would accept it or not, the genre's self-reflexivity and willingness to critique society by its own referents makes it a legitimate heir of the tradition of critical engagement that defined Adorno's oeuvre, and that of his Frankfurt School colleagues. Indeed, there are few happy endings or "spurious harmonies" in the music put out by serious metal musicians I have encountered across the Muslim world. Instead, their art moves far from "mere" diversion or entertainment toward a living embodiment of the type of aesthetic politics that Adorno tried hard (perhaps vainly) to remind the rest of us that the best music must possess.

As Adorno would have wanted, the artists in these metal scenes see their music as illuminating the "absurd, blindly violent element of the system" (2002, p. 158)—whether it's the global system, the regional system, the local/national system, or the religious/cultural system from which many feel ostracized or estranged but which they refuse to abandon. For them and him, music is understood as having the capacity, and function, of expressing "modernity's highest order of truth": the "truths behind reality's masks"—the mask of neocolonialism, neoliberalism, neopatriarchy and the violence of late capitalism that sustain all three (Adorno, 2002, pp. 96-97, 101; Smith, 2006). And they, like him, understand that the two worst ways to confront that violence are, on the one hand, to suffuse their critique with such an "extreme consciousness of doom" that it threatens to "degenerate into idle chatter," or, on the other, to enter the full chain of commodified cultural production, and in so doing "collaborat[e] with culture as its salaried and honoured nuisance" (Adorno, 1983a, p. 34; Adorno and Tiedemann, 2003, p. 147).

The violence and its underlying truth is perhaps best revealed in the song and video for "Baptize," by the Iranian group Arthimoth. The baptism here is into the mind-numbing and soul-deadening conformity of the official culture and ideology of the Islamic republic. As the band meticulously plays through several complex, rapid fire guitar-bass melodies over blast-beats, the video[2] shows a young man being tied to a chair and his skull being sawn open in what looks like the laboratory from an old horror film. At this point electrodes are placed on his brain and someone shouts repeatedly into his ear. Ultimately, after a mouse has nibbled at his brain, the top of his skull is sewn back on and he stumbles out of the frame into the darkness, as a "good Iranian."

Given the level of atonality in the song, there is the chance that Adorno might have appreciated the intense level of musicianship and the skill with which the message is delivered. At least he would have recognized the sense of "moral obligation to reflect the truth" of the conditions in which the band, like others I've encountered, are living (Witkin, 1998, pp. 3-5). If he observed the Iranian scene more broadly, or those in surrounding countries, it would be clear to him that it is not reducible to a mere stylistic choice or a profit motive (in fact, the police arrested the band members and video production team as it was being edited. Only by luck did they miss one copy, which was put on YouTube as soon as they were released from custody). He would see that like him, most of the members of these scenes instinctively despise corporatized and/or normalized mass culture and its effect on their societies (see Adorno, 1983a, pp. 31-3; Helmling, 2005).

Perhaps most important, even if he didn't fancy the music, he would have to appreciate how the artists attempt to navigate the almost invisible line separating commodified music that submits to the culture industry and serious music that reveals some of society's most basic, but normally veiled contradictions. "We play heavy metal because our lives are heavy metal" is how one of the founders of the Moroccan scene described his motivations to me (interview with author, Sicily, June, 2005; see LeVine, 2008, ch. 1; Witkin, 1998, p. 179). And to this day his music remains informed both by a serious critique of the larger cultures he inhabits, and by the desire to record and perform it in front of the largest possible audiences.

The various levels at which the metal scenes I've discussed operate clearly define them as a phenomenon and even an epitome of globalization in its broadest, cultural sense. Yet despite such a pedigree, heavy metal has yet to be considered a legitimate form of "world music" by most scholars of the genre or professionals in the industry (as I write these lines, the 2009 WOMEX, or "World Music Expo" is

---

[2]    Available on YouTube: http://www.youtube.com/watch?v=qNav2lzd-TQ, accessed April 7, 2011.

taking place in nearby Copenhagen, and once again heavy metal is almost entirely absent from the expo).

One could understand why when the concept was first introduced in the 1980s, before metal's global spread was understood, it would have been largely ignored. At that point, industry executives, looking for a better way to market their music, developed and deployed the term "world music" to describe music that "comes from elsewhere but [is] sold as a familiar package" (Frith, 2000, p. 306). More broadly, the genre came to define commercially available music of non-Western origin and circulation, or the music of dominated ethnic minorities within the Western world. As it developed, the most popular exemplars of the genre often blended so-called "traditional" indigenous and Western styles, tonalities, rhythms, and instrumentation (Frith, 2000, p. 305). Specifically, ever since the huge success of Paul Simon's 1986 *Graceland* album, featuring his (much criticized in some quarters) collaborations with South African and other nonwhite American rock artists, world music has been defined by the conscious blending of and hybridity between styles associated with different cultures, creating an aesthetic and sonic "creolization" that is very much part of the larger processes of deterritorialization and disembedding that are at the core of contemporary globalization. Indeed, we could perhaps label the musical process involved as "post-hybrid." By post-hybrid I mean a deeper hybridity, one that moves beyond the surface hybridities of more commercialized cultural and sonic intermixings, and in so doing addresses the core concerns of critics such as Spivak, who argue that when all the talk of hybridity makes everything seem hybrid, the underlying imbalances of power that shape so many processes of hybridization (imperialism, capitalism, etc.) are lost from view (Hutnyk, 1998, pp. 412-13). Not only does the hybridity of the metal scenes in the Middle East not lose the centrality of imbalanced power that shapes them—indeed, that is one of the most important generators of the music—but it is precisely in the groups and scenes where critiques of power and its abuses are most present that the sonic hybridity is more innovative and revealing of new identities that transcend, or move "beyond," both East and West toward something more holistic and positive (Ascherson, 2004; LeVine, 2008, pp. 253-76; Pieterse, 2009, pp. 87-9).

This dynamic can be seen in the rise across the Muslim world of new syntheses of various genres of metal and indigenous musical styles, instrumentation, and tonalities, much of them covered by the rubric "oriental death metal." Such post-hybridities in fact betray what could be termed (chronologically speaking) a "pre-hybridity" at the core of the music's history, returning to the medieval era across the Muslim world when in places such as al-Andalus Muslim, Christian, and Jewish musicians regularly interacted and performed together, in the process helping to create a diverse body of musical styles, from Jewish liturgical music to baroque, and later rock 'n' roll, that still bear their stamp for those who know how to listen properly.

That the universally acknowledged founders of this genre are the Israeli (Jewish) metal band Orphaned Land, whose fan base in the Muslim world is strong enough that fans from countries like Saudi Arabia and Jordan have had the band's logo tattooed onto their body, reveals how powerful and creatively destructive of old, religiously, nationally, and ethnically exclusivist identities and discourses the music has become. Adopting the terminology deployed by the ethnomusicologist Steven Feld, we can describe oriental death metal as a move away from the kind of "schizophonia" characteristic of much modern music, which splits sounds from their sources and brings them together in a deterritorialized synthetic landscape (usually through the process of sampling and other production techniques), and towards the more positive form of schismogenesis, which is a more regenerative interaction between various styles that produces truly new, hybrid forms of music in which the resulting whole is greater than some of the constituent stylistic elements (1994, pp. 263-74).

Of course, all music is the product of constant movement and innovation, even—especially—the most traditional (Frith, 2000, p. 311). Walter Benjamin understood this well when he explained that "the uniqueness of a work of art is inseparable from its being imbedded in the fabric of tradition" (1936, Section IV). Two very different experiences from musicians two generations removed support this notion. The first was relayed to me by the lead singer of the pioneering Turkish rock band Moğollar, founded in the late 1960s, who while talking backstage at a festival at which we were both performing, pointed to the band on the stage whose blending of Middle Eastern and rock elements I'd just complimented, and said, "You think mixing Eastern instruments over rock grooves is new? We were doing that forty years ago ... That's how long globalization has been going on. But the key for us is that we never just copied the West. It was always us taking what we heard to a new level. That's why we still can play in front of 20,000 people after all this time" (quoted in LeVine, 2008, p. 265).

The second quote comes from a young Egyptian extreme metal singer from the band Beyond East, who had brought me to the desert behind the Pyramids in Giza to show me where he'd first "screamed brutally" in exhilaration after outrunning the police who were chasing him because of his obvious metal attire. When I asked him how American music influenced his own, he exclaimed with a combination of anger, sadness, and pride, "For you we are all riding camels, wearing *gelegiyas* ... and we are Pharaohs. Fuck off ... Step away. We know you, we love you. ... We love America and your music. But ... you get it?" As his voice trailed off he shrugged his shoulders, half in anger and half in despair. He didn't need to elaborate further, as his sentiment betrayed his deep fatigue from having spent his adolescence and adult life having to fight against both homegrown repression and an American-dominated global system that devalued him economically, culturally, ethnically, and religiously at every turn.

**The Rebirth of Rock's Aura**

I have already argued that these scenes can reasonably be considered aesthetic heirs to the critical philosophical tradition of the Frankfurt School. They also embody a reversal of one of the most important disruptions to aesthetic/cultural production brought on by the consumer culture studied by the school's most outstanding members. Specifically, the uncommodified, digitized reproduction and circulation of the music characteristic of these scenes reflects a return of the "aura" of authenticity whose loss is brought on by the process of capitalistically and technologically driven reproduction and circulation, as described (and lamented) by Benjamin in his seminal "The Work of Art in the Age of Mechanical Reproduction" (1936). This is a crucial development, for in so being these scenes can be understood as fulfilling a core requirement for challenging cultural—and through it, social and political—hegemony. What's more, the multifarious stylistic differences between scenes in different Muslim countries highlight the often overlooked nuances of difference within and between their respective cultures.

Indeed, today we have moved far beyond the "mechanical" in the reproduction and circulation of the music, and the industries upon which it depended. On the one hand, the digitalization of musical reproduction and circulation with the internet allows for an even more rapid deterritorialization and transmission, but this in turn makes the reembedding that much faster as well. At the same time, because it's hard to play it live and certainly almost impossible to make this music a commodity except for the most lucky, there is a real return to the aura lost a century ago. And because the scenes are so performative, in returning the aura the musicians are also returning the ritual to the music that Benjamin argues was lost with its mechanical reproduction and commodified circulation (the description he uses is "emancipation of the work of art from its parasitical dependence on ritual"; 1936, Section IV). The ritualistic nature of the heavy metal performance—as with most forms of music—accounts for why many artists and religious figures alike have commented on the resemblances between the "performance" of heavy metal in the Muslim world and religious rituals (LeVine, 2008).

In interviewing Bruce Dickinson, frontman for Iron Maiden (interview with author, Irvine, Calif., May, 2008), one of the most important heavy metal groups in rock history (and undoubtedly the most popular metal group in the Muslim world), I described my experience of seeing Iron Maiden at their first ever performance in the Arab world, at the 2007 Dubai Desert Rock Festival. It was one of the most powerful concerts of my life—twenty thousand screaming Arab/Muslim metalheads from all over the Muslim world, some of them in tears for much of the concert. The gathering of metalheads from so many Muslim countries led one of my friends, the founder of Hate Suffocation, to label the festival the "Mecca" of Middle Eastern metal. I asked Dickinson what he thought was behind that reaction and he replied that "Maiden fans are like a giant family. You can meet a fellow fan anywhere and it's like you're family." This is an especially apt description considering so many metalheads feel estranged from their actual families, never mind larger cultures.

The "familial" foundation of Iron Maidendom might seem ironic considering the imagery of the bands is suffused in extreme violence, with lyrics focusing on death, war, destruction, and even Satanic themes. But it brings to light one of the most interesting comments common among Middle Eastern metal fans. To paraphrase one Iranian fan: "You can't imagine how a music about death can affirm life" (interview with author, Tehran, April, 2007). This view highlights how metal fulfils one of the most interesting functions assigned by Adorno to immanent criticism: to engage in a "negative dialectical" maneuver that ultimately produces the positive synthesis, or hybrid, of identities described above. As Adorno predicted, under the conditions of late capitalism, the best art, and politically the most effective, so thoroughly works out its own internal contradictions that the hidden contradictions in society can no longer be ignored ([1970] 1997). This process is described by Adorno as a "negative dialectics"; that is, the first step in producing a critical yet positive alternative to the current culture industry and the dominant culture it serves. It is, as Adorno describes it, a postnational or multinational dialectics, i.e., a mode of thought capable of analyzing and decoding the world of post-Cold War, multinational capitalism. It is a "non-identity" (*Nicht-identitaet*) that offers a way forward toward a more holistic future.

What is crucial here is that this affirmative process moves beyond the easy hybridity that defines commercial world music, one that is based on schizophonia, toward the much greater level of feedback with the forms upon which the music is constructed, and a cumulative and regenerative interaction and reaction that produces the "schismogenesis" described above—a peculiarly productive process whose roots return all the way to the interaction between Jewish, Muslim, and Christian musicians in the medieval courts of the Mediterranean and Arabo-Persian worlds.

It is through this process that music reclaims its aura in the Benjaminian sense. If Benjamin felt the "work of art reproduced becomes the work of art designed for reproducibility" (1936, Section IV), the small, marginalized and subaltern context in which much of the metal in the Muslim world has been produced returns the immediacy and aura to it. In so doing, at least this form of music stops being the herald of a new stage in the organization of capitalism (through the repetitive mass production of all social relations), but rather a new challenge to it, if not a transcendence of it. And while Adorno might not have approved, in behaving thus the scenes described here, like other "do it yourself" underground music scenes, share many characteristics of Adorno's notion of critically engaged modern art as "social monads" ([1970] 1997) whose unavoidable internal tensions express the equally unavoidable conflicts within the larger social and historical processes from which they arise and to which they belong.

**Warriors in a Musical Jihad**

It is not surprising that as fascism rose to power across Europe and especially in Germany, Adorno and other members of the Frankfurt school began to despair of the possibility of achieving the kind of progressive societal change they'd been working toward through politics. In the place of directly political and economic critiques, Adorno came to believe that it was not politics, but art, and particularly music, through which the critic could "posit an 'otherwise' to the present" (2002, p. 70). In fact, Adorno never gave up his belief that contemporary society has the resources to alleviate the suffering it perpetuates. Because of this, his "negative" dialectical movements had a utopian reach, one that would involve the reconciliation between humans and nature and humans with each other (Adorno, 1983b, p. 11). One can see a similar optimism, however sober, in the fans and artists of the metal scenes of the Muslim world, who against numerous forces—the inheritance of colonialism, corruption, authoritarianism, and patriarchal control—are converting their musical communities into spaces where they can carve out a bit of autonomy, if not freedom from oppressive governments and cultures alike.

For Israeli oriental death metal pioneers Orphaned Land, Adorno's vision is reflected in their song "Ocean Land," where the unending intercommunal conflict that has plagued their homeland is resolved through a new flood. As lead singer Kobi Farhi sings:

> Tears do flow, yet can't conceal
> This land is barren, it does not feel
> Our self-made slaughter
> By our own hands
> Here lies the orphaned land ...
>
> Suddenly lightning strikes the earth
> It marks the sign of my rebirth
> Seeds of love from myself evolve
> This cannot be living—without (your) safety
>
> The rain keeps on falling
> Filling the dried land.
> It drinks the purity of life
> (The) land starts to grow.

The members of Orphaned Land have no illusions about their music changing the contours of the Israeli-Palestinian conflict, which is why they refrain from writing overtly political songs even though none of the members have completed their compulsory army service (something very few Israeli men don't do). Instead, they use their music to open the minds of their fans, and when a young fan emails them asking for advice on what do to about the army, they explain how they handled the situation.

A little over 100 km to the north, in Beirut, a new political party, Hezb al-Rock, was born out of the ashes of the 2006 Israel-Hezbollah war. The name plays on that of the much more popular and powerful movement turned political party Hezbollah. But where Hezbollah's iconic banner features a hand holding an

AK-47 thrust into the air from the calligraphy of the group's name, in Hezb al-Rock's banner the hand is holding a guitar (in fact, it's a B.C. Rich guitar, one of the iconic heavy metal guitars) while making the "metal horns" with the second and fifth finger.

From what I've heard from the party's small cadre of supporters, Hezbollah was not too happy about the obvious critique embedded in the name and artwork of its doppelgänger. But in Lebanon today there is enough space that even a party that directly challenges the core symbols of the country's most powerful—and potentially violent—political force can slowly pry open the public sphere to new ways of imagining Lebanon's future, and the region's. Across the Mediterranean, in Casablanca, metalheads who only half a decade ago were arrested or beaten for walking down the street in metal attire now move about freely in even more extreme goth outfits, including full make-up, and dance next to hijab-wearing teenage girls at metal festivals drawing more than 100,000 people.

Across the region, metalheads are acting, not merely as "immanent critics" of their cultures, but as "cultural physicians" (Ahern, 1995), trading—sometimes literally as in the case of doctor turned rock star Salman Ahmad of the Pakistani supergroup Junoon—stethoscopes for guitars in order better to reach, and in so doing, heal, the many political, social, and even spiritual ills of their societies. These young people are, as more than one musician has put it, warriors in a musical jihad, whose goal is to win greater acceptance for themselves while, if possible, helping to make their societies at large a little more open, tolerant, and perhaps even just.

It may not be the large-scale social revolution hoped for by generations of critics past, but it's a start, and reflects an organic collective of musicians and fans who, along with their music, clearly warrant the protections under the still evolving body of international human rights law. Most important, the rapidly evolving music and scenes are linking them in ever-widening networks with artists and fans worldwide, together with whom they are creating a "world" music that will be much harder to commodify or co-opt by those in economic and political power than its predecessors, in their countries or the global ecumene more broadly. If you close your eyes and open your ears, you can almost imagine Adorno and Gramsci headbanging along to the music.

Chapter 6

# The "Dangerous" Folksongs:
# The Neo-folklore Movement of
# Occupied Latvia in the 1980s

Valdis Muktupāvels

In Soviet-occupied Latvia in the late 1970s and 1980s, two different sociocultural currents existed in folk music. The first, folkish folklorism or staged folklorism, was formed as representative of Soviet cultural policy, and was officially supported and oriented toward the stage.[1] The other current, the neo-folklore movement, emerged spontaneously as a grassroots movement; balanced between recognition and nonrecognition, it focused on the individual and was aimed at the preservation and popularization of traditional culture.[2]

## Folklorism and Soviet Cultural Policy

The formation of folkish folklorism was to a large extent connected to Soviet cultural policy and especially to the amateur art or the so-called *samodejatel'nost'*. Broad masses of people were involved in artistic activity which was decided mainly by ideological slogans such as "art belongs to the people," and which was, in turn, realized at all levels of cultural life. The connection between this type of amateur art and the Soviet cultural administration after World War II is precisely characterized by Arnolds Klotiņš:

---

[1]  Folkish is taken from the German *volkstümlich*, which describes a sensibility characteristic of ordinary people, especially peasants of the past. In this chapter, the term "folklorism" refers to a totality of all different expressions of how traditional culture is interpreted in the context of modern culture.

[2]  The "Neo-folklore movement" is a term used in Latvia and other Baltic countries, specifically Estonia and Lithuania, to denote the sharp and extensive rise of interest in folklore traditions during the 1970s and 1980s. The term also describes practical forms of actualizing folklore in daily life and in the expressions of amateur art that accompanied the spiritual awakening of the people and their fight for the restoration of independence at the beginning of the 1990s.

With the help of an organised amateur arts movement, propaganda had the chance to influence even those people whom it could not reach via the systems of education, official employment or military service. Special departments for the coordination and control of the amateur arts functioned within the cultural institutions of the trade unions, which themselves were subject to municipalities, the state and the communist party. In order to attract new participants, special competitions and shows for amateurs learning different arts were organised. Participation in some kind of amateur group became almost compulsory to all who were not engaged in other social activities; at least, under certain conditions, this kind of involvement lifted the suspicion of being disloyal to the regime. (2002, p. 111)

Another ideological slogan defining socialist culture was "art is international by its contents and national by its form." This suggested the adoption and display of different elements of local culture, or so-called "national characteristics," which can be viewed as a request for formal "folkishness." Without the promotion of systematic in-depth studies in the field of folklore, a kind of superficial and consumer attitude toward traditional culture developed in the sphere of amateur art. Soviet ideology, which permitted only "progressive" (i.e., reflecting the class struggle) elements, also had a distinct impact on the practice of folklorism. Folkish ornaments in Stalinist architecture, stylized folk costumes in ideologized mass events, folkish motives in music, and glorifying the regime were formal elements with a local "smell" used in different forms of specialized arts and expressions of professional culture. In fact, this kind of folklorism was an instrument of ideological influence and with the aid of amateur art it was applied to broad masses of people. The goal of Soviet folkish folklorism was ideological influence, transformation, socialist indoctrination, and, of course, control of the people.

*Forms of Soviet-Era Folkish Folklorism*

Typical expressions of staged folklorism were folk dance ensembles, folk music instrument orchestras, and *kokles* ensembles (see Figure 6.1). The number of adults involved in folk dance ensembles at the beginning of the 1980s was more than 30,000, or about 1.3 percent of the population, and when including school children this number could be easily doubled. Additionally, the number of those participating in folk music instrument orchestras and *kokles* ensembles was more than 1,000. The singing of choral arrangements of folksongs was also practiced in amateur choirs and vocal ensembles. For the purpose of the representation of "folk culture" at festivals and other events, such as the decade of Latvian literature and art in Moscow in 1955, so-called ethnographic ensembles were organized. This type of ensemble presented live, continuous local forms of vocal or instrumental folk music, which were arranged and partly transformed under the auspices of professional culture activists, producers, and choreographers and subsequently performed on stage. On the one hand, members of an ethnographic ensemble were bearers of live local traditions, but on the other they could lead their activities only within the ideological framework set by the totalitarian system, and they had to glorify the kolkhoz system as well as express their joy about the happy life in the Soviet Union.

Figure 6.1    Latvian folk music instrument and folk dance ensemble Sakta at the end of the 1950s. Photographer unknown, from the personal collection of Elmārs Zemovičs

*The Birth of the Neo-folklore Movement in the Late 1970s*

Another current emerged in response to global cultural processes in the second half of the twentieth century. This was influenced by postmodernist, anti-industrialist, neopaganist, environmentalist, and feminist movements as well as by the folklore revival movement.[3] The latter emerged spontaneously as a more or less personally motivated approach to the heritage of traditional culture; typically its adherents focused on the study, preservation, and use of dialects, customs, and crafts, different forms of oral folklore and musical instruments, and they paid special attention to the most archaic forms of heritage. Constructing alternative models of living and thinking, the new movement existed in opposition to the majority opinion and thus it can be viewed as a counterculture. In the free world, this counterculture adapted more or less legal forms, whereas in the context of Eastern European totalitarian systems it preserved its informal status for a considerably longer period. The folklore revival movement of the 1970s-80s is also identified as a neo-folklore movement, thus recognizing its new approach toward the study, inheritance, and interpretation of folklore heritage. In its difference from previous

---

[3]    The main spheres of dissident Aesopian language in Soviet art were Baroque, Latin (and Western Christianity), Oriental (Far Eastern) mysticism, avant-garde and new wave folklorism. For more on this, see Brauns (2002).

forms of folklorism, the new movement was oriented not so much toward staged performances of folklore as toward the introduction of folklore into the personal sphere, making heritage a part of individual life. Therefore it was sometimes called "lifestyle folklorism," while informally the participants of this movement were named "folklorists."[4]

## The Different Expressions of the Neo-folklore Movement

Because totalitarian systems do not tolerate the existence of free, uncontrolled subsystems, the neo-folklore movement had to adopt legally permitted forms of social and artistic activity in Soviet-occupied Latvia. Hence only accepted forms of folkloric performance, a choral concert, a folk music instrument ensemble, or a folk dance ensemble, existed. Besides, the system of the so-called "culture houses" accommodated another part of folkloric activities such as amateur groups practicing different folk crafts like weaving, embroidery, and so on. Within the neo-folklore movement a new form—folklore ensembles or *kopa*—became established.[5] For administrative purposes, folklore ensembles were treated by official bodies as other amateur art units: they were placed in the same category as choirs, dance ensembles, and so on and they had to perform regularly on stage in a "culture house" which had a salaried artistic director. All public performances of the ensemble had to be organized in accordance with general norms regulating concert activity. Ensembles were required to have an approved concert time, place, and program, as well as a list of musical pieces, and any text spoken during the concert would have to be cleared too. The body approving such programs was the Folk Arts Centre, a structural unit within the Ministry of Culture, with its professional censors who strictly looked after ideological correctness. Nonetheless, the *kopas* more and more resembled clubs or groups of like-minded friends interested not so much in staged concerts as in informal activities aimed at the preservation of traditional culture. They were focused more on the collection, study, practice, and dissemination of "authentic" folklore materials such as songs, dances, instrumental music, and, above all, the seasonal and lifecycle traditions of peasant society. These members of folklore ensembles learned traditional crafts and made jewelry, dresses, belts, or musical instruments. As a rule, the *kopa* was open to people of different ages, sex, occupation, artistic potential, and education, in contrast to dance ensembles, where it was usual to have all members of the same size and age. Apart from performing on stage, groups usually arranged informal celebrations of still existing calendar festivities or revived extinct ones. They also served the local community in arranging wedding, baptism, or funeral ceremonies in traditional ways, or by adding certain traditional elements to existing forms.

---

[4]    For more on this, see Muktupāvels (2000, pp. 393-6).

[5]    The term *kopa* is a Latvian neologism for "ensemble," one specifically related to the neo-folklore movement.

Most importantly, they did all this through personal motivation, just for themselves or in a circle of friends or families; folkloric activities became part of their lifestyle and thinking.

One of the most influential folklore ensembles, from the late 1970s onward, was Skandinieki. Soon they were followed by smaller or bigger *kopas* all over Latvia: Senleja, Madonas Skandenieki, Savieši, Dandari, and others. Some folklorically significant events, such as the 125th anniversary of the composer and folk music collector Andrejs Jurjāns in 1981, or the 150th anniversary of the collector and classifier of folksong texts Krišjānis Barons in 1985, promoted the rise of dozens of new *kopas* everywhere, from villages to provincial towns, not to mention the capital.

*The Transformation of the Concert Situation*

Though folklore ensembles had to adjust their public activities to the norms of Soviet cultural life, often they successfully managed to evade or even ignore them. One such norm was connected to public artistic performance, which was usually treated as a concert. Yet folklorists tried to avoid by any means using the word "concert," replacing it with such words as *tikšanās* (meeting), *vakarēšana* (an evening with singing), *sadziedāšanās* (singing together), and *sadancošanās* (dancing together). At other times the specific name of the event, be it a seasonal or any other traditional celebration, was used, such as *apjumības* (harvest festivity), *bedības* (funeral celebration), and so on. Furthermore, members of folklore ensembles tried to avoid unnecessary scenic elaborations as much as possible. Instead they tried to be natural and to communicate informally with the audience and among themselves. So they called each other by name, spoke to their friends and acquaintances in the audience, shared their instant feelings and impressions, or expressed their remarks and opinions.

It was also important to diminish the distance between performers and audience. This could be done in different ways, notably by finding the proper disposition of the ensemble. Hence folklorists performed their activities not on the stage, but in front of an audience, on the same level as it were. It was quite usual for performers to stand in a circle, facing each other, but not the audience, thus accentuating the reality instead of the artistic conditionality of the performance. Often they tried to involve the audience either in singing or especially dancing, which was very effective. In such cases folklorists showed the basic steps and movements, started to dance themselves, and then invited all to dance. Note how the activities of one such folklore ensemble, Savieši, were characterized in the weekly *Dzimtenes Balss*, a Soviet official propaganda newspaper, aimed at émigré Latvians:[6] "Members of the *Savieši* ensemble do not make a concert in the usual

---

[6]     The intention of the newspaper was to depict Latvia as a free, uncontrolled and happy society, and certainly free of totalitarian influence. Therefore descriptions of different events were more or less transformed to fit the intention. Fortunately for propagandists, the

sense, they rather arrive as guests, involving the public in the performance and merging in one rhythm and tone" (Burgmeistere, 1982). Frequently the concert exceeded its time limit simply because the joint singing and dancing could go on and on. The situation was also used to appeal to all who were present to become active in the preservation and study of cultural heritage, to collect local songs, tales, stories, and beliefs, to make musical instruments and also to revive old customs. The more responsive listeners were eager to get involved in the folklore movement and sometimes a new local folklore ensemble emerged as a result. Ilga Reizniece, one of the very active folklorists of the early 1980s, remembers, "I had a feeling, that a concert is not enough, people want to do something themselves, they want some continuation" (Personal interview with author, February, 2006). As an alternative to public performances, informal private meetings, developing into house concerts, were also arranged (see Figure 6.2). A free, informal atmosphere could be experienced at such events, which was unusual in the case of public events. And quite naturally these events provided a space for the fusion of traditional music with free, meditative musical forms.

Figure 6.2    Informal house concert in Riga in 1982. Photo by Ilmārs Blumbergs

performances of folklore ensembles or other events within the neo-folklore movement had a free, informal spirit and thus could be described in the newspaper without significant "elaboration."

*Spontaneity, Creative Use of a Situation, Improvisation*

Rejecting concerts as a format for folkloric performance, folklorists tried to create various situations where songs, dances, and traditions would fit organically into modern contexts. Such situations included joint singing in public events or evening parties, or dancing and games in seasonal celebrations, or perhaps a house concert. Certain kinds of folklore were successfully included in social events such as folk crafts fairs. Sometimes, besides the "official" organized stage there was spontaneous singing in small groups, games or dancing, or humorous singing contests between craftsmen and visitors, and very soon all this became a traditional part of such events. In the face of the usual government practice of total control of cultural life in that period, all these small performances could not be foreseen, planned, and officially approved. They were in fact illegal and certainly not permitted from the point of view of the official system. Yet the totalitarian system was unable to cope with such situations, basically because of their spontaneity and frequency, and also because of their integration into common daily matters. However, in 1981 officials of the Ministry of Culture of the Latvian SSR were informed about the unofficial, not permitted, activities of folklore ensembles, and in some cases certain punitive measures were taken. Such a situation occurred when the folklore ensemble Savieši went on an unofficial trip to Lithuania, and together with their Lithuanian friends arranged a public celebration of the midsummer solstice. A secret informer reported this public event to the Ministry of Culture of the Latvian SSR. Consequently the whole event was treated by Ministry officials as an illegal performance and the ensemble was faced with the possibility of suspension of its activities should a similar case occur. Yet a year later, when the neo-folklore movement involved more and more people and its activities became less and less controllable, officials had to treat such cases with greater tolerance.

In contrast to the staged dance groups or choirs, who usually conducted their performance in accordance with the state approved program, folklore ensembles often experienced situations when a random impulse could divert the event in an unforeseen direction. For instance, honoring the wish of somebody in the audience, the ensemble could sing a song which was not in the program. An eager public response could cause an improvised singing contest between the ensemble and the audience or, say, the demonstration of a traditional custom could develop into a real celebration. The repertoire of the most talented and experienced folklorists was usually broad and varied enough to choose songs, games, dances, or other narratives for any situation or to choose the most fitting texts for the mood, season, or topic of the event. Such practices were recognized by folklorists as corresponding to the essence of traditional music and as a continuation of traditions, an advantage over the staged folklore groups with their characteristically rigid, unchangeable repertoire.

*Authenticity*

*The meaning of "authenticity" for folklorists* "Authenticity" became one of the conceptually most important and essential keywords of the neo-folklore movement. With the help of this almost magic word a clear line was drawn between the spheres of folkish folklorism and the movement. While the members of staged dance ensembles or folk music instrument ensembles based their artistic activity on folklore materials arranged by composers, choreographers, and other stage professionals, the activists of the neo-folklore movement focused on folksongs, dances, and customs from the living tradition. For the former a folksong or a folkdance was a mere source for a composition, artistic arrangement, or stylization; for the latter it was important to respect the style of the traditional singer, or, if field recordings or published materials were used, to reproduce them as close to the original as possible.

Members of staged folkish ensembles perceived all kinds of folklore texts as anonymous and/or part of an impersonal tradition, and they therefore used generalizing terms like "Latvian folksong" or "Latvian folkdance," and in concerts or in different kinds of promotional materials always mentioned the composer, arranger, or choreographer of the respective piece. They also ignored dialects and other local peculiarities or used them only for artistic expression or stylization. Folklorists, on the contrary, presented, whenever available, the name of the narrator, singer, or musician who had produced the original text and from whom it was recorded. Furthermore, in communication with the audience, folklorists also tried to introduce details about the song, dance, or fairy-tale such as when and where it was recorded. Whenever possible they also related interesting facts about the person from whom the recording was made, thus adding personal touches to the folklore text and thereby revealing something more about the personality of the creator or inheritor of this text.

Authenticity provided the neo-folklore movement with the dimension of age-old tradition and helped to create the feeling of a time and space that had existed before the Soviet and other occupations and which could be identified by everyone as their true, original, and rightful inheritance. In this way the criteria of authenticity were symbolic road signs pointing away from the Soviet reality of the 1980s. Such authenticity turned out to be unacceptable to the guardians of Soviet ideological space, who showed their dissatisfaction clearly in numerous publications and in personal communications. Thus, in an ideological campaign initiated by the KGB and aimed at the leader of the Savieši ensemble, one designed to illuminate his ideologically dangerous position and to provide ideological procurement, an article "Par avotu tīrību" (On the Purity of Sources) was published in the communist daily *Cīņa*, where a "leading folklore specialist," B. Dambrāns, sarcastically wrote:

> The efforts to celebrate "authentic" midsummer solstice according to "the most ancient traditions" and "on the hill of pagan idols" is a self-delusion, as one can

get to this hill by bus, not by walking with primitive leather shoes on … The illusory escape into the past is nothing but a refusal of the nation's rich history, it is self-denial, cowardice, denial of the problems of real life. (1984)

Concerning "denial of the problems of real life," the "leading folklore specialist" was right because denial of Soviet reality and all its problems was silently and unanimously accepted as the main task of the neo-folklore movement. As for "cowardice," this perhaps pertains more to the author of the article who chose not to reveal his real name.[7]

*The practice of the "open" voice*    Among the different components constituting an authentic performance style, the manner of singing emerged as particularly important. Choral arrangements of folksongs were sung by choirs and vocal groups accompanying staged dance ensembles in the style characteristic of professional choral art, and sometimes even the *belcanto* style of fine art music was employed. In contrast, folklore ensembles cultivated as different a manner of singing as possible. Without proper knowledge of the stylistics of traditional singing, this different singing manner was reduced to the use of "open voice," in contrast to choral "tempered" singing. Nevertheless, though it had a resemblance to the ethnographic singing manner, singing with the "open" voice realized its main function: it positioned the singers in a certain sociocultural segment. The main characteristics of this segment were archaic versus modern, simple and natural versus refined and artistic, challenging and active versus conformingly calm. This practice was characterized in rather negative terms in the newspaper *Cīņa* in 1985:

> The singing and performance manner of the ensemble is quite disputable. Perhaps to refute the view about our forefathers as reserved, quiet people, the members of *Skandinieki* ensemble behave provocatively freely, not shyly, sometimes even offensively. And such is their singing—always constantly loud. It is possible to listen to one song, and afterwards a terrible monotony is overwhelming. (Hausmanis, 1985)

It is clear that establishment officials would have been delighted if folklore had remained merely a subject of academic research and a source of inspiration for socialistic (indoctrinated and controlled) art, or a supporter of harmless and sentimental emotions.

*Traditional versus modernized musical instruments*    From the end of the 1940s, in folkish folklorism concert practice special "modernized" or "improved" instruments were introduced. By adapting the symphony orchestra paradigm, with its string, brass, woodwind, and percussion instrument sections, groups

---

[7]    There was no "leading folklore specialist" with the name B. Dambrāns at that time in Latvia.

were created from traditional instruments, with substantial modifications to their construction, tuning, and diapason. The new instruments were used to make either a folk music instrument orchestra or smaller ensembles. Rooted in the Russian *balalaika* and *domra* orchestra tradition of the end of the nineteenth century, this practice was considered an important cultural form in Soviet amateur art. Expressing folkishness, such a practice existed in all Soviet republics and was introduced into the occupied Baltic states (Vertkov et al., 1975, pp. 14-15). The best-known result of folk music instrument modernization in Latvia is the concert *kokle*, an instrument which was played not only in folk music instrument orchestras but in numerous *kokle* ensembles as well. The whole modernized *kokle* family—soprano, alto, tenor, and bass modifications—were constructed shortly after the end of World War II, in 1947.[8]

Instruction on the concert *kokle* became part of the curricula in music schools, music colleges, and the only folk music department then operating in Latvia. *Kokle* ensembles were organized in many provincial culture centers: they became an integral part of festive public and official occasions, including official Soviet celebrations of "the Great October Socialist Revolution," Soviet Army day, and so on. Such celebrations typically included the appearance of *kokle* players, dressed in stylized and uniform folk costumes together with elements that emphasized "folkishness"—long artificial braids, massive crowns, and other suitable accoutrements. An exaggerated seriousness, replete with ideology, meant that a rigid atmosphere dominated these events.

Distancing themselves from such institutionalized forms of folk music, participants of the neo-folklore movement strictly refrained from using modernized musical instruments. Instead they focused on traditional instruments, from the simplest reeds to bagpipes or zithers. In reviving these instruments all possible documented sources and living traditions were studied. In the event of there being insufficient local information, the necessary impetus for reviving these instruments could be found through turning to neighbors—Lithuanians, Estonians, or others. Thus, the lost tradition of birch bark playing was revived, thanks to some visiting German folklorists who taught musicians how to make and play bark instruments. Or, in the case of bagpipes, it was the Estonian revived piping tradition that provided impetus in Latvia.[9] Besides being played at public performances, these instruments were eagerly played at dance parties, different social events, calendar celebrations, and festivals, as well as just for self-enjoyment. In particular, traditional *kokles* with seven to 12 strings gained the broadest acceptance, whether played solo or as an accompaniment to singing, whereas violins, bagpipes, and drums constituted the core of a dance music group.

---

[8]   Other instruments—duct flutes, hornpipes, box-shaped fiddles—were "modernized" as well, but the result was not so successfully accepted in musical life.

[9]   For more on this, see Paterson (2005).

*Syncretism*

Participants of the neo-folklore movement intuitively felt the destructive aspect of the professional, art-based approach to traditional culture. Something of the kind had existed in the nineteenth century, when folklore was generally treated as a mere literary text, and the melody of a traditional song was treated as a mere musical text. As a counterweight to this, the idea of syncretism was eagerly accepted and circulated among folklorists in the 1980s. For them syncretism denoted the original coexistence and unity of text, music, movement, symbolic meaning, and functional context. Practically, folklorists took documented descriptions of calendar or lifecycle customs as the matrix and filled it with appropriate songs, games, dances, sayings, and music. Such restored customs were presented to an audience in a concert situation, or they could be included in real life, especially for the celebration of calendar festivities (see Figure 6.3).

Figure 6.3    Celebration of midsummer solstice by the Savieši ensemble and friends in 1983. Photo by Gunārs Janaitis

Folklorists did not feel it necessary in a concert situation to present calendar or lifecycle traditions in detail and usually the presence of any traditional event was marked symbolically. For example, instead of presenting all midsummer solstice customs in sequence, folklorists might incorporate only symbolic signs of midsummer solstice such as crowns made of flowers and herbs on their heads, just to mark the event. Additionally they would sing appropriate songs, share folk wisdom in the form of beliefs, and engage in plays and dances. This was different to the practices of the folkish staged dance groups, who also called on traditional customs—weddings, calendar celebrations, and so on—but only in order to create a plot or story, and subsequently during their performance to present this story. Hence, while folklorists tried to revive traditions and introduce them into their lives, members of the staged folkish ensembles perceived these traditions as artistic works from the past which were not modern and not worth paying attention to. Thus folklorists could grasp the humanistic dimension of traditional culture and continued to maintain the traditions.

## The Neo-folklore Movement as a Counterculture

The different expressions of the neo-folklore movement clearly identify it as a subculture. Though it was congruent with legally accepted cultural forms, the movement at the same time existed in opposition to folkish folklorism, which was significantly supported by the official cultural system. To a certain degree, then, the neo-folklore movement can be viewed as a counterculture. In support of this proposition some quite clearly formulated anti-Soviet positions can be discerned among folklorists alongside their focus on values of the pre-Soviet period, and, more generally, the propagation of views at odds with official ideology.

### *The Political Engagement of Tonality*

Expressing the optimism required by Zhdanov's[10] aesthetics meant totalitarian art had to be a kind of mobilizing agent of the working class, which was necessary for the implementation of the goals of the Communist Party; a poetical formulation of these goals—"towards new fights and new work victories, towards the dawn of communism"—was in circulation. Such an ambience significantly influenced the staged expressions of folkish folklorism, turning this kind of amateur art, just like so many others, into a tool of ideological manipulation. This is how the "new Soviet Latvian songs" were characterized by Marxists Roberts Pelše and Jānis Niedre, compilers of the "Latvian Soviet folklore" collection *Latviešu padomju folklora*:

> These are songs about the new, fresh and active Soviet reality. These are songs about the great leaders of the Soviet people, V.I. Lenin and J.V. Stalin, about the new socialist democracy. These are songs about our high culture … about the diverse and intense life of the new Soviet citizen, about the bright reality of socialist life. (1986, pp. 12-13)

---

[10]   Stalinist politician, developer of the Zhdanov Doctrine that governed Soviet cultural activities in the late 1940s and later.

To present this "bright reality" and to express the optimistic, mobilizing intonations, certain artistic methods were created and established in various spheres of amateur art. In the case of staged folkish dances, this practice is characterized by Arnolds Klotiņš: "The leaders of dance groups were instructed to incorporate into their choreographic folklore faster tempos, higher jumps, brilliant, never-fading smiles on the dancers' lips, etc." (2002, p. 112). Vigorous, artificially cheerful moods dominated both the vocal and the instrumental spheres of folkish music, and it is not surprising that the use of major tonality became established as a norm of its kind.

A different approach was established within the sphere of the neo-folklore movement, especially in its initial stages. In building their repertoires, members of folklore ensembles preferred the most archaic part of traditional music: recited songs. Predominantly, these songs are in neither a major key, nor a minor, while their emotional content is very limited and the scope in which they can express the mood of the singer or situation is insignificant. From this point of view, the singing of a folklore ensemble was neither optimistic nor vigorously mobilizing. Regarding other types of folksongs, there was a clear tendency to prefer melodies in minor tonality. This tendency was especially characteristic of music by small, meditation-oriented ensembles, such as Iļģi. Their album *Zemgales dziesmas*, recorded in 1986, has six songs, and all are in a minor key, or with dominating minor harmonies in the instrumental accompaniment. How such music was censored in that period is exemplified by how Roze Stiebra's animation film *Man vienai māsiņai*, based on folkloric motifs, was for a long time denied permission to be shown. The reason for this turned out to be the film's soundtrack, recorded by Iļģi, which made an impression upon ideological censors as being too sad and evoking a mood of contemplative ritualization; besides, the responsible producer, Jānis Brants, who was also in charge of ideological control, felt there was too much pessimism radiating from the film. In a further example, in 1981 the executive administrator of the Folk Arts Centre, Broņislavs Juškēvičs, clearly pointing out that sad, pessimistic moods are incompatible with Soviet reality, refused permission to some young musicians to perform certain songs, arguing that singing sad songs is inappropriate for a graduate of a Soviet university.

*Temperance and Vegetarianism*

A certain dose of idealism was characteristic of the neo-folklore movement, especially in its initial period. Particularly relevant here are attitudes toward alcohol. Heavy drinking habits in Soviet society and the resulting degradation were informally perceived as a consequence of Sovietization. Therefore, abstinence from alcohol was regarded as a form of otherness, or as a demonstration of one's individuality, which made the abstainers different from the main mass of Soviet people. A significant portion of folklorists accepted this position and used their folkloric activity to promote similar views. In this context, the song "Tādi vīri kungam tika" (The Master Likes Men), popularized in the early 1980s by Artis

Kumsārs, the leader of the Madonas Skandenieki ensemble, should be examined. A translation of the song goes: "The master likes men who drink beer and brandy. Now all you scatterbrains, listen and obey, the overseer is happy! They drank away their land and their fathers' horses. Now all you scatterbrains, listen and obey, the overseer is happy!" The message contained in the song and in its performance was clear: by accepting common heavy drinking habits one is losing the spirit of resistance and protest. Not surprisingly, this song was eagerly picked up by folklorists as well as by a much larger audience and was sung on many different occasions.

Vegetarianism played a similar role to temperance: it demonstrated individuality and spiritual independence. Certain difficulties might arise, however, were someone to proclaim and publically promote ideas of vegetarianism. Though vegetarianism could point toward a healthy, natural lifestyle, its practice raised suspicion in wider society about the cultivation of religiosity or interest in spiritual teachings, and this, of course, drew the attention of the KGB. Thus, vegetarianism turned out to be too radical and its supporters could be viewed as a counterculture within a broader counterculture of folklorists. This is why KGB agents, in their instructional and prophylactic activities aimed at vegetarians, involved "neutral" persons, who were in fact KGB collaborators charged with publicly denigrating the practice of vegetarianism. Ironically enough, the stereotypes found in Latvian traditional culture, with its northern, meat-eating habits, were put to good use. So in keeping with the opposition to vegetarianism a "former teacher, J. Smilga,"[11] wrote a letter to the leader of the Savieši ensemble, who was a vegetarian at the time:

> Is our folklore meant for monkey-business, national sectarianism and narrow-mindedness! Does it instruct our people to wallow naked in the dewy grass on St. John's morning! Those are songs, customs and beliefs of working people, and not the supplement to some rituals of foolery! And this craze with eating— was the ancient Latvian—a good-working and harmonious man—a vegetarian or a Hindu ascetic?! (personal letter, January, 1985)

*The Cultivation of Anti-Soviet Sentiments*

Public performances by folklore ensembles were often used to propagate views and convictions that differed from the officially accepted position. By recontextualizing folklore texts, conventional expressions, motifs, signs, and symbols, the audience was offered a certain message, commonly understood by all present, but never fully verbalized. There was a kind of non-verbal consensus that matters vitally important for people's lives should not be named directly. Thus, for example, during a performance by the Skandinieki ensemble in the early 1980s, the idea of the de-occupation of Latvia was easily expressed with the help of a traditional, but

---

[11]    This seems to be a pseudonym of a KGB agent or collaborator.

slightly altered recipe against cockroaches: "To get rid of cockroaches, one has to utter: 'The red lords, from now on you have no place here!' And then one should put them into an old shoe and drag them across the border (originally [across the threshold]), without looking back."[12]

Some hidden meanings could be easily expressed with the help of certain song genres. Ilga Reizniece admits that the "strongest" songs of the early 1980s were war songs or songs with mythological content (personal interview February, 2006).[13] Reizniece was the leader of the Bizīteri ensemble, who lost the patronage of the Latvian Music Academy just because they sang war songs.[14] To properly understand the message carried by Latvian war songs at that time one has to recall how Soviets tried, through intense brainwashing, to substitute local or Latvian patriotism with Soviet patriotism. A national fatherland could not exist in Soviet ideology, but it existed in folksongs, particularly in war songs, which therefore meant that they posed a serious threat to the establishment. The flagship of the Latvian neo-folklore movement, the Skandinieki ensemble, composed their first program of war songs in the second half of the 1970s, and the members of the ensemble remember the program aroused strong patriotic feelings. The emotional content of certain songs was clearly felt as an appeal to voluntary self-offering for the sake of people's liberty.

Another example of the neo-folklore movement adopting the role of anti-Soviet agent is the album *Latvian Folklore: Ceļatiesi bāleliņi!*, published by Latvian émigrés in Hamburg in 1986. It contains selected recordings of recognized folklore ensembles of the first half of the 1980s, including work by Iļģi, Skandinieki, Sendziesma, and Bizīteri. The album cover displays a recognizable outline of Latvia, composed of bright stars on a dark background—a clear, symbolic picture of hope and longing for an independent Latvia. Furthermore there is a clearly visible reference to the publisher on the album's back cover, the ominous acronym KGB, which stands for "Kultūras Glābšanas Biedrība" (Society for the Saving of Culture); thus the publishers draw attention less to themselves than, in a sarcastic manner, to those they consider the biggest enemy of Latvian culture. (See Figure 6.4.)

---

[12]  This is taken from a Skandinieki performance at the beginning of the 1980s and is reproduced by the author from memory.

[13]  Latvian traditional war songs are contemplative rather than offensive in character. The usual motifs of these songs are recruiting, the horrors of war, hope for survival, protective magic, longing for the bride, the home, or the native country.

[14]  According to the norms regulating cultural life in the Soviet period, every artistic unit should have its parent institution which is responsible for its activities.

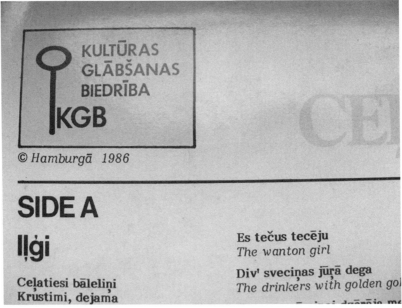

Figure 6.4    Front cover and detail of the back cover of the LP *Latvian Folklore: Ceļatiesi bāleliņi!*, published by KGB (Kultūras Glābšanas Biedrība) in Hamburg in 1986. By permission of Ģirts Zēgners

## Conclusion: The Neo-folklore Movement and the Singing Revolution of 1987-91

Though the followers of the neo-folklore movement did not outnumber the participants of staged folkish folklorism, the cultural significance and the social and political influence of the neo-folklore movement grew to be much greater than that of the folkish folklorism, especially in the second half of the 1980s, when it became one of the catalysts of the singing revolution. During this period, the people's movement against the Soviet system took more definite shape, several peaceful, nonviolent mass demonstrations took place, and the spirit of resistance was strongly supported and uplifted through singing. A significant cornerstone of this liberation process was the folklore festival *Baltica '88*. The festival was initiated in 1987 in Lithuania as an event through which the musical and choreographical folklore of the three Baltic nations could be presented to a broader public. Though the intention was to present only true, genuine folklore, both currents of folklorism—the staged folkish folklorism and the neo-folklore movement—were present on an almost equal basis at the first festival in Vilnius. But only a year later, when public awareness of the importance of de-Sovietized cultural heritage became stronger, the neo-folklore movement in its different expressions won the leading position at the festival in Riga. Furthermore, one of the symbolically most important events in the liberation process took place during the festival: the national flag, which was strictly banned during the whole Soviet period, was for the first time displayed publically again (see Figure 6.5).

Figure 6.5    National flags displayed publicly during the street procession of the folklore festival *Baltica '88*. Photo by Pēteris Korsaks

It is not surprising that even the publication of traditional music recordings had a touch of political symbolism at that time. While the first LP of the Iļģi ensemble, *Pieśni łotewskie*, published by the Poljazz company in 1989 in Poland, contains only orphan songs and wedding songs, the cover carries a clear political message: through a small hole in a brick wall one can see the Monument of Liberty. Thus, the neo-folklore movement positioned itself clearly at the centre of political activities that finally led to liberation from the Soviets and the reestablishment of national statehood in 1991.

Chapter 7

# Yugoslav and Post-Yugoslav Encounters with Popular Music and Human Rights

Rajko Muršič

In October, 2009, the Croatian Minister of Foreign Affairs, Gordan Jandroković, sent a note to the Swiss embassy in Zagreb to protest against the decision of the Swiss authorities to ban a performance in Switzerland by the well-known Croatian rock singer Thompson (Marko Perković) (Ivanović, 2009). Marko Perković/ Thompson, who started singing while a member of the Croatian defense forces in 1991/92, took his stage name from the Thompson machine-gun used in the war in Croatia. A couple of days after Jandroković had sent his note, the Croatian Prime Minister, Jadranka Kosor, supposedly seriously considered dismissing the minister. Although she refrained from doing so, the incident is proof enough that music can become an important political issue, and that such incidents may question or change our points of view. Although I have occasionally been active in defending freedom of expression in music (see Muršič, 1999, 2000), I sympathized with the Swiss government's decision. This was a situation that effectively demonstrated that we cannot advocate unchangeable universal principles of freedoms and rights. Why?

Only two months before the incident, while giving a presentation on popular music and its political implications in the former Yugoslavia, I played one of Thompson's patriotic songs ("Duh ratnika" [The Spirit of the Warrior]) to an audience of non-Croatian-speaking students and asked for their opinion. It was perceived by the students, who sincerely enjoyed it, as a very nice rock ballad. Some of them considered it just another love song. To some extent, I agreed. Then, after presenting them with some other examples of music from the 1990s period, when war ravaged the region, I played the song again, this time accompanied with video footage. After a few seconds it became clear to everybody that the song was not just about love, but about a very specific kind of love: love of a country. In glorifying the *Ustaše*, Croatian war heroes who in World War II collaborated with the Nazis, Thompson's "love song" acquires a fascist patina. For someone who is not a Croatian nationalist to have enjoyed the song, only to discover its meaning is not what they thought, this could present quite a dilemma.

Thompson is a product of the violent breakdown of the Yugoslav socialist federation. Taking his music as the mark of a structural shift from nationalism, or postnationalism, to "pop-nationalism," his example may not be as threatening as it at first seems. Using nationalist symbolism in a pop milieu, pop-nationalism substitutes hard chauvinist-nationalist sentiments for just another pop charade. With its aestheticized ritual it can transform nationalist emotions, power, and "truth" into a pop event, providing the stage for the catharsis of accumulated postwar public sentiments and concerns in facing structural uncertainty about future "nationhood." However, there is no guarantee that such pop music will not be used for real nationalist and chauvinist mobilization. After all, the same music could be used in immensely different ways.

New musical styles that articulate widespread needs and aspirations with the minimal level of artistic expression are a common response to war and postwar trauma. Just such a style—dubbed "turbo-folk" in 1988 by Montenegrin singer and author Antonije Pušić (known as Rambo Amadeus)—appeared during Yugoslavia's dissolution. The "cathartic" function of this turbo-folk had the potential to lead to two radically opposed outcomes: on the one hand, this pop-nationalism expressed in patriotic popular music and in an unrestricted mélange of sex, hedonism, splendor, and "supermodern traditionalism" could provide symbolic attachment without any profound "real-political" consequences; on the other it could not only stimulate nationalist sentiments but provoke acts of intolerance, ethnic hatred, and violence.

Is this a situation that was specific to the former Yugoslavia? Considering Bulgarian *chalga*, Turkish *arabesk*, and other similar genres, it is more likely a rule than an exception. After all, "pop's 'offence' can bring to light problems that might otherwise not gain attention" (Cloonan, 1996, p. 34). Since Walter Benjamin warned about aestheticized political rituals and their sublime power, it is well known that partying, having fun, and the expression of mutual sentiments through song can play a crucial role in the success of populist, (neo)nationalist, and fascist movements. Indeed, by the power of ecstatic interpellation, anger and aversion to "others" are often expressed by those who feel socially excluded from their own society (by social rank, age, and territorial distance from the centers of power) through ongoing symbolic and ideological struggles in support of their own people.

Thompson's example reveals important points to be considered when analyzing music and its relationship to human rights. First, music alone—that is, as humanly organized sound (Blacking, 1973), or as a nonverbal sound game (Muršič, 1993)—never carries its inherent meaning; it is its social context, use, intentions, and additional carriers of meaning that make a piece of music a meaningful means of communication (or at least a shared experience). Second, when music is being used to mobilize the masses, there is always the possibility of it being used in opposite or alternative ways. Third, when music is being used as a means of political mobilization, defense, identity-making, or even torture, social situations need also to be considered as crucial in its understanding, not just the musical material itself. More simply put: it is not music but people who harm other people. The question though is, are harmful acts any different if people use music as a means of violence?

## Music as an Act of Violence

Despite the fact that music, especially military and court music, has been used to mobilize masses since time immemorial—and many examples of the power of music are found in ancient myths—music scholars have only very recently started to examine the use of popular music as a means of violence (Johnson and Cloonan, 2008). With its nonverbal appeal and sound structure, music is very powerful. It can even reach the existential core of individuals as social beings, affecting them profoundly with subtle cumulative effect at physiological, psychological, and aesthetic levels.

Making music is, in essence, making sense of a cacophonic experience by turning manifold social experiences into symbolic commonalities with other "insiders." This role is often ascribed to "the stranger within," who can manage to cultivate fields of identification and a "more complete experience of Self" (Port, 1999, p. 292). Such strangers within, members of marginal and often suppressed minorities, are often important as the carriers of musical traditions (Merriam, 1964, pp. 123-44). In the case of Yugoslavia such minorities were the Roma and, especially after the turbulent 1960s, the youth.

The Roma played wedding music on instruments popular in particular places and at particular times. They would use string instruments in the north and brass instruments in the south. Among the brass orchestras worth mentioning are the Feat Sejdić Orchestra, the Boban Marković Orchestra, and the Kočani Orchestra, and among musicians the king of Roma saxophone from Skopje, Ferus Mustafov. One of the first big stars of Romani ethno-pop was Esma Redžepova, with her magnificent voice, later joined by Šaban Bajramović and other Romani singers. Esma Redžepova is an active member of the Lions Club, sponsor of the Romani Women's Association "Esma," and was named an ambassador of the United Nations for refugees. In 2002 she was nominated for the Nobel Peace Prize. With its appeal, music could make a significant contribution to the struggle for Roma emancipation. Nevertheless, the Roma are still waiting for true recognition as equal citizens in European countries.

In the former Yugoslavia (as in other countries) Roma musicians are seen as people who play their music with great pleasure. While urbanized and industrialized people who moved from the countryside were seen as unable to enjoy their lost "traditional" music in the same way that their forebears had, Roma musicians, by continuing to play their music, were able to continue enjoying it. An oppressed and stigmatized minority, who didn't choose to be marginalized, Roma are considered to play music "with heart." However, it is their suppressed social position that is believed to be what makes them seemingly more "musical" than the dominant population. The same could be said of African Americans in the United States. Recent appropriations of hip-hop and rap, and more distant appropriations of reggae, among worldwide "colored" populations, including, for example, Bulgarian gypsies (cf. Rice, 1996, p. 196; Silverman, 1996, p. 243), prove that music can be used as a means of gaining or promoting self-confidence.

Very similar observations can be made regarding youth as a permanently marginalized group in industrialized societies. For example, Slovene youth turned to Yugoslav or Balkan popular music at a time when their own no longer gave them what they were looking for: for them, "Yugo rock" or "Balkan rock," as it was called, preserved what Slovenian popular music did not: identification with passionate and authentic music.

As a collective symbolic activity, playing or listening to music has manifold social implications, but it cannot be taken as a magic wand with which to change society's ills. Though music is essentially a social phenomenon, it is not possible to master its social impact. Only exceptionally are its social effects predictably encoded into the music, but even in these cases (anthems, jingles or other advertising music are possible examples), universal social consensus about its meaning is hardly to be established. Consequently, when considering music's social effects, the contextual dimensions in which the meaning of music is socially achieved need also to be taken into account. If, for example, certain music intervals are officially forbidden, as indeed some were at the time of Shostakovich's well known struggles with the Soviet authorities, and a composer chooses to employ them, it is not the intervals or other music materials themselves that are subversive, or even the imposition by others of meaning upon the composer; it is the decision of the composer who opposes the regulations that gives rise to the charges of subversion.

## Music in the Time of War

The dissolution of Yugoslavia was violent. During more than a decade, war and conflict dictated daily life, having dramatic effects on the popular music of the region. With the first armed conflicts, the popular music market was effectively destroyed. Nonetheless, exchange of music between the republics was never completely halted. And although audiences were changed along with dramatic changes in the popular music infrastructure, especially within the public and commercial media in the region, the idea of common popular music survived.

Throughout the 1990s it was almost impossible for Serbian bands and performers to perform in Croatia, as much as it was for Croatian groups and singers to play in Serbia. After the fall of Slobodan Milošević in 2000, however, the situation changed, though not as fast as expected. In 2002, for example, a Belgrade magazine, *Ilustrovana Politika*, wrote that an unofficial ban on playing Serbian artists was still in force at national radio and television stations in Croatia. Meanwhile, big Serbian (or former Bosnian) stars like Ceca, Zdravko Čolić, or Goca Tržan were privately very popular. Similarly, while the Croatian singer Severina was frequently played by the Serbian media (Gajić, 2002), Dalmatian superstar Oliver Dragojević still claims he will never again perform in Serbia no matter how much he's offered—not even for 200,000 EUR, which was possibly the largest amount paid to any singer from the area to perform in Belgrade (Gajić, 2002). Leaving aside noncommercial acts, one of the first singers to perform in Croatia after the war was Serbian Bajaga (Momčilo Bajagić) with his band Instruktori, promoting his album *Zmaj od Noćaja*. It has been claimed that Bajaga and Instruktori sold more albums in Croatia than in Serbia (Gajić, 2002). Đorđe Balašević was another of the first mainstream Serbian acts to perform in Croatia after the fall of Milošević. In Slovenia too, Serbian musicians were the first to be invited to play after the country gained international recognition. Back in 1992, however, only those who did not support Milošević were booked. Interestingly, among the concert audiences of singers like Đorđe Balašević or Bajaga, who regularly performed in Slovenia, there were perhaps more Croatian attendees than Slovene.

War and armed conflict affect society more dramatically than perhaps any other kind of exceptional circumstance. When grenades fall and arms are fired around one's home it is impossible simply to dismiss the fact. After the initial shock, everything changes. For a musician, too, it is almost impossible simply to stand by and pretend that nothing is happening. When armed conflict begins, how an individual becomes involved in the conflict is essential: as a victim, as a helpless observer, as an aggressor, and so on. But whatever happens, it is impossible to remain silent. Consequently, musicians from the former Yugoslavia reacted to the conflicts in many different ways. The majority of Slovene and Croatian musicians reacted to the atrocities as the victims of aggression, or in solidarity with their co-citizens, while their fellow Serbian musicians, especially the younger ones, found themselves in a much more difficult position: some rejected the violence and organized antiwar events, others responded individually to the atrocities, some remained silent and waited, others supported their country's regime, some emigrated before or during the conflicts, others defended "Yugoslavism." Whatever choice they made, it was impossible to pretend that nothing had happened. And even if popular musicians tried not to get involved, they could not avoid the facts of everyday life in their surroundings, which were in many cases marked with unprecedented violence, first in Croatia and then in Bosnia and Herzegovina. While it is impossible to make a general assessment of musicians' responses to the war, after almost two decades since the beginning of the conflict, and almost a decade since its end, it is more or less clear that popular music became actively involved in the processes. The following sections present some examples "from the field."

## Bosnia and Herzegovina

Bosnia and Herzegovina was one of the cradles of Yugoslav rock music, starting with the first famous Yugoslav rock band Indeksi, followed by the most successful Yugoslav rock group ever, Bijelo Dugme, and the famous "new primitivism" of the 1980s in the form of bands such as Zabranjeno Pušenje and Elvis J. Kurtović. Among alternative acts were SCH and the art group Zvono. Bosnia and Herzegovina was also an important center of Yugoslav pop and ethno-pop. The singer Zdravko Čolić attracted an audience in the 1970s and made his comeback (from Belgrade) in the 2000s when he sang in all parts of the former Yugoslavia. In the 1980s, the extraordinarily popular Lepa Brena paved the way for turbo-folk.

At the beginning of the war in Bosnia and Herzegovina in 1992, newly-composed folk music was for a while "expelled" from all electronic media in Sarajevo. Nevertheless, cassettes were smuggled across the front lines in both directions (Šavija, 1998). During the siege, for younger Sarajevans the creation of alternative culture was the only means to keep urban culture alive (Šavija, 1998). Thus in the 1990s, during and soon after the war, the most vivid alternative cultural scene to emerge in all the former Yugoslav cities, with several dozen rock bands, art groups, culture magazines, and fanzines, did so in Sarajevo (see Janjatović, 1997; Šavija, 1998; Jeffs, 2005). This music scene was documented on the compilations *Rock Under the Siege* A and B, released by the independent radio station Radio Zid. Furthermore, rock concerts, many of which had been organized during the siege of Sarajevo, were in many instances the first events that proved life was returning to normality after the war. The concert performed by Croatian and Bosnian acts in Skenderija, Sarajevo, on December 28, 1996, entitled *Pjevajmo do zore* (Let's Sing until Dawn) was one such positive sign (Sinclair and Janjatović, 1997).

Further positive signs can be read in other developments and achievements in the music world. At the end of the 1990s, commercial domestic ethno-pop, influenced by Serbian turbo-folk, merged with pop (Andree Zaimović, 2004, p. 163). The pop-music-oriented *Glorija*, published simultaneously in Zagreb and Belgrade, became one of the most widely distributed magazines in Bosnia and Herzegovina (Andree Zaimović, 2004, p. 164). On May 7, 2001, five years after the Dayton Peace Agreement, national public radio service BH Radio 1 was among the first national institutions established in postwar Bosnia and Herzegovina, which had been divided into two entities, the Republic of Srpska and the Federation of Bosnia and Herzegovina, and further divided into cantons (Andree Zaimović, 2002, p. 125). Much later, in late 2009, public support was mobilized for the defense of the radio station Radio 202 which was about to lose its frequency, but which was finally incorporated into the newly-established Sarajevo city radio and television.

One of the most serious problems Bosnia and Herzegovina faced after the war, a problem deeply related to its popular music, was the massive exodus of educated people. It is estimated that around 300,000 university-educated people (Andree Zaimović, 2002, p. 126) left the country in the decade after the dissolution of socialist Yugoslavia. Many musicians found new residence in Croatia, Serbia, Slovenia, other European countries, or in the United States. Hence one of a number of exciting Bosnian rock acts, Culture Shock, comes from Seattle.

In the 2000s many exciting alternative acts also appeared. Among them perhaps Damir Avdić (sometimes under the name Balkan Psycho) from Tuzla produces the most poignant and profound lyrical and artistic reflection of postwar Bosnia. Also of note is Vuneny from Mostar.

## Croatia

Croatia was undoubtedly a center of the Yugoslav popular music industry. It had a vivid postwar jazz scene (Boško Petrović is of especial note in this regard; see Vrdoljak, 2008) and produced the majority of domestic pop songs. The Zagreb Song Festival (since 1953) introduced great singers and songwriters such as Ivo Robić, Vice Vukov, Tereza Kesovija, Oliver Dragojević, Severina, and others, and composers and directors Miljenko Prohaska and Nikica Kalodjera (Luković, 1989; Vrdoljak, 2008). Zagreb was home to the first Yugoslav rock singer Karlo Metikoš (Mat Collins), the first domestic rock album (Grupa 220's *Naši dani*), and many successful bands, such as Time, Parni Valjak, Prljavo Kazalište, etc. (see Janjatović, 1999; Mirković, 2004).

During the war in Croatia, the vast majority of Croatian musicians responded to the atrocities with projects and songs directed at the war. The most well-known song was the late Tomislav Ivčić's "Stop the War in Croatia." It had international appeal and reached the Top 10 in Australia. On the compilation CD *The Best of "Rock za Hrvatsku,"* which accompanied an edited volume on music during the war in Croatia (Pettan, 1998), we find peace songs, militant songs, and others. Among these, perhaps the most interesting is "E, moj druže beogradski" (Hey, My Belgrade Comrade), in which the singer, Jura Stublić of the famous new wave group Film, directly addressed his former Belgrade friends for not openly opposing the war in Croatia.

Although the Croatian media attempted to promote the preferred urban forms of popular music as Croatian, in opposition to the "rural" forms of ethno-pop as Serbian, this divide was not proven in the field. Many Croats preferred ethno-pop, while many Krajina Serbs preferred rock. Some militant Croatian musicians, such as Marko Perković/Thompson, intending to mobilize audiences for war (see Pettan, 1998, pp. 24-5), used Balkan rock (or Yu-rock) as a background to the image of self-confident fighters, although they were actually at the same time fighting against something they conceived as "Balkanism."

During and immediately after the war very few bands from Croatia were willing to perform with Serbian artists. When in late 1992 the alternative band Vještice performed for peace in Prague with their Serbian antiwar friends, they faced public discontent. Among the bands that tried to avoid disputes with their Serbian friends, or were critical of Croatian nationalism, were punk and post-punk bands Kud Idijoti, Fuck off Bolan, Let 3, Dark Busters, and others (Sinclair and Janjatović, 1997). After the war, Croatian musicians did not perform in Serbia until the fall of Milošević in the year 2000. Among the first were Alka Vuica (Janjatović, 2000) and the superstar singer Mišo Kovač. The first artist from Serbia to perform in Croatia after the war was well-known anti-Milošević alternative singer and songwriter Rambo Amadeus (Janjatović, 2000).

## Macedonia

Due to the difference in language and Macedonia's geographical distance from other centers, the country's popular music scene produced only a few famous bands and singers, including the jazz-rock group Leb i Sol, Roma singer Esma Redžepova, and pop singer Ljupka Dimitrovska. After the dissolution of Yugoslavia, new talents, acceptable to all regions in the former Yugoslavia, appeared. Two examples, DD Synthesis and Anastasia, both used folk elements in their new musical synthesis. Another, who rose to superstardom, was Toše (Todor) Proeski. His untimely death in 2007 prompted perhaps the first display of unanimous sentiment in audiences from all over the former Yugoslavia who united to show respect for this artist's work and efforts, among which were charity and activism for peace.

The alternative music scene in Macedonia began to grow only in the last decade. When the national radio and television network RTV Macedonia wanted to cancel Kanal 103, a semi-autonomous station that played primarily alternative and noncommercial music, the response of its listeners and civil society in general was very strong. It is possible this event further stimulated development of the local alternative music scene with excellent bands such as Foltin, PMG Collective, Bernays Propaganda, and others coming to the fore.

## Serbia (and Montenegro)

Despite being the capital of Yugoslavia, Belgrade was not the country's most important popular music center. However, the first famous Serbian rock group, Siluete, hailed from there and was followed by supergroups Yu Grupa and Smak. Then, in the early 1980s Belgrade exploded with new wave groups including Šarlo Akrobata, Idoli, Električni Orgazam, and Ekaterina Velika (see Janjatović, 1999).

Together with domestic pop, a new hybrid style had developed in the late 1950s, combining a couple of decades of older local adaptations of popular music in towns—the so-called *starogradska pesma* (old-town song)—with pop, jazz, and rural traditional music, producing a local ethno-pop genre called *novokomponovana narodna muzika* (newly-composed folk music). Based on the specific use of accordion and melismatic (Oriental) vocals, it further developed with the introduction of modern pop, until it became a dominant music genre in the early 1990s when it developed into what is now known as "turbo-folk."

In the late 1980s, a sharp division was established between the audiences attached to ethno-pop music, the so-called "narodnjaci," who would mostly follow nationalist ideals, and domestic rock, which took another direction, more openly cosmopolitan and antinationalist. Some would claim that the dividing line was between rural and urban cultures, although the division was not so clear. For example, some musicians, such as Boris Kovač, who took their inspiration from traditional music, did not follow this nationalist path at all, while some Serbian rockers, most notably Bora Đorđević from Riblja Čorba, "dived head-first into the nationalist waters" (Janjatović, 1999, p. 33). Turbo-folk, or neo-folk (Dragičević-Šešić, 1994), fused "love songs and older folk tunes" with contemporary dance music in an explicitly or implicitly ethnic Serbian manner (Monroe, 2000).

If the development of turbo-folk was directly related to Serbian nationalist politics in the 1990s, and nonnationalist rock was vehemently marginalized with the destruction of alternatives (Gordy, 1999), two events, both related to rising international interest in music festivals, exemplify these strands in post-Milošević Serbia. The first is the annual festival of brass bands in Guča (near Dragačevo) in central Serbia. The festival offers a very strange mix of ecstatic music performances, dance, heavy drinking, and the gathering of fans of Romani brass bands. At the same time it is an exhibition of Serbian nationalist relics. The second is a more cosmopolitan event that brings the most exciting popular music acts to Serbia: the Exit Festival. This festival is the result of urban youth opposition to the Milošević regime throughout the 1990s. In the summer of 2000, students and youth activists from Otpor (Resistance) organized a festival in Novi Sad which lasted 100 days. Since 2001 the festival has been organized annually in the Petrovaradin fortress across the river Sava. It very quickly developed into one of the most exciting summer festivals in Europe with strong urban and multicultural characteristics (see Žolt et al., 2004; Bizjak et al., 2005). The festival boasts a very broad range of modern popular music. It is a gathering, it is fun, but it is also the main symbol of modern, nonnationalist, urban Serbia. Furthermore, the Exit Festival also gives space to presentations from civil society projects and nongovernmental organizations.

It is well known that the student movement Otpor was closely related to cosmopolitan rock promoted by the independent media. For more than a decade, Radio B92, the student station Radio Index, and the network of independent radio stations had an important role in the continuing struggle against Milošević's regime. Many musicians, at least for a while, especially if they wanted to speak out, left the country. However, during protests against Milošević in 1996, protesters who had shifted their social engagement from the political field to carnivalesque "spheres of culture, personal identity, individual style, spare time and everyday life" (Milić and Ćičkarić, quoted in Grlja, 2002. p. 41) sang an adaptation of the Beach Boys' "Surfin' U.S.A." by pop band Eva Braun, entitled "Serbia Whistling" (Sinclair and Janjatović, 1997). That year, unfortunately, the street noise—including whistles, shouts, and the beating of pans—that protesters employed did not help. Nevertheless, independent releases, such as the compilation albums *Nas slušaju svi, mi ne slušamo nikoga!* (Everybody Listens to Us, We Don't Listen to Anybody) and *Ovo je zemlja za nas?!? Radio Boom 93 (1992-1997)* (Is This Country for Us?) (Sinclair and Janjatović, 1997), did have a profound effect on people who did not accept the predominantly nationalist call and resisted further. The compilation *Korak napred 2 koraka nazad* (Step Further, Two Steps Beyond), with adaptations of old Yugoslav hits, even helped pave the way to a warming of relations between Croatia and Serbia (Janjatović, 2000). Prior to this, while the Serbian media had not banned Croatian music, it was not being played as frequently as before the war. However, at the beginning of the NATO bombing of Serbia in March, 1999, the majority of radio stations stopped playing music in English (Pančić, 1999).

## Slovenia

Despite being a small republic, Slovenia played an important role in the development of Yugoslav popular music. In Ljubljana the first Yugoslav jazz ensembles (Jazz Negode in 1922) were formed and the first jazz festival was organized in Bled in 1960. Rock band Kameleoni achieved Yugoslav recognition in the 1960s while in the 1970s the lyrics of the underground band Buldožer faced censorship. In the late 1970s, a very strong and politically conscious alternative scene developed, not only with punk rock, but with many post-1960s movements in culture and arts, as well as with new social movements. As a consequence, during the 1980s it was possible to follow step by step the processes of liberalization and the ongoing questioning of the limits of expression. Early punk and alternative new social movements helped pave the path toward democratization. The leading ideas of the growing new civil society were the abolition of the death penalty and the abolition of so-called "verbal crime," Article 133 of the Civil Penalty Code, that could see someone jailed merely on the basis of his or her public expression of thoughts that might disturb the public.

Many other human rights and basic freedoms were promoted through processes that were closely related to music activism, such as environmentalist activism and new spiritual movements, and, perhaps the most important and symbolically powerful, gay and lesbian movements. These movements are the main reason why at the end of the 1980s Slovenian politics was not overwhelmingly nationalist. Popular music, especially alternative rock and other kinds of underground music, played a major role in these processes. Having said that, examples of new patriotism and nationalism were to be found in popular music as well (Agropop), though even these might have been interpreted ironically (Barber-Keršovan, 1999).

Soon after June, 1991, in particular, a certain amount of music censorship existed in the media, and it was very difficult to hear songs in the Croatian and Serbian languages on Slovene radio stations. However, the media blockade in Slovenia did not last for long. Some media, like independent Radio Študent, played music from Serbia and other parts of the former Yugoslavia all the time. On September 16, 1991, Radio Študent launched a legendary show in the Croatian/ Serbian language: *Nisam ja odavde* (I Am Not from Here), initially titled *Balkan urnebes* (The Balkan Pandemonium), was partly nostalgic, partly activist, and partly devoted to refugees.

After the war in Slovenia, and during the wars in Croatia and Bosnia and Herzegovina, it did not seem opportune to invite Serbian acts to play in Slovenia. At the beginning of 1994, Bajaga and his band Instruktori were refused visas, and only after the intervention of the then Slovenian president Milan Kučan were the visas acquired. It was not until February, 1996, that Slovenian bands (four of them) visited Serbia, and in May of the same year four Serbian bands (Love Hunters, Nothing but Logopedes, Svarog, and Goblins) responded in kind (Janjatović, 1996). The interruption in the exchange of music had somehow been unexpected, because many Slovenian citizens originated from other Yugoslav republics. Before the dissolution of Yugoslavia, these citizens were stigmatized and named "južnjaki" (the southerners), "bosanci" (bosnianers), or "čefurji" (a derogatory term for migrants from other former Yugoslav republics). One pop singer, Robert Pešut, also known as Magnifico, turned this stigma around with his album *Kdo je čefur* (Who is *čefur*). In the past few years it has become fashionable for Slovenian youth to act as stigmatized "čefur," and in 2009, the writer Goran Vojnović was awarded the national prize for the novel *Čefurji raus!* (*Southerners Go Home!*). Music and popular culture proved to be powerful tools in turning stigma around and empowering minorities.

## National and Cosmopolitan Popular Music in the Light of Human Rights and Freedoms

That Serbian turbo-folk was popular in Croatia and Bosnia and Herzegovina even in the most tragic times of war is extremely interesting. Not only did civilians listen to it, but also mobilized soldiers who would appropriate music from behind the enemies' lines and use it for their own purposes. This popularity was coterminous with the unprecedented burst of creativity among the people in areas of conflict. The Croatian rock singer Thompson and the Serbian neo-folk singer from Croatia Baja mali Knindža (Mirko Pajčin) are typical examples of the spontaneous wave of militant popular music that flourished at the time. They sang songs entitled "Serbs Aren't Afraid of Anyone," "Tears Aren't for Serbs," "Kosovo Is Our Soul" (Baja), and "Because We Are Croats," "The Spirit of the Warrior," and "Shut the Gun" (Thompson), among others.

With imagery in the music videos of "nouveaux riches, gangsters, beautiful girls, femmes fatales, luxurious interiors, and fancy cars" (Kronja, 2004, p. 8), turbo-folk not only became the dominant popular culture in Serbia, but spread to other countries in the region, including Bulgaria, Albania, Macedonia, Bosnia and Herzegovina, Croatia, and Slovenia. The most popular acts would play for audiences of thousands. In 2002, the most popular Serbian singer in Croatia was Ražnatović Ceca and "even soldiers in Croatian barracks listened to her" (Gajić, 2002). Belgrade based TV Pink, established in 1994, became the most important center for the promotion of turbo-folk. In 2009, much remained the same: in Croatia, Svetlana Ceca Ražnatović was still by far the most sought after Serbian performer. However, although she was announced the No.1 "folk music" star in

Croatia (according to the website of her Croatian fan club[1]), she continued to claim that she would never perform there.

Despite proclamations of freedom of expression in the former Yugoslavia and the world over, some bands still face censorship. The primary motives for suspension of freedom of expression are public moral and religious issues. The Croatian band Let 3, for example, is well known for provoking outrage, including by sometimes performing nude on stage. Indeed, their performance on the program "Tistega lepega popoldneva," on Slovenian national television on November 11, 2006, was censored, and their performance in Travnik (Bosnia and Herzegovina) was banned (Jaušovec, 2007).

When using a human rights framework to understand cultural movements, it is important to remember that universal human rights were introduced into the international language of law only after World War II was concluded and the human atrocities that were perpetrated therein were revealed. These declared human rights are the lowest possible denominator from which it is possible to deduct something we can comprehend as the universal human existence underlying the dignity of each individual human being. Thus the provisional notion of "human rights" relates to manifold dimensions of human existence. The Universal Declaration, however, was a political compromise, and hence it supports only basic freedoms without explicitly rejecting censorship and other "softer" ways of regulating freedom of expression.

Music, as well as other kinds of art, transcends and rises above the particular "and reaches for the universal" (Ostertag, 2009, p. 8). Ostertag's *Yugoslavia Suite,*[2] performed by American artists Bob Ostertag and Richard Board in Slovenia and Serbia immediately after the NATO bombing of Serbia in October, 1999, as well as concerts in Sarajevo in 1995 by U2 and (the internationally renowned and somewhat controversial Slovenian avant-garde group) Laibach, efficiently transcended dead-end situations in the region without having any immediate impact. This is how music affects social life. It is an essential part of new social movements, especially the carnivalesque rebellion of youth against the constraints of nationalist politics or against global capitalism. The organization of protest concerts (see Grujičić, 1999), the adaptation of pop songs, chanting on the streets, the release of antiwar compilation albums, and carefully chosen music played in the media all proved to be relatively effective ways of mobilizing the youth in the former Yugoslavia, especially in Serbia. The famous line of the antiwar song "Slušaj 'vamo!" (Attention!) by Rimtutituki, comprising members of Električni Orgazam, Partibrejkers, and Ekaterina Velika, declares "we don't want folk music to win." This was not merely a statement about aesthetic preferences (Žolt et al., 2004, pp. 373-4), but a clear declaration of resistance to the homogenization of cultural space in a modern European country. Given the limited appeal of this

---

[1]    http://ceca-fans.bloger.hr/, accessed July 30, 2009.

[2]    See http://bobostertag.com/music-liveprojects-yugoslaviasuite.htm, accessed May 27, 2010.

song, and of rock music in general, music journalist Petar Janjatović would claim that "rock was absolutely never a real force here," though many people in Serbia believe that "Milošević was brought down by rock and roll" (Janjatović and Rogošić, quoted in Mijatović, 2008).

Some rock musicians are still involved in breaking the barriers between countries. In August, 2008 a monument to Bob Marley was erected in the Serbian village of Banatski Sokolac. The statue was unveiled by the famous Croatian rock musician Dado Topić (Time) and Serbian reggae rocker Jovan Matić (Del Arno Band), and the event was accompanied by a concert by Croatian and Serbian bands. However, the common belief that "rock is engaged in the music of rebellion" is clearly unfounded (Grujičić, 1999). No music in its essence is rebellious or supportive of a regime. The Serbian movement Otpor adopted rock music as its common music expression with groups like Eyesburn, Love Hunters, Atheist Rap, Kanda Kodža i Nebojša, and Darkwood Dub. And when the ethno-pop (*narodnjak*) star Dragan Kojić Keba expressed his desire to participate in an Otpor protest, he was rebuffed (Grujičić, 1999). In contrast, some rock and pop singers openly joined the nationalists, for instance Serbian and Croatian rock singers Bora Đorđević and Marko Perković (Thompson). In 1992, ethno-pop singer Zoran Kalezić, pop singer Vladimir Savčić Čobi, and rock singer Bora Đorđević came together to sing "U boj, ustani, Srbine moj!" (To Fight, Arise, Oh My Serb!).[3] Montenegrin singer Zoran Kalezić explained: "We can't expect Sloba [Milošević], [Vojislav] Šešelj, or Arkan to Sing! They'll do some other things, and we'll sing" (Tarlač, 2003).

Together with the escalation of war in Yugoslav republics, traditional music forms were revived and were either considered as markers of national or regional exclusiveness or as a means of military mobilization (*gusle* singing in the Dinaric region,[4] for example). It is well known that the political leader of the Bosnian Serbs, Radovan Karadžić, performed as a *gusle* singer (Tarlač, 2003). However, it is less widely known that all parties in the conflict revived *gusle* singing. In 1998 the international authorities in Bosnia and Herzegovina were supposedly preparing an Act banning *gusle* singing events in the Republic of Srpska, because they would promote ethnic hatred and celebrate war criminals (Milojević, 2007).

Music has always been used, in some form or another, not only as a mobilizing force, but also as a weapon aimed at the "enemy." Serbian patriotic neo-folk singers, though not so different from the Croatian and Bosnian variants, with their megalomaniac and mythomaniac expressions of kitsch, sang about "Kosovo, Serbia, God, tradition, territory, faith, blood, land, pride, children, spite, love, language, hearth, graves, traitors, fights, and borders" (Tarlač, 2003).

---

[3]  A version of the song can be viewed on YouTube: http://www.youtube.com/ watch?v=2yOlp91IMQY, accessed April 9, 2011.

[4]  *Gusle* singing is a musical form comprising the singing of epic songs accompanied by the single-stringed instrument after which the form is named.

Yet surprisingly the production of offensive music in the former Yugoslavia has not been limited to the locals. In 2005, under the name Shiptare Boys, Norwegian KFO soldiers recorded the song, "Kosovo," a kind of a bad joke with an anti-Serbian message which scandalized the Serbian public.[5]

## Conclusions

Freedom of expression and freedom to associate in public, together with freedom of the press and of other forms of public communication and expression, shall be guaranteed. Each person may freely collect, receive, and circulate information and opinions. Except in such circumstances as are laid down by statute, each person shall have the right to obtain information of a public nature, provided he or she can show sufficient legal interest as determined by the statute. These are basic principles declared in the Universal Declaration of Human Rights. Why should popular music be excluded from these principles? Popular culture is, after all, as Noam Chomsky and others have repeatedly argued, "Integral to the construction of consent for the dominant ideologies of the West ..." (Monroe, 2000). In his writings on freedom, John Stuart Mill claimed that there is no interest in banning words or the gestures of people unless they can cause harm to others (Cloonan, 1996, p. 12).

Freedom of expression and unrestrained creativity in popular music are essential constituents of modern democratic society. Together with other forms of freedom, freedom of artistic expression is the essential basis for a democratic and tolerant society. Wittgenstein's frontiers of one's language, which become frontiers of one's world, are constantly changing. The question is whether the actors are approaching an open or closed universe.

---

[5]   See http://www.youtube.com/watch?v=cpu8IQH4B9U, accessed April 12, 2011.

## Chapter 8

# Víctor Jara: The Artist and His Legacy

### John M. Schechter

It seems nothing short of incongruous now to consider that the martyred musician, Víctor Jara, who was born into a peasant family outside Santiago, Chile, in 1932, approached adulthood with the goal of becoming an accountant. Not surprisingly, he soon tired of accountancy and his following flirtation with a seminary and the possibility of priesthood also failed to take a hold. Indeed, it was only after a period in the army that he found his true vocation in music. Trained initially as a theater director, Jara gradually developed notable skills as a guitarist and emerged as a great composer-singer-guitarist of the Nueva Canción song movement in Chile. He served as director of the pathbreaking musical ensemble *Cuncumén*, and he would acknowledge the influence of Violeta Parra (1917-67), researcher into Chilean traditional musics, multifaceted artist, and pioneering figure of Chilean Nueva Canción. In July, 1969 Jara was co-winner of the first prize at the Primer Festival de la Nueva Canción Chilena, held under the sponsorship of the Catholic University, Santiago. This, as Jan Fairley makes clear, was a significant award as the festival "brought together groups of musicians and soloists who represented a broad spectrum of folk music that could be heard in Chile at the time." Jara's victory with "Plegaria a un labrador," Fairley continues, "legitimized the music and work of a new generation of musicians who not only reacted against the limits and prejudices of traditional 'tourist' folk, which sentimentalized and idealized rural life, but who were also through their music committed to social and political change" (1984, p. 109). In 1970 Jara relinquished his career as theater director and became a practicing musician. Beginning in 1971 he traveled throughout Chile and Latin America as a cultural representative of the government of Salvador Allende. Juan Pablo González summarizes Víctor Jara's contributions and ultimate martyrdom: "Jara was a passionate and vibrant cultural activist of the Chilean left, and many of his performances and songs were directed towards students and workers. A charismatic and popular figure, he was murdered following the military coup d'etat of 11 September 1973. His music and commitment to the ordinary people of his country and their cause has brought him to worldwide audiences" (2009).

Many writers have treated Víctor Jara and Violeta Parra together, as co-participants in Chilean Nueva Canción, with Parra as a pioneer in that movement. Martha Nandorfy compares the philosophical stances of these two artists, noting that, where Parra "rail[ed] against functionaries, bureaucrats, and politicians, in short, against government, and Jara ... oppos[ed] the ruling class through organized party politics—both fought to defend cultural survival, recognizing that social justice and human rights must be defined and defended within popular culture" (2003, p. 203). Jane Tumás-Serna, after commenting that Parra and Jara "modeled new song on the folk culture and music of Chile" and that "both folksingers have become nearly mythical figures since their untimely and violent deaths due to their role in political protest and the centrality of their music in the politicizing of the people," notes that both great artists "composed protest songs that became a permanent part of Chilean culture," "[they] took the traditional 'folk' songs of the countryside and combined them with modern lyrics," and they "Infused the music with intense emotion." The result was a "musical hybrid of the past with the present" (Tumás-Serna, 1992, p. 146).

My focus here is on Víctor Jara, the musical artist, as well as on his multidimensional legacy after his 1973 murder. His is a legacy which owes much to his work with the truly disadvantaged. In her biography of her husband, Joan Jara notes that by the mid-1960s, Víctor's songs were clearly becoming motivated by his empathy with Chile's underprivileged, by his sensitivity to injustices, and by his determination in songs such as "Preguntas por Puerto Montt" to decry these outrages (1984, p. 98). Joan Jara emphasizes the positiveness of Víctor Jara's greater vision, his avowed faith in the might of love, of freedom, of the person who is content and at peace (1984). For all these reasons, my approach in this chapter is explicitly interdisciplinary. I first examine four of Jara's songs for their music-compositional techniques and resources, for their use of text, for their formal structures, and for their overall stylistic traits. I seek to understand these songs as carefully crafted artistic expressions designed to foreground specific, divergent motivating messages: biographical intent, ethnographic reenactment, a plea for worker solidarity, and metaphorically expressed Marxist sentiment. The chapter continues with a view to examining several aspects of Jara's legacy: the well-known rock group of the Chilean political and musical underground Los Prisioneros as heir to the heritage of Violeta Parra and Víctor Jara; the Swedish political/rock group Hoola Bandoola Band and their song about Jara; and allusions to Víctor Jara, discovered in songs composed/performed by iconic figures of folk and popular music, such as Arlo Guthrie, Holly Near, and U2.

"Angelita Huenumán" was composed by Víctor Jara in 1969.[1] According to Joan Jara, she and Víctor met Angelita Huenumán during a journey to Mapuche country in southern Chile around 1964 (1984, pp. 91-6). In this song, Víctor Jara sketches a musical biography of this Mapuche blanket-maker, incorporating aspects of her natural environment and the kinetic activity that earns her a livelihood. The song is in strophic form, and its textual focus is on her hands—in both literal and figurative senses: "Her hands dance in the hemp"; "Angelita, in your weaving, there is time and tears and sweat, there are the anonymous hands of my own creative people." The song's text—in which the first two strophes sketch the natural surroundings of the Pocuno Valley where the weaver resides—reveals

---

[1]     All dates are those listed in Acevedo et al. (1996, pp. 352-3).

arch form, a structure in which some textual aspect(s) at the beginning appear also at the end. In this case, there are two instances of this construction: the phrase, "Vive Angelita Huenumán" concludes both the first and the last stanza; and, the second stanza and the final one are identical. Figures of speech are diverse and effective: simile ("like a bird in a cage"; "like the wings of a little bird"), metaphor ("the red blood of the *copihue* flower"[2]), personification ([the finished blanket] "sings for the highest bidder"), and synecdoche ("Angelita, in your weaving ... there are the anonymous hands of my own creative people"). We shall return to the red metaphor, in our discussion of Jara's song, "El pimiento."

In "Angelita Huenumán," Jara evinces his identification with the masses— with the untold numbers of creative rural artisans—of his own Chile: "... of my own creative people," as he puts it. In his perceptive analysis of this song, Peter Gould, whose 2002 study bore the title: "'Mi Pueblo Creador': Remembering Víctor Jara," comments as follows:

> ... the word ["pueblo"] means more than it appears to. It is a collective noun that can refer to the specific group of people Víctor comes from: workers, or Chileans, or campesinos. But to get it right, you have to think of a collectivity from which no individual stands out—as in the "first people," as some indigenous Americans referred to themselves historically. It is almost as if you were speaking of one organism, one pair of hands, one creative force: not "my creative people," but "my People, the Creator." In other words, the source of all the common generative strength that Angelita or Víctor borrow a little of, when they create an individual work of art. In other words, a tremendous identity moving in, and out of, the artist's hands. (2002, p. 177)

Musically, "Angelita Huenumán" is in pentatonic mode: D-F-G-A-C, within D minor. Harmonically, one emerges with a strong sense of bimodality: relative minor juxtaposing with relative major: D minor/F major, with cadence on the subtonic of C major. It should be noted that both melodic pentatonicism and the particular use of this relative minor/relative major bimodality, harmonically, are characteristic of Andean traditional musics, both those Indigenous and those mestizo.[3] In short, in "Angelita Huenumán" we find, for prominent aspects of text usage and musical depiction, the following: biographical intent, strophic form, arch-form structure, profuse and diverse figures of speech, literal and figurative focus on the hands, harmonic bimodality, cultural pride in/identification with the anonymous masses of rural artisans of Chile.[4]

---

[2]    Mapuche: *copihue*, the national flower of Chile.

[3]    For three examples and analytical discussions of bimodality in Ecuadorian *sanjuán*, Peruvian *wayno*, and Ecuadorian *albazo*, see Schechter (2009, pp. 436, 449, and 465).

[4]    Many of these same aspects also emerge in Víctor Jara's song, "El lazo." I have previously analyzed Jara's "El lazo" in some depth (Schechter, 2002, pp. 388-91). Note also my analysis of Jara's song, "El aparecido" (Schechter, 2009).

In "Despedimiento del angelito," the ethnographic reality is extended to the point of ethnographic reenactment. I have noted in an earlier essay (Schechter, 1999b, p. 434) how in this song Jara presents with care the atmosphere of a Chilean child's wake, complete with appropriate guitar rhythmic patterns and harmonies, melodic shapes, and actual words/phrasing—all capturing the musical structures and textual phrases of the *versos* performed at actual Chilean children's wakes (compare María Ester Grebe's transcription of a *verso* "Por Despedimento" at Grebe, 1967, pp. 93-7). Grebe discusses the fact that *versos a lo divino* use the *décima* form often, in Latin America, with the following *décima espinela* rhyme scheme: ABBAACCDDC (1967, p. 28; she provides various *a lo divino décima* examples on pages 29-33, with page 31 offering two *décimas* "for 'angelitos' [dead children]: in Farewell").[5] Víctor Jara, in his "Depedimiento del angelito," utilizes this *décima* form, with a twist: he deploys three *décimas* but within each he *repeats* the second *B*—thus generating "11-line" *décimas*.

Grebe has commented upon the fact that one can typically find, in Chilean *versos*, the use of Mixolydian (flat VII) harmonies; she considers this employment of the Mixolydian mode a modal "harmonic archaism" traceable to the sixteenth-century Spanish *villancico* (1967, pp. 59-61, 77). Jara's ethnographic reenactment intention, in his "Despedimiento," extends to his use, harmonically, of Mixolydian mode—but also of Lydian and Ionian ("major") modes.[6] Lastly, Jara attends to local Chilean dialect, as well: he uses *maire* (mother) and *Alto Paire* (Great Father, God), instead of *madre* and *padre*. In nations such as Ecuador, Venezuela, and Chile, adult poet-singers present at the *velorio del angelito* (infant wake, a joyful occasion)[7] take the role of the deceased child or infant and bid "farewell" (*despedimiento*) to its "mother" on the child's behalf, as "I" (i.e., the deceased infant) am on "my" way to Heaven.[8] By virtue of his

---

[5]  This form of the *décima* is attributed to Vicente Espinel Gómez Adorno (1550-1624), the Spanish poet, novelist, and musician.

[6]  Chile is the repository of other archaic European traditions, emanating from the Middle Ages and/or Renaissance, such as the presence of female harpists accompanying folk musics, the use of the *rebec*, or *rabel* (an early violin-type of three strings, played at the thighs) for certain *tonadas*, and, also in *tonadas*, the presence of linked strophes (Schechter 1992b, pp. 22-3, 39, 208; Moreno Chá, 1999, pp. 251, 252). Diana Nieves has analyzed (1991, pp. 55-66) and transcribed (pp. 122-7) Jara's "Despedimiento"; she discusses the song's poetic scansion, the structure of its melodic motives, its antecedent-consequent periodic structure, its modal usage (Mixolydian and Lydian), and its distinctly multimetric character of rhythm and meter. Her transcription is followed by a schematic harmonic diagram, in which the fundamental chordal structure is elucidated.

[7]  See Schechter (1983, 1994, and 1999a), for full discussions of this music-ritual, including its underlying philosophy of celebration.

[8]  My side-by-side comparison of Jara's text, in "Despedimiento del angelito," with the words from an actual Chilean *verso* "Por despedimento" (Grebe 1967, pp. 93-6) reveals how Jara faithfully utilizes the same turns of phrase that appear in *versos* sung in the natural context of a Chilean child's wake (Schechter, 1999b, pp. 434-5). One notes that

faithful recreation of the natural-contextual setting of a Chilean child's wake, both musically and textually, Jara renders homage in a different fashion to the practices of his rural Chilean neighbors.

In 1950, on the advice of a priest in whom he found he could confide, Víctor Jara entered the seminary of the Redemptorist Order in San Bernardo, a town south of Santiago; he remained for a period of two years. In "Plegaria a un labrador" ("Supplication to a worker"), Jara penned a call for worker solidarity, which owed much to phrases drawn from the Lord's Prayer. In Joan Jara's explanation, "Plegaria" served as

> ... a call to the peasants, to those who tilled the soil with their hands and produced the fruits of the earth, to join with their brothers to fight for a just society. Its form, reminiscent of the Lord's Prayer, was a reflection of Víctor's newly reawakened interest in the Bible for its poetry and humanist values, at a time when a deep understanding was growing between progressive Catholics and Marxists in Latin America. (1984, p. 131)

In its artistic style, "Plegaria" both conforms to and stretches Jara's earlier practices. It reveals the use of arch form, in that the second stanza, while beginning "Stand up/ And look at your hands/ Take your brother's hand so you can grow," is nearly exactly recapitulated in the final stanza, with only the last line being modified. One locates simile ("Blow, like the wind blows the wild flower of the mountain pass"; "Clean, like the fire, the barrel of my gun"). Once again, now profoundly, there is focus on the *hands*—not those of a blanket-weaver, but those of workers.

Musically one perceives a juxtaposition of two minor modes: Dorian (in the opening melodic motif) and Aeolian (in the melody of the stanzas). Yet Jara begins to innovate. While "Plegaria" opens in the key of E minor, for the first two stanzas, he then offers a *tonal shift* (unprepared) to the *parallel major*, E major, for the exhortations that occupy the center of the song—the *prayers*, themselves. And that tonal shift into the parallel major corresponds with the bright optimism of the text, at that point: "We'll go together, united by blood; the future can begin TODAY." The middle section of the song, which conveys and builds the emotion of this artwork, sees, harmonically, a persistent Mixolydian alternation, between the tonic of E major and its subtonic key, D major. Complementing that now-established modal usage, in Jara's oeuvre, is the startling deployment of the emotionally charged major-major-seventh chord, here built on the subdominant root of A major, that harmonic color perhaps dramatically conveying the idea of *plea*.

As the emotion and the tempo—the urgency—of "Plegaria" build, toward the end of the middle section, so Jara then pulls the string, for the concluding ("Stand

---

Violeta Parra likewise captured an analogous child's-wake *despedimiento*, in dialect, in her *décima*, "Madre mía, no me llores" (Parra, 1970, pp. 131-2). "Farewell" verses, such as these documented for selected Latin American child's wake music-rituals, have roots in the early Christian era (Rush, 1941, pp. 185-6).

up/ And look at your hands") recapitulating stanza, now *shifting* again *back* into the original key: E minor. This serves to unify the song (E minor/E major/ E minor), creating the effect of an "harmonic arch"—E minor framing the song, as a whole—thus reinforcing the textual "arch" of the repetition of the second stanza. In short, the final stanza is a synthesis of the "old" and the "new": harmonically a return to the original key, but retaining the urgent *Presto* tempo generated in the middle section. Peter Gould seeks to "imagine" the nature of the audience whom Víctor Jara might have had in mind with "Plegaria" when he suggests that Jara

> was singing to the poor and indigenous ... to the growing group of music and theatre artists he belonged to, and to the growing ranks of Allende supporters. ... And in a way he may also have been singing to the elite power structure, first calling them to come across, but, if they would not, daring them to retaliate against him by singing in a wide range of challenging voices, daring them to a punishment he would—everyone would—later underestimate. (2002, p. 156)

In sum, Jara has created a remarkable, effective work of art in "Plegaria." The established stylistic traits of arch form, simile, focus on the hands, and use of multiple different modes coexist with powerful new approaches: a worker-solidarity "plea," based on the Lord's Prayer; parallel minor alternating with its parallel major, for expressive purposes; a concluding climax of true power, juxtaposing original key with "new," rapid, tempo; a message directed to a notably broad listening public—both potential supporters and likely detractors. One can clearly understand the reasons "Plegaria" was singled out for award, at the 1969 First Festival of Chilean New Song.

Jara's "El pimiento" (1965) is a fitting song with which to conclude this analytical segment as it encapsulates many of the musical and textual stylistic signatures we have singled out in this chapter. Ostensibly, the song speaks of a red pepper bush, blooming in the desert of the Chilean north, the enormously arid Atacama Desert, considered, at its core, the driest place on earth. Jara uses the red pepper bush and its profusion of fiery red fruit-pods as a metaphor for Marxist sentiment. The song text, like the plant itself, is filled with red: "When your branches bloom/ It is a fire"; "Spilling so much red/ Completely red/ completely red"; "You should continue blooming/ Like a fire." There are allusions to the plant's working beneath the ground: "No one sees it working/ Underneath the soil." At the mid-point of Jara's song, one hears a departure from the melodic and harmonic activity, a play of percussive sounds (the *kena* at one point recapitulating the minor-pentatonic outline of the song), in an unsteady, if occasionally rhythmic, character. The Atacama Desert is the region of Chilean mining, and it includes the Chuquicamata open-pit copper mine (the world's largest). The spring of "El Pimiento," is also in a region of some 11 different mines. The sounds audible at the mid-point of Jara's song—heard just prior to "No one sees it working/ Underneath the soil,"—allude to the *roots* of the pepper plant, working beneath the soil, while also being suggestive of miners working underground. In listening to these sounds, one can imagine sounds of digging and hammering.

Musically, Jara employs fundamentally the D minor pentatonic scale (scale-degrees: 8-7-5-4-3-[1]), with an interesting treatment of scale-degree 6: it is at times *raised*—creating the Dorian mode, at other moments *lowered*—creating the Aeolian mode: thus, a harkening back to Jara's accustomed multiple modes. The bimodality we saw earlier, in "Angelita Huenumán," is once again in evidence: D minor/F major. Again, too, we encounter metaphor and simile: "When your branches bloom/ It is a fire"; "You should continue blooming/ Like a fire." The underlying revolutionary message appears in the final stanza; here, the red (fruit-pods; Communist flag, with hammer) and the underground labor (plant roots; miners) meet: "You should continue blooming/ Like a fire/ Because the north [of Chile]/ Is all yours/ Fully and completely/ Fully and completely." Jara suggests that "you" workers, in the northern Chilean mines, should continue blooming (appearing together, organizing), for the north of the country [can be] all your own. Where "Plegaria" embodied a call to worker solidarity via the Lord's Prayer, here, in "El Pimiento," we find an analogous, now metaphoric, call to worker solidarity. In short, in "El Pimiento," we see Jara utilizing his principal stylistic tools encountered to date: pentatonic scale, harmonic bimodality, multiple modes, figure of speech (metaphor and simile), call to revolution.

## Post-1973: The Multidimensional Iconic Role

*Chilean Rock Group: Los Prisioneros*

In Chile, the artistic legacy of Víctor Jara continues in the Chilean political and musical underground, particularly in the rock group Los Prisioneros, heirs to the legacies of Violeta Parra and Víctor Jara. Patricia Vilches has discussed how this ensemble, from a working-class neighborhood of Santiago, came together as a group in 1979, then emerged on the Chilean rock music scene in roughly 1984 (2004, pp. 197, 205). In the early years, the songs of these young rockers were not aired on official radio, yet they quickly became one of the most-listened-to ensembles of the Chilean musical/political underground (Vilches, 2004, p. 205). Vilches notes the linkages between Los Prisioneros and Parra and Jara, among these the contestatory nature of the song lyrics. Both Nueva Canción and rock emerged at the same juncture, the 1970s, each disturbed by political happenings in Chile during that time.

Vilches asserts that Jara's name is fully identified with the collective memory of the political campaign and subsequent government of Allende's Unidad Popular, during which the goal was to obtain for the working classes the cultural benefits that had earlier been the privilege of the few (2004, pp. 200-201). Vilches states that Jara, as early as his 1962 song, "¿Qué sacó rogar al cielo?," expresses empathy—and an indisputable link—with the dispossessed (2004, pp. 201-2).

Those who support Los Prisioneros hear in their song lyrics—in an emotional, visceral fashion—the historical memory of the epoch of Chile's military junta, in their country. Ensemble leader Jorge González also shares with Jara an urgency to inform his listeners, through his songs, about the historical/ideological processes of the Chile of his own day (Vilches, 2004, pp. 204-5). Vilches compares Jara's song, "Movil' Oil Special" to Jorge González's lyric, "La voz de los '80," stating that both expressions call upon the youth of the political Left to support revolutionary processes in Latin America (2004, p. 205). According to Vilches, Jorge González believes that, today, in Chile, historical/ideological movements have conspired to eliminate the "Left" of earlier years (2004, p. 207). With this in mind, listening to Los Prisioneros today offers an "historic journey of committed music" (Vilches, 2004, p. 209), dating from the era of Salvador Allende.

*Songs Alluding to Víctor Jara*

Holly Near (b. 1949) deployed music to espouse political causes, often before others did so. Her musical career blossomed in the 1970s; her engagement with topical lyrics, however, echoed the political song of Phil Ochs and Tom Paxton of the prior decade. "It Could Have Been Me," released on *Holly Near: A Live Album* (1974) was penned in response to the Kent State University shootings of students in May, 1970. It contains three stanzas, with an introductory and thence periodic choral refrain. Stanza two reads: "The junta took the fingers from Víctor Jara's hands/ They said to the gentle poet, 'Play your guitar now if you can!'/ Well Víctor started singing until they shot his body down/ You can kill a man but not a song when it's sung the whole world round." The recording begins with Near's spoken introduction: "In May of 1974, when I was invited to sing at a memorial event for the four students who were killed at Kent State, Ohio, and, ... I stood there in a field and listened to those bells toll, very quietly, for a long time ...," at which point, she begins to sing the choral refrain. Until the concluding chorus, the entire song is sung *a cappella*, in a Moderato tempo, and it is set in the key of D major. Her melodic line employs a full heptatonic major scale, and the harmonic scheme employs chords of the tonic, dominant, subdominant, supertonic, mediant, and submediant. The musical accompaniment (bass and piano) enters, in a rousing concluding chorus, which is sung twice, with an extension ("I can, too") the second time. This accompanied choral conclusion is lively, rhythmic, and syncopated.

Near's message is one of homage to those who gave their lives for the cause of freedom, as the ending of the choral refrain indicates: "But, if you can work (die, sing, live) for freedom, freedom, freedom, freedom, If you can die for freedom, I can too." Her citation of Víctor Jara's final torture in the stadium broadly echoes this message: written in 1974, "It Could Have Been Me" was penned within a year of Jara's death and clearly made a great impact on Holly Near. In the refrain "And it may be me, dear sisters and brothers, before we are through ..." one cannot help but feel, here, a premonition of death akin to what Jara, referencing

Che Guevara, conveyed in "El aparecido."⁹ We shall see, later in this chapter, how the Arlo Guthrie/Adrian Mitchell song "Víctor Jara of Chile" partakes of this same ominous foreboding, now of the death of Víctor Jara, himself. Indeed, in the final line of "Plegaria," Jara conveyed some of this same premonition—for himself: "We'll go together united by blood/ Now and in the hour of our death."

U2's song "One Tree Hill" appeared on their CD *The Joshua Tree* (1987). At least two of the YouTube recordings of this song¹⁰ carry spoken dedications to Bono's friend, Greg Carroll, and the song's 1987 CD liner notes, following the song's text, carry the inscription: "(Greg Carroll's Funeral, Wanganui, New Zealand, 10th July)."¹¹ The song contains the lines: "And in the world a heart of darkness, a fire zone/ Where poets speak their hearts, then bleed for it/ Jara sang—his song a weapon/ In the hands of one/ Whose blood still cries/ from the ground/ He runs like a river runs to the sea ...." Bono references Joseph Conrad's terrifying *Heart of Darkness* (1902), to convey the fearsomeness of the situation where "poets speak their hearts, then bleed for it"—exactly what Jara did, in "Plegaria," ultimately paying for these and many other unvarnished expressions with his own life. Unquestionably, song was, for Víctor Jara, "a weapon," and, as this chapter seeks to clarify, his "blood still cries from the ground." Musically, the harmonic palette of "One Tree Hill" is sparse, relying (in the tonic of C major) upon tonic, subdominant, and subtonic (B flat major), the subtonic being set against the subdominant. The prominent use of B flat major in a song decidedly in C major suggests the Mixolydian, a mode Jara foregrounded in "Despedimiento del angelito" and "Plegaria a un labrador."

Swedish progressive political rockers Hoola Bandoola Band, another group who kept the Jara flame burning, achieved significant commercial renown in the 1970s. Mikael Wiehe, who along with Björn Afzelius led the band, translated Dylan's songs into Swedish and composed widely known progressive songs; one of these, "Vem kan man lita på?" (Who Can You Depend On?), created a satire on alleged selling-out by John Lennon and by Bob Dylan (Eyerman and Jamison, 1998, pp. 152-3). Other Wiehe songs addressed the CIA, the sinking of the *Titanic*, freedom of expression, and the struggle for justice. According to Ron Eyerman and Andrew Jamison (1998, p. 153), "One of [Wiehe's] best songs with Hoola Bandoola, a eulogy over the Chilean folksinger, Víctor Jara, well expressed the international solidarity, but also the broader political ideals, of the [Swedish]

---

⁹ For my analysis of Jara's "El aparecido," with its motivating message of glorification of a revolutionary hero, Che Guevara, whom Víctor Jara had met briefly in 1960 (Jara, 1984, p. 52), see Schechter (2009, pp. 418-21).

¹⁰ http://www.youtube.com/watch?v=6xqjsP9Un8I; http://www.youtube.com/watch?v=QprWe_kqliE, both accessed September 11, 2008.

¹¹ Greg Carroll died in a motorbike accident in Dublin. See U2 FAQS.COM (accessed September 11, 2008) for reporting on the background of the "One Tree Hill" of the song's title, and on the relationship between Greg Carroll and U2.

progressive music movement." They provide the following song text excerpt, in English:

> There are many who do tricks
>> For those who hold onto power.
> And there are many who grovel for crumbs
>> At the tables of the rich.
> But you made your choice, to sing for the many.
> And you laughed at the promises
>> And threats of those who rule.
> Yes, Víctor Jara you gave voice
>> To the prisoner's longing for freedom
> And for those who believed in a future
>> With only people in power.
> And you gave strength and courage
>> To the trampled-upon's dreaming.
> But for the rich and the few
>> You sang out your disgust. (Eyerman and Jamison, 1998, p. 153)

These Hoola Bandoola Band "Víctor Jara" lyrics echo sentiments we have now discovered in Jara's "Plegaria a un labrador" ("you made your choice, to sing for the many").

Originally performed in Swedish, the song has six verses, with an introductory and intermittent, flute-dominated instrumental section. One hears (in the key, C minor) verses 1/3/5 in: tonic-dominant-tonic, then V/III-III, then V/V-V; verses 2/4/6 in: tonic-dominant-tonic, then V/iv-iv-V-i. The harmony of the instrumental sections similarly (to the harmony of verses 1/3/5) enacts a play between the mediant key (E flat major—the relative major key) and the original tonic, of C minor. In other words, Hoola Bandoola Band's "Víctor Jara" harmonically exploits the bimodality of relative minor/relative major alternation, which is exactly what we discovered in Víctor Jara's "Angelita Huenumán" and "El Pimiento," and what we noted was characteristic of traditional musics of the Andes region of South America.

The song "Víctor Jara of Chile" is a collaborative effort of Arlo Guthrie (composer/performer, b. 1947) and Adrian Mitchell (1932-2008). Mitchell was a prolific and popular British poet/dramatist known for works with a strong social conscience. After working as a journalist, he became a freelance writer, penning works for adults and children; his oeuvre includes novels, plays, libretti, and poetry. His poem, "Víctor Jara of Chile," appears in his anthology, *The Apeman Cometh: Poems by Adrian Mitchell*, published in 1975, two years after Víctor Jara's murder in Santiago. The performance poet/songwriter Trev Teasdel described the song as "one of the most powerful protest songs ever written and probably not as well known as it deserves. It began as a poem by one of the top British poets—Adrian Mitchell and Arlo Guthrie was inspired to set the poem to music to great effect in my opinion."[12] The song functions as an icon for the style and content of several Víctor Jara songs analyzed earlier in this chapter.

First, Adrian Mitchell's "Víctor Jara of Chile" is strophic in form, and it is a ballad, a tale. In this sense, though it resonates with Víctor Jara's "Angelita Huenumán," Mitchell's ballad adds a refrain: "And his hands were gentle/ His hands were strong." This recurring refrain focuses on Jara's hands, now, where Víctor Jara's own songs ("Angelita Huenumán" and "Plegaria") had also centered on the hands: those of a skilled rural artisan, and, those of workers called to unite. The biographical intent of Jara's "Angelita Huenumán" is replicated here, too, in Mitchell's poem: he effectively sketches the life of Víctor Jara, from his childhood, through his adult musical battles on behalf of workers to his final torture and martyrdom. Similarly, the arch form we discovered repeatedly in Jara's songs is likewise found in "Víctor Jara of Chile": the first quatrain, together with its refrain, is repeated at the poem's conclusion.

Beyond broad formal matters, Mitchell attends even more closely, to Jara's own expressions and life experiences. In the sixth quatrain of his poem, he writes: "... He [Jara] sang: take hold of your brother's hand/ The future begins today," which is a quote from Jara's "Plegaria," second stanza. Mitchell's fifth quatrain, "He sang about the copper miners/ And those who work the land/ He sang about the factory workers ...," recalls "El Pimiento" and "Plegaria." In his second stanza, Mitchell's line "Víctor Jara was a peasant ... [who, as a boy] sat upon his father's plough" both conforms to the lad's actual experience (Jara, 1984, p. 25) and echoes Jara's text, in his song, "El arado." Likewise, Mitchell's depiction, in stanza three, of Víctor's presence, as a lad, at the occasion "When ... one of [the neighbors'] children died/ His mother sang all night for them/ With Víctor by her side," is both faithful to the actual facts—as Joan Jara recalls: "Víctor used to go with his mother to other houses in the village when, as happened all too often, a baby died ... the all-night wake was a festive occasion ... Half asleep and half awake, Víctor curled up on the floor beside his mother as she sang ..." (1984, pp. 25-6)—and resonates with the sentiments of Jara's own song, "Despedimiento del angelito," discussed earlier in this chapter.

Perhaps more profoundly, we find, in "Víctor Jara of Chile," the premonition/ prediction/description of the death of a Communist/Socialist cultural icon, eerily akin to Jara's own song, "El aparecido." In a similar vein, Adrian Mitchell drafts, in his poem, stanzas that depict the life of Víctor Jara, who, in a September 28, 1961, letter to Joan Jara described his own absorption in Communism (Jara, 1984, p. 66). The ghostly notion of premonition is paramount in both poems/ songs. "El aparecido" depicts a man being warned to run, for he will be killed; a man being intentionally pursued, a man whose head is being finished off "By ravens with talons of gold," which is a reference to the wealthy and powerful. Mitchell's "Víctor Jara of Chile" likewise builds, in a climactic fashion, toward

---

[12]   http://trevteasdelsongs.vox.com/library/post/victor-jara-written-by-adrian-mitchell -arlo-guthrie.html, accessed August 27, 2008.

the moment of Víctor Jara's being "caged" in the stadium, and recounts vividly his ultimate isolation in that mass of humanity, his torture, and his assassination by the military of the September, 1973 coup. Indeed, the notions of building to climax and condemnation at impending/actual murder evident in Jara's "El aparecido" are highlighted by Adrian Mitchell in his poem.

Arlo Guthrie composes the music for Mitchell's "Víctor Jara of Chile" (Jara and Mitchell, 1976, pp. 12-13). Guthrie's 1978 recording, with Shenandoah, is a ballad, Moderato, in 4/4 meter, with identical music for each verse. There is a decidedly plagal thrust to the harmonic setting, with (stanza one) the subdominant harmony (IV) present on the words, "lived," and "fought," in the verse, and, in the refrain, "his hands were strong," creating a plagal cadence. Looking more closely, we find something that clearly echoes Víctor Jara's own harmonic usage: *modality*, specifically, in this instance, Mixolydian mode. We recall Jara's recourse to modal harmony in his "Despedimiento del angelito," his "Plegaria a un labrador," and his "El Pimiento." In both "Despedimiento" and "Plegaria" he used the Mixolydian mode. Here, in Arlo Guthrie's setting of Mitchell's poem "Víctor Jara of Chile" the only chords *other than* the expected tonic (D major), dominant (A major), and subdominant (G major; see above paragraph) in the song's key of D major are *E minor* and *B minor*. These two chords are at once striking—being in the minor, in contrast to the major of the three structural chords—and Mixolydian, in character: E minor is located immediately following D major, thus the Mixolydian relationship of a whole-step (major second), E to D; and, B minor is placed immediately before the dominant, A major, thus the Mixolydian relationship of a whole-step (major second), B to A. The E minor and B minor chords are not prepared by any form of secondary-dominant harmony—they are, therefore, all the more striking in impact. By their unprepared and isolated nature (each one is sounded but once), they generate much of the power and emotion latent in Arlo Guthrie's song. In many different dimensions, the Adrian Mitchell/Arlo Guthrie "Víctor Jara of Chile" is iconic of the life, philosophy, political orientation, and artistic structures and techniques of Víctor Jara the poet/composer/performer.

Among Jara's artistic stylistic signatures, then, we find an identification with the Chilean masses—artisans, miners, workers of all stripes; a rallying cry to revolutionary ideals—worker solidarity, urging miners to unite; formal structures employing Lord's-Prayer template and strophic schemes; focus on the hands; multifarious figures of speech; arch form in stanza, melody, and/or harmony; harmonic use of modal structures, often multiple modes in the same song; the bimodality of juxtaposed relative minor/relative major scales; melodic pentatonicism; encapsulating traditional rural Chilean speech and practices—modal-scale-usage, dialect, and child's-wake "Farewell" verse.

Like his music, Jara's legacy emerges as a prism of diverse angles; this chapter has elucidated the following ones: the 1980s emergence, in Chile, of Los Prisioneros, a rock group in the politically committed mold of the songs of Jara and Parra, specifically reenacting the biting satire of some of Jara's great expressions;

the explicit reference to Víctor Jara in four distinctive expressions by noted figures and ensembles of the contemporary West: Holly Near, U2, Hoola Bandoola Band, and Arlo Guthrie/Adrian Mitchell. These four analyzed songs echo with Jara's broader messages; with the foreboding of death seen in Jara's "Plegaria"; with Jara's willingness to speak his mind, to speak out for what he believed (U2's "One Tree Hill": "Where poets speak their hearts, then bleed for it"); with Jara's decision "to sing for the many" (Hoola Bandoola Band song, "Víctor Jara"); with Jara's own biography; and with Jara's stylistic signatures: strophic form, focus on the hands, arch form, figures of speech, modal harmony—specifically, Mixolydian mode and harmonic bimodality. In short, Jara's has been a deep, multichanneled legacy, a stream that, as one examines it closely, broadens into a rich, verdant, and powerful river. All this is testimony to the craft and strength of his artistry.

## Chapter 9

# No Country for Young Women: Celtic Music, Dissent, and the Irish Female Body

Gerry Smyth

On January 31, 1984, a 15-year-old girl named Ann Lovett left school after morning lessons and made her way to a field outside the small town of Granard in County Longford in the Republic of Ireland. In the field was a shrine to the Virgin Mary. At around 4.00 p.m. she was found by a passing schoolboy, lying in the grass beside the dead body of a baby she had attempted to deliver alone and unaided. Ann Lovett died later that day from blood loss and exposure. The event shocked the local community and the island (separated into the northern and southern states) as a whole. One of the interventions within the ensuing debate was made by a Dublin-based performance artist named Nigel Rolfe, who presented a lyric entitled "Middle of the Island" to Christy Moore, one of Ireland's most successful folk singers. Moore set the lyric to music and included the song (with vocal accompaniment from Sinéad O'Connor) on his 1989 album *Voyage*. Two of Rolfe's lines encapsulate the shock and anger of the moment: "Everybody knew, nobody said"; "It was a sad, slow, stupid death for them both."

The death of Ann Lovett was immediately acknowledged, and has continued to be regarded in the years since, as a pivotal moment in modern Irish history. The event encapsulates a struggle between modernity and tradition which many perceive as the island's central ideological conflict throughout the modern era. That struggle, as well as the debates attending it, are also to be found in "Middle of the Island"—in its musical and lyrical discourses as well as in a number of other factors bearing upon the "meaning" of the song. In short, the scandal of Ann Lovett's tragic death, as well as this particular musical response to it, are locked in to some of the most compelling moral, political, and cultural issues besetting modern Ireland. It is the task of this chapter to describe those issues, and to identify the nature of the relationship between the "primary" event and the "secondary" musical response which it generated.

## The Female Body and the State

On September 7, 1983, when Ann Lovett was about 17 weeks pregnant, the people of the Republic of Ireland approved by referendum a constitutional ban on abortion. This event represents just one moment within a much longer history in which the Irish state attempted to assert control over the female body (Ward, 1991; Flynn, 1993). After independence in 1922, a church-state partnership claimed jurisdiction over all matters relating to the female body, including sex, sexual health, reproduction, and legal status. Failures to adhere to the Irish feminine ideal were strongly sanctioned, both officially and in vernacular culture (Coulter, 1993; Daly, 1997). There were strong taboos against pre-marital sex and adultery. Single motherhood could have especially dire ramifications—at least for the mother. Divorce and "artificial" contraception were banned, although the more "liberal" wing of the establishment pointed to the sops of legal separation (once duly sanctioned by the Catholic hierarchy) and the so-called rhythm method (a "natural" contraceptive system to which many Irish people of the late twentieth century owe their existence).

Feminism and bourgeois revisionism began to make inroads into Irish life during the 1960s, although this was predominantly an urban, middle-class development (Foster, 2007). The principal effect of this was to excite strong establishment reaction, which in turn precipitated the abortion and divorce referenda of the 1980s and 1990s. These issues were forced by elements (sponsored, once again, by the institutions of church and state) which retained an investment in enshrining once and for all a set of values which (so they believed) constituted an immemorial Irish identity, especially the role and representation of the female body in relation to that identity. If, during the late summer of 1983, the debate throughout the Republic of Ireland on the Eighth Amendment was both rancorous and far-reaching, the outcome was never really in any doubt: the people voted to accept it by a majority of two to one (Hesketh, 1990).

This was the context within which Ann Lovett lived her short life. Even as her own body was in the process of changing, she would have been confronted—in the media, at school, in the community at large—with an array of frighteningly prescriptive discourses relating to the use and disposal of the Irish female body. Eventually, the state into which she had been born decided that it retained control over her body, its functions, disposition, and capacities. If, as the poet W.B. Yeats famously proclaimed, the Ireland of his day was "no country for old men" (1981, p. 217) the fate of Ann Lovett was a disastrous demonstration that the same place was not a particularly salubrious country for young women in the late twentieth century.

## Music in Ireland in the Late Twentieth Century

"Middle of the Island" is clearly *about* the death of Ann Lovett, and thus by extension *about* the array of sociocultural discourses (religious, familial, educational, medical) which created the context within which that execrable event occurred. It is also a very particular kind of cultural event in itself, however—a song—and as such, it is necessary to approach it with an awareness of the traditions within which certain musical discourses emerge and develop. There are in fact three recognizable, though overlapping musical discourses discernible within "Middle of the Island," which I would like to describe briefly before moving on to examine the song itself.

Since its "discovery" and institutional ratification in the late eighteenth century, traditional music had emerged as one of the principal cultural signifiers of Irish identity. "Traditional music" comprehends an identifiable body of material which includes dance tunes of various kinds (with the reel and the jig predominating) and a song canon combining influences from an ancient Gaelic poetry tradition with a ballad repertoire accumulated over centuries of international exchange (O'Boyle, 1976). Traditional music also comprehends a particular set of musical values which determine instrument selection and technique, text structure, the dynamics of ensemble performance, etc., as well as a set of extra-musical precepts which impact significantly upon how the music is produced and consumed (Vallely, 1999, pp. xv-xviii).

Traditional music's position as an easily recognizable sonic representation of Irishness was consolidated by the development of a complex infrastructure throughout the nineteenth and twentieth centuries (including various amateur and academic initiatives) which guaranteed it a crucial role within Irish cultural life. After 1922, it became one of the tasks of a newly independent state to nurture this cultural practice in which, so it was widely believed, some inalienable sense of Irish identity was embodied (White, 1998; Smyth, 2005, pp. 18-24).

As with so many other areas of Irish life, this model of traditional music began to come under pressure with the advent of mass media during the 1960s and the emergence of a general revisionist sensibility within the public sphere. As the meaning of Irishness changed, in other words, so the function of those cultural practices which embodied Irish identity were obliged to change also. It was one of the signs that things were changing (and not necessarily for the better) that a widely-practiced and much-valued "traditional" discourse fused in all sorts of ways with various elements (musical and otherwise) which, precisely because of their "foreign" status, were categorically suspect to a church-state establishment.

Music is particularly amenable to influence; ultimately, it refuses to adhere to the prescriptions laid down in nonmusical agenda (those geared towards state or subject formation, for example). Music is always adapting, anticipating, remembering, welcoming, suggesting, gesturing, metamorphosing—it is always somewhere and something other than we would wish it to be. That in large part constitutes its perennial fascination. It should thus come as no surprise that traditional music provided a crucial site for the contention between tradition and modernity which came to characterize Irish life during and after the 1960s, nor that such debates should be understood to have implications which impact upon every aspect of Irish life, both contemporary and historical.

The singer-songwriter Christy Moore was exposed to Irish traditional music as he was growing up in Kildare (a predominantly rural county at the time, southwest of Dublin) during the 1950s and 1960s. At the same time, like so many other young Irish people of the period he would have been aware of the folk movement which was gathering pace in the United States and the UK. At an early stage, the idea of North American folk music connoted the performance of material (traditional ballads in the main) adapted from the immigrant Celtic and Anglo-Saxon communities. During the first half of the twentieth century, however, the idea of folk music had incorporated a number of identifiable influences (acoustic blues, for example) and modifications (an emphasis on topicality and vaguely leftish leanings) (Reuss, 2000; Mitchell, 2007). By the 1960s the iconic figure of the international folk movement was the hard-traveling, guitar-toting white male, a figure upon whom Woody Guthrie was the defining historical influence, and for whom early Bob Dylan was the modern avatar (Cohen, 2002).

As an Irish folk singer, Christy Moore could be expected to perform material from the native tradition with which he was so familiar. So it proved on an early album entitled *Prosperous* (1970), which included a range of traditional material including indigenous and adapted British ballads. However, the album also included original songs by Moore, one song by Dylan, and one by Guthrie himself. In fact, Moore's career profile (including his association with the seminal bands Planxty and Moving Hearts during the 1970s and 1980s) has by and large adhered to the template laid down on *Prosperous* in as much as he has continued to perform a blend of traditional and topical material—the latter a combination of self-penned and purpose-written ballads.[1] He has also become identified as a kind of contemporary protest singer, something once again which has been adapted from the folk profile of Guthrie, early Dylan, and the American folk movement of the 1960s. Over the course of a 40-year career Moore has performed a range of material characteristic of what might be described as a generally left-wing engagement with the modern world. He has sung about "dissident" topics ranging from nuclear power to witches, from the Spanish Civil War to American industrial relations. He has performed material by politically engaged artists such as Morrissey, Elvis Costello, Jackson Browne, Willie Nelson, Joni Mitchell, and Bono, while also being claimed as an influence by various younger Irish musicians possessed of a vaguely dissenting profile (such as Shane MacGowan, Damien Dempsey, and Sinéad O'Connor). Christy Moore is, to all intents and purposes, the nearest thing contemporary Ireland has had to a high-profile protest singer.

Part of this identity is constituted in terms of a specifically sonic discourse. Moore retains a musical identity that is "folky," by which I mean lo-tech and oriented toward live performance. He plays most of his material on acoustic guitar, using a capo to enable him to perform the songs using chords related to his favorite G shape. Although occasionally employing acoustic accompanists (such as his

---

[1]    See http://www.christymoore.com/discography.php (accessed August 7, 2009) for a list of Moore's recorded repertoire.

friends Declan Sinnott on guitar and Donal Lunny on bouzouki), Moore's recorded repertoire clearly adheres to a "folk" aesthetic in so far as the foregrounded lyrics are mediated by his distinctive vocal style, while the modest musical arrangements constantly gesture toward the ideal of live solo performance. The one occasion on which Moore deviated significantly from that aesthetic was on *Voyage*, the album containing "Middle of the Island." Moore's own comment on this release is instructive:

> I got my head turned here by Warner suits. They came to my home and sat there telling me I should remix the album. An A & R wanker who fell asleep during the meeting, a big shot from London, the head of WEA Ireland, my manager and me. I listened to these shysters and took their counsel and allowed my album to be remixed. It was a rash and regrettable move on my part and to this day I regret it—but I learned.[2]

One of the reasons why Moore may have allowed his head to be turned from what he believed to be his core values was the emergence of a new style of "Irish" music during the 1980s. In 1988, Moore's label WEA released an album entitled *Watermark* by the Irish artist known as Enya. The latter was in fact Eithne Ni Bhraonjin, one time member of the family band Clannad who became well known in Ireland during the 1970s performing a blend of traditional and jazz music, and who had scored a Top 10 hit in the UK in 1982 with a single entitled "Theme from *Harry's Game*." If that track introduced the possibility of a new form of sonic Irishness, it was the worldwide success of *Watermark* a number of years later, spearheaded by the single "Orinoco Flow," that brought the genre known as "Celtic" music to a mass market.

"Celtic" music constitutes an important subgenre of the "world music" marketing phenomenon that emerged in the later decades of the twentieth century (Stokes and Bohlman, 2003). This style is possessed of a highly distinctive sonic signature, characterized by lush, layered soundscapes which are themselves the result of intense studio work involving a combination of "real" and synthesized instruments. These technical values support a thematic function which is generally at a distance from the modern world. The lyric of "Orinoco Flow," for example, invites the listener to "sail away" in order to experience the different values associated with a range of exotic locations removed in space and time from "normality": the Yellow Sea, Avalon, Fiji, Babylon, etc. Music and lyrics combine to produce a mood that is clearly intended to be ethereal, other-worldly and New Ageish—a species of "Celtic" spirituality, in fact, understood by its adherents to be at odds with a prevailing Western system in which material success is the implicit index of happiness.

---

[2]  The comment may be found in the "More Info" section of the notes on *Voyage* at http://www.christymoore.com/discography.php, accessed August 7, 2009.

Christy Moore was not the only artist to feel the force of a sound that has become perhaps the foremost sonic signifier of Irish identity in the years since "Theme from *Harry's Game*" and *Watermark*. Such a development has been subject to widespread criticism, however, and on a number of grounds. For one thing, so-called "Celtic" music has been critiqued as an attempt on the part of various critical and commercial institutions to posit a connection between quite diverse musical practices—not only Irish, but a whole range of supposedly affiliated regions and nations, including Scotland, Wales, Brittany, and Gallicia. In some accounts "Celtic music" encompasses everything from Alan Stivell to U2, rendering any attempt to describe a cogent impetus informing the music as highly questionable (Melhuish, 1998; Skinner Sawyers, 2000).

The key to its ideological status, however, is encoded in the seemingly unproblematical use of the word "Celtic," a term with a long and troubled career in Irish cultural history (Smyth, 1996). Serious problems are bound to arise whenever a cluster of cultural practices and themes becomes attached to a specific ethnic or racial discourse. Despite its undoubted novel status in commercial terms, it remains the case that "Celtic music" is composed, performed, and received in terms of long-established discourses which emphasize "Celtic" difference from mainstream or "ordinary" experience. Especially in relation to Ireland, "Celtic music" in fact serves to reconfirm certain stereotypical notions regarding an essential national recalcitrance toward modernity, and an innate—at times, indeed, almost a biological—difference from other cultural formations.

The phenomenon of "Celtic music" represents a lucrative niche market in which certain experiences are offered to those willing to invest—emotionally, culturally, and financially—in the notion of some inherent Celtic spirituality which is supposedly at odds with the modern world. Like all ideologies, Celticism is enabling in terms of subject-formation: it offers the individual a way to experience, to be and to act in the modern world. Like all ideologies, however, it also represents an attempt to conflate cultural and natural discourses, to convert a set of historical contingencies into an identity, and to invite subjects to claim that identity as their own.

**"Middle of the Island"**

By the time Moore came to record *Voyage*, traditional, folk, and Celtic music were established elements within Irish popular music. Like all his albums, *Voyage* contains a mixture of material.[3] It was, nevertheless, a departure for him, and one which he came to consider as a false step. The title track is a slow, sentimental

---

[3]     *Voyage* was produced by Donal Lunny, and was recorded at three Dublin studios in the early months of 1989. Notable musicians who contributed to the album include Mícheál Ó Súilleabháin (future head of the Irish World Music Centre at the University of Limerick), singer Mary Black, Paddy Maloney of The Chieftains, and Elvis Costello.

love song organized around an increasingly strained nautical metaphor. The inclusion of another love ballad (Ewan McColl's "The First Time Ever I Saw Your Face," widely perceived as a modern popular "classic") is perhaps another indication of record company pressure. There are also topical interventions such as "Musha God Help Her" (about Dublin's contemporary underclass) and "Farewell to Pripchat" (about the Chernobyl disaster). The album contains four songs by Jimmy McCarthy, a well-known songwriter from Cork and a popular performer in his own right. Of these four, only "Missing You," on the theme of Ireland's latest "lost" generation of emigrants, is a "typical" Moore song; the others are more ambitious (lyrically, structurally, and musically) than had been his wont up until this point. The same is true of "Deportees' Club," purpose-written for the album by the British-Irish rock artist Elvis Costello, and a song which contributed to Moore's reputation as a serious artist possessed of cross-over potential.

The signature status of "Middle of the Island" is established by the fact that it is the last sequenced track on the album. The song lasts four minutes and five seconds. Its B flat minor key is unfriendly for the acoustic guitar (even one with a capo on the first or the sixth fret). Twelve seconds of electric slide guitar (0.06-0.18, played, untreated apart from slight reverb, by Moore's long-time collaborator Declan Sinnott) help to establish a yearning, melancholy atmosphere from the outset. Besides this, however, the track comprises only four distinct "voices." The first is that of a Prophet-5 synthesizer played by Donal Lunny (who also produced the album). This is an analogue keyboard instrument developed in the United States during the late 1970s, and capable of sophisticated polyphonic effects. Lunny has used it extensively since the early 1980s whenever he wishes to introduce drama and texture into what would otherwise stand as standard acoustic ballads. Such was the effect it had when he played it on "Ride On" (another Jimmy McCarthy composition), the seminal track from the album of that title released in 1984, and still Moore's most successful release. Such was the effect, also, when Clannad used the Prophet to create the brooding, eerie soundscape of "Theme from *Harry's Game*." This instrument's use in Irish music stands as a clear indication of the way in which innovative technology can be deployed to create discursive effects which are in some respects opposed to technology, in terms of both their ethos and their wider cultural impact.

The melody of "Middle of the Island" is not, as suggested by Moore on his website, "sung a cappella to a drone," as there are in fact clearly discernible chord changes (provided by the Prophet) from B flat minor to F major and E flat minor, as well as harmonic overtones throughout. Nevertheless, the melody clearly seeks to evoke something brooding and primordial, and it is interesting to observe how Moore and his fellow musicians set about creating this effect. The melody of "Middle of the Island" claims allegiance with the traditional Gaelic singing style known as *sean-nós*, which translates as "old style." *Sean-nós* is rooted in the social, cultural, and linguistic systems of the Gaelic world (Vallely, 1999, pp. 336-45). It refers in the first instance to a style of unaccompanied singing which is characterized by a great number of technical and contextual protocols, the complexity of which only prolonged exposure and study can comprehend. These include subtle tone quality, rhythmic variation, phrasing, and (most recognizably to an outsider) pronounced melodic ornamentation. Despite this, it is a style in which communication is valued above technique, and in which emotion and personality are the yardsticks of a successful performance.

So-called "Celtic" music has developed a kind of vulgar *sean-nós* element which endeavors to invoke the emotionality and intimacy of a traditional performance through the use of various studio techniques. On "Middle of the Island" this is provided by the "drone" from the Prophet (although, as suggested above, the sound produced by that instrument in this instance is in fact no such thing), by the "close miking" of Moore's voice (creating a breathy, almost confessional performance), and through certain vocal techniques on the part of the singer himself. Moore's singing voice is recognizably Irish, in terms of both his accent—on words such as "years" (0.53) and "herself" (1.33)—and his pronunciation, as for example when he sings about "de middle of de island" (1.21). Indeed, it is an important aspect of his "folk" persona that Moore refuses to modify his accent for the purposes of singing, and that the "Irishness" of the vocal medium through which the text is communicated accords with the "Irishness" encoded with the lyrical and musical content of the text itself. Beyond this, however, at various points throughout the song Moore introduces vocal trills, on the words "Tuesday" (0.42), "for" (2.18), "knew" (2.30), and "island" (3.02)—the effect of which is to claim intertextual allegiance with *sean-nós* and its specialized sociocultural dispensation.

A third "voice" is provided by a bell which is actually composed of two clearly discernible sounds, one a deeper and more resonant "gong," the second a brighter ringing note. The bell, which enters after seven seconds and repeats thereafter at approximately five-second intervals throughout the track, has a programmatic function in as much as it is intended to invoke a sound (a "passing bell") which has been associated with death since medieval times. Despite Celtic music's alleged recalcitrance vis-à-vis "the real world," the intention here is clearly realist and mimetic: the song is *about* death, therefore the musicians produce sounds which *signify* death for a listener who will be more or less familiar with its sonic conventions.

The final "voice" on "Middle of the Island" is provided by Sinéad O'Connor, a singer well known for her outspoken views on a wide range of issues. O'Connor has in particular become noted as a critic of the Catholic Church in Ireland and what she understands to be the repressive moral regime under which generations of Irish people, and Irish women in particular, have suffered. O'Connor's presence on "Middle of the Island" oscillates between two related yet distinguishable discursive functions: one oriented toward her extra-textual public persona, the other toward her role as a character "inside" the song, as it were. This in turn is linked to certain key aspects of O'Connor's wider identity. In iconographical terms, O'Connor operates between two recognizable paradigms: one sensitive and vulnerable, the other aggressive and militant. These paradigms, moreover, are directly related to O'Connor's singing style, which, as Keith Negus describes it, is characterized by

> the use of two distinct voices: a more private, confessional, restrained, and intimate voice; and a harsher, declamatory, more public and often nasal voice that she frequently slides into a snarl or shout. There is often a tension present throughout many of Sinéad's vocal performances, between a more vulnerable and uncertain voice, and a more imperative and assertive voice. (1995, p. 221)

This tension may be heard on many of her recordings, including the version of "Nothing Compares 2 U" which was a number one hit in the UK and the United States in January, 1990. On "Middle of the Island," O'Connor restricts herself by and large to the former voice—one that is, as Negus says, "private, confessional, restrained, and intimate" (1995, p. 221). When she enters on the line "It was a sad, slow, stupid death for them both" (2.09), doubling Moore's melody line an octave higher, her voice is located quite far back in the mix. The purity and thinness of her voice at this stage, when contrasted with the foregrounded resonance of his, suggests the idea of female vulnerability which is a central element of the lyric. At such points, I suggest, she becomes discursively identified with Ann Lovett herself. Something of O'Connor's more aggressive public persona emerges in her delivery of the emotive words "sad, slow, stupid death" when she repeats that line on her own a little later (3.10). Once again, however, the anger subsides and the voice fades into a kind of "girlishness" during the words "for them both" (3.22). The voice which articulates the final line (and it is instructive that Moore has withdrawn by this stage)—"Everybody knew, nobody said"—is both part of the world *inside* the story (Ann Lovett) and part of the world trying to make sense of that story (Sinéad O'Connor).

I have been quoting lines from "Middle of the Island" throughout the above analysis without really discussing their meaning, but of course words represent a crucial aspect of every song. The first thing to note is that, in apparent contrast with the complex musical discourses at work throughout the piece, Nigel Rolfe's lyric seems disarmingly simple and straightforward. The words relate the tragic story of Ann Lovett in a few lines, describing how the 15-year-old went to a shrine in a field somewhere in the midlands to deliver her own baby, and how she and her baby died there. The language is predominantly descriptive rather than interpretative or analytical; it uses simple, relevant words and structures to relate what happened rather than metaphor, analogy, or other rhetorical devices. The partial exception is the line "It was a sad, slow, stupid death for them both" which employs alliteration to emphasize the point. Even then, however, the opinion is all the more striking for the relevant straightforwardness of its expression. The words "sad, slow [and] stupid" have no great resonance here beyond their primary signification; they are all relative terms (how sad is "sad"?), yet they have a currency which renders them perfectly serviceable in everyday discourse. The lyric of "Middle of the Island" is thus on one level fully in keeping with the banal reality of Ann Lovett's needless death.

There may appear to be a tension, then, between the music and the words of "Middle of the Island," the former multidimensional and allusive, the latter one-dimensional and realist. There are, however, at least two aspects of the lyric which complicate such an interpretation; moreover, the relative importance of these aspects to the text as a whole (the opening line of the lyric and the title) points to an underlying complexity which belies the impression of linguistic simplicity.

The opening line, "Everybody knew, nobody said" (0.20-0.34), is repeated twice later in the track, the first time (2.26-2.42) by both singers singing an octave apart, the second time (3.27-3.46), with a slight melodic variation, by O'Connor. Such repetition signals the importance of this utterance within the linguistic economy of the song; it also establishes a discursive binary between "everybody" and "nobody," and between knowing and saying. On one level, "everybody" refers to the local community among whom Ann Lovett lived and died; likewise, "nobody" refers to the absence of anyone from that community who was willing to address the situation before it reached its crisis. The listener recognizes this indictment, and acknowledges the moral culpability of those who "knew" but refused to "say." As it is repeated a second and then a third time (the latter, as we have observed, by a voice identified with the victim), however, the indictment extends beyond the local community. Now it encompasses not only a mimetic subject located within the world of the song, but also an extra-narrative subject, the listening community, located ostensibly "outside" the drama described in the lyric, but in fact fully implicated in its moral failings. "Everybody" *means* everybody: those who were blamed and those who did the blaming, those represented within the text and those consumers protected by the privilege of the "off" switch on their playback systems.

The same point obtains with reference to the spatial discourse which structures the lyric. The words "grotto" and "field" defer to the discourse of localism noted above. It was, after all, "just a field" in which Ann Lovett died. It appears as if the listener is being invited to observe and enjoy the irony of the fact that such a shocking event could take place in locations which have a benign (occasionally a comic) cultural resonance.[4] With the introduction of the line "In the middle of the island," however, there is a shift from a local perspective (one limited to the apprehension of the senses) to a much larger one in which, once again, the listener is implicated. As the focus zooms out, moreover, geography segues into morality. The words "the middle of the island" register in a geographical sense, certainly, in as much as the town of Granard is located in a part of the Republic known

[4]   In a country in which Mariology was traditionally engrained, the location of Ann Lovett's death next to a grotto of the Virgin Mary was regarded as particularly poignant. The "moving statues" phenomenon, during which thousands of people throughout the island claimed to have witnessed statues of Mary levitating, occurred during the summer of 1985. On gender and landscape in Irish cultural history, see Nash (1996, 1997).

as "the midlands." However, it also registers in a moral sense, invoking a kind of imaginative heartland in which the core values of the whole community have been tested and found wanting. Thus, to call the song "Middle of the Island" is to signal not only the geographical centrality of the event (with all that that entails in terms of traditional values), but also, and more importantly, the significance of Ann Lovett's death as an indictment of the moral health of the wider community.

**Conclusions**

"Middle of the Island" stands as an exemplary instance of the troubled relationship on which the present volume is focused: that obtaining between popular music and human rights. Its primary resonance has a particular geopolitical focus, however, in terms of modern Irish history. As suggested at the outset of this chapter, many of the issues which have animated the debate regarding post-revolutionary Irish identity may be observed within this particular song. On one level the text invites interpretation as part of a clearly dissident discourse, opposed to many fundamental aspects of traditional Irish identity. Moore, O'Connor, and Rolfe may be said to inhabit the broadly revisionist public sphere which emerged within Ireland during the last decades of the twentieth century, and which was intent on deconstructing the precepts, as well as exposing the silences, of the world into which they had been born. Most centrally, the song appears to be an indictment of the attitude which allowed, indeed encouraged, a patriarchal church-state establishment to define the role and representation of women within that world. The artists draw on different cultural traditions and utilize different musical techniques to expedite their (re)vision. These traditions and techniques carry their own ideological resonances, however, some of which support the dissident stance, some of which undermine it. While the debates as to strategy and the effectiveness of cultural interventions continue, however, one fact remains: Ann Lovett would have been 40 by the time this chapter is published.

# Chapter 10
# Long Live the Revolution?
# The Changing Spirit of Chinese Rock

Andreas Steen

Zhongnanhai, Zhongnanhai ... Zhongnanhai, Zhongnanhai
Zhongnanhai, Zhongnanhai ... I only smoke Zhongnanhai
Zhongnanhai, Zhongnanhai ... I can't live without Zhongnanhai
Zhongnanhai, Zhongnanhai ... who smoked my Zhongnanhai?

"Zhongnanhai" is the title of a popular post-punk song from Beijing's music scene, composed and performed by the band Carsick Cars.[1] "Zhongnanhai" (central and southern lakes) is also the name of a popular cigarette brand as well as a complex of buildings in Beijing, in close proximity to the Forbidden City, which serves as the headquarters of the Chinese Communist Party and the Central People's Government. Thus, the term "Zhongnanhai" is synonymous with the leadership and government administration of the People's Republic of China (PRC).

Relatively outspoken political wordplay like this is rare in Chinese rock today, especially when a song is recorded in Chinese. However, Carsick Cars defuses possible trouble by insisting on singing only about the cigarette brand. Fans appear to advocate this meaning by throwing cigarettes on stage when the band starts to perform the tune. This choice is typical among the new generation of rock musicians in Beijing, where, as the band's 24-year-old lead singer and guitarist, Zhang Shouwang, claims, he is not alone in being interested only in his friends, his music and writing, and "not about revolution, but about everyday life" (Foo, 2009). Beijing's underground usually stays away from politics. After all, it is hip, professionally organized, commercial, and partly moving "overground." This is an underground that is being promoted and taken around the globe by foreign professionals, and Carsick Cars is only one act among many. The band even played three concerts with Sonic Youth in Europe, and has become so popular at home that Zhang Shouwang appeared on the front cover of the Chinese glamour and celebrity magazine *Esquire* (*Shishang xiansheng*) in May, 2009.[2] The magazine features Zhang in an interview with Michael Pettis, a finance professor at Beijing University, who owns the rock venue D-22 and operates the independent record

---

[1]    "Zhongnanhai" appears on the band's debut album *Carsick Cars* (2008).

[2]    See: "Michael Pettis interview of Carsick Cars' Zhang Shouwang," www.danwei. org/music/on_zhang_ shouwang.php, accessed July 12, 2009.

label Maybe Mars (Bingmasi) in Beijing, a label that has released two Carsick Cars albums and recently helped to organize a concert tour of the United States.[3] The band exemplifies the changing image and popularity of rock in China; it also illustrates a new message as well as the possibilities provided by global and commercial networks for this musical genre in China today.

Rock music (*yaogun yinyue*) in China began in the northern capital Beijing in the early 1980s. Since then, rock musicians have often been perceived of and promoted as the authentic voice of the suppressed creative individual, and as a protest from below. In popular discourse, their obvious counterpart—if not enemy—became the commercialized "southern" popular and light music (*liuxing yinyue*) of Hong Kong and Taiwan, called Canto-Pop, Mando-Pop, or Gangtai music. Against the background of the latter's nationwide popularity and commercial success, Chinese rock developed along a more diverse and controversial path. It matured in the liberalizing atmosphere of the post-socialist cultural environment of the 1990s, and responded in various ways to the forces of globalization, commercialization, consumerism, new nationalism, and self-censorship. Similar to other forms of art and cultural production, rock also engaged in a complex and creative relationship with the PRC's revolutionary heritage, confirming that "[i]f Chinese society experienced modernity as revolution and socialism, Chinese postmodernity is to be grasped not only in its relationship to modernity in general but also in its relationship to a socialist and revolutionary modernity" (Dirlik and Zhang, 1997, p. 8).

Today, Chinese rock is played in many Chinese cities and includes a broad range of music styles. Musicians articulate themselves in music journals, newspapers, books, films, concerts, festivals, on TV shows, via the internet, and at charity concerts, e.g., for the victims of the disastrous Sichuan earthquake of 2008. Beijing is still the centre of Chinese rock; the *Encyclopedia of Chinese Rock 'n' Roll* (Li Hongjie, 2006) lists 180 Beijing musicians and bands, and their CDs. In practice, Beijing offers a repertoire of three or four generations of rock musicians in a dozen venues. These generations are characterized by different social backgrounds, experiences, and musical preferences; together they form an underground, an alternative culture of individual creativity and protest, divided into different scenes, and embedded in—if not bound to—a specific discourse of "revolution/rebellion" (*geming*).

### Revolution I: New Spirits and New Voices United in Protest

The Chinese Communists' rise to power is usually traced back to the heroic Long March (1934-35), which ended at the revolutionary base camp Yan'an, Shaanxi Province. From there, Mao Zedong successfully organized the war against Nationalist and Japanese forces and also defined the future role of culture in his

---

[3]   The two albums are *Carsick Cars* (2008) and *You Can Listen, You Can Talk* (2009). See also www.maybemars.org.

influential "Talks about Literature and Art" (1942). Following the founding of the PRC in 1949, his concepts were put into practice: culture (including, of course, music) became an instrument of politics. The process reached its climax during the "chaotic ten years" of the Cultural Revolution (1966-76). Several years later, the musician Liang Heping would point out in a BBC documentary (dir. Greg Lanning, 1990) that both China and the West had their revolutions in the 1960s. There was, of course, a difference between adoring Mao Zedong or The Beatles, but in the end both revolutions destroyed old authorities and opened new spaces of individual freedom for young people. However, by the time the first rock bands appeared in Beijing, Mao had died (1976) and John Lennon had been shot (1980). In the meantime, Deng Xiaoping initiated the PRC's reform and open-door policy. Consequently, after foreign acts like Jean Michel Jarre (1981) and Wham! (1985) had been invited to perform, in the spirit of "We Are the World" (released March 7, 1985), and in the "International Year of Peace" (1986), the musician Cui Jian (b. 1961) rose to fame with his song "Nothing to My Name" ("Yiwu suoyou"). He soon became China's *enfant terrible*. Truly revolutionary, dressed in the uniform of a PLA-soldier, decorated with the Communist red five-corner star, which later became his symbol, he released the country's first rock album in early 1989: *Rock 'n' Roll on the New Long March (Xin changzheng lushang de yaogun)*.

The "New Long March" alluded to Deng Xiaoping, who used the metaphor of the exhausting and highly glorified old "Long March" of the Red Army to prepare China for the hardships of the reform period. The Long March was a popular symbol for successful revolution, because it ignored people's status, power, and profession, swept away all enemies and finally won. Inspired by this spirit and by the meaning of Chuck Berry's "Roll over Beethoven" (1956; The Beatles, 1963), Cui Jian began to spread rock as a new means of self-expression and liberation. As he later recalled, rock musical was seen as a very serious music form, which he thought gave people a specific feeling, consisting of self-confidence (do not lose yourself), naturalness (do not force yourself to do things you do not want to do), and freedom (liberate yourself) (Cui and Zhou, 2001, pp. 56-7, 79; also Song, 2006). In short, whereas the Long March had liberated China, the New Long March would liberate the economy and rock music would liberate the individual.

The sensation and popularity of rock music as a new outlet for individual expressions of unity, anger, and hope in 1989 can hardly be overestimated. After Cui's album was released as *Nothing to My Name (Yiwu suoyou)* in Hong Kong and Taiwan in April, 1989, not only the PRC, but these regions as well experienced a "Cui Jian Fever" (*Cui Jian re*). Moreover, the Tiananmen movement of 1989 not only multiplied the production and impact of musical protest and songs for democracy in Hong Kong (Lee 1992; Ho, 2000), it also inspired the political use of pop music in greater China and turned rock music in Beijing from a marginal underground phenomenon into a new urban youth culture, especially among students. Aside from Cui Jian, bands like Tang Dynasty (Tang Chao) and Panther (Hei Bao) already existed, and new bands like Breathing (Huxi), the all-female band Cobra (Yanjingshe), and Zang Tianshuo's 1989 were founded during the summer. Yet Cui Jian was the most visible musician, and he even performed a few songs on the Square. His uncompromising expression of "individuality" (*gexing*) turned him into a hero and an idol for many young Chinese. In practice, he combined Western instruments and rock beats with traditional Chinese melodies and instruments, accompanied by powerful lyrics that were shared by almost everyone. His song "Nothing to My Name" unexpectedly became the students' anthem on Tiananmen Square in 1989 and has remained his most popular song. More generally, his lyrics were well-phrased and allowed generous space for interpretation. They addressed love and insecurity, vast and rapid changes that were difficult to cope with, the lack of proper feeling (*ganjue*) and the hypocrisy (*xuwei*) present in Chinese society. The level of admiration for him is illustrated by the slogan on the banners waved by young fans at his concerts: "Long Live Cui Jian" (*Cui Jian wan sui*), a sentiment formerly reserved for Mao Zedong. However, while Cui Jian provided young audiences with a radically new musical and social experience, his status was a provocation, and subsequently rock music was officially regarded as a subversive and threatening musical practice.

Nonetheless, immediately after the crackdown in June, 1989, government officials were still ambiguous about this music form. Two events suggest that 1), the government also saw that rock could be used as a means of pacifying anger among China's youth, and 2), officials were beginning to demonstrate a somewhat liberal position toward new trends. In February, 1990, musicians and likeminded friends organized the so-called Beijing Concert of Modern Music, which featured six rock bands over two days, and was attended by 18,000 people each day. The audience was young, enthusiastic, and wild, and left officials with what was called the "rock problem" (*yaogun wenti*). Meanwhile, Cui Jian had been given permission to perform in 10 Chinese cities, provided that he promoted the "Asian Games" and donated one million Yuan. Taking the opportunity, he promoted the tour as the Long March of rock music in China. His lyrics, outfit, and terminology were inspired by revolutionary symbols, idealism, and Long March rhetoric; cities where concerts were held became known as "liberated areas" (*genjudi*). The tour was cancelled after only four concerts, but it demonstrated the popularity of rock music's "rebellious spirit" (*fanpan jingshen*) outside Beijing and gave a strong push to the already visible rock fad among urban youth (Steen, 1996, pp. 136-48; Baranovitch, 2003, pp. 36-42). This episode ended the first period of rock in China. Wrapped in and equipped with well-known symbols of China's socialist revolutionary heritage/history, Cui Jian had successfully spread the self-liberating message of rock in China. However, for the next few years he was only allowed to perform at private "parties" in Beijing and abroad. Outside China, the foreign press, in attempts to help their audiences in the West to understand his status, dubbed him the "Bob Dylan," "John Lennon," or "Bruce Springsteen" of China (Figures 10.1 and 10.2).

Figure 10.1    Cui Jian, 1990. Courtesy of Cui Jian and Beijing East West Music &
Art Production Co., Ltd

Figure 10.2    Cui Jian, 1990. Courtesy of Cui Jian and Beijing East West Music &
Art Production Co., Ltd

**Revolution II: Musicians, Markets, and Audiences in Transition**

The cultural condition of the "post-Tiananmen era" was largely determined by the push for far-reaching market reforms, initiated by Deng Xiaoping in early 1992 (Lu, 2001; Zhang, 2008). What came to be known as "socialism with Chinese characteristics" opened the market to all kinds of national and international commercial activities and supported the rise of a new leisure and consumer culture that was considered nonthreatening to Party hegemony (Barmé, 1999; Wang, 2001). The 1990s is often perceived as a period of decline in rock culture, because the revolutionary "rock spirit" (*yaogun jingshen*) of the late 1980s had dwindled away into disillusionment amid the newly developing world of commerce, pop, and consumerism. For example, Hao Huang (2003, p. 190) speaks of the "Post-Tiananmen Blues." In retrospect, we may speak of a period in which Chinese rock struggled between globalization and localization on the one hand, and the transformation of China's society and its cultural industry on the other.

The decade began with an unexpected and highly debated "Mao Fever," which reflected peoples' dissatisfaction with the reform process and a popular nostalgia for the revolutionary past. It reached its peak in 1993 when the country celebrated Mao's hundredth birthday. The most popular music item of this period was a cassette entitled *The Red Sun* (*Hong taiyang*, 1992), a compilation of revolutionary songs from the Mao period, accompanied by a modern disco beat. Produced by the Shanghai Record Corporation, it sold millions of copies, including pirated copies, and resulted in several new releases in the following years (Barmé, 1996; Baranovitch, 2003, p. 48). The *Red Sun* phenomenon demonstrated the commercially successful fusion of the PRC's revolutionary heritage and modern popular culture. Equally astonishing were new releases of jazzy tunes from Old Shanghai, which for almost half a century had been dismissed as bourgeois and pornographic. As formerly heavily disputed ideological differences were washed away, musical genres of the twentieth century began to appear together in music stores for the first time since 1949. Alongside these changes two contrasting developments affected the world of Chinese rock: foreign commercial interest and support on the one hand, and decreasing consumer interest and sales figures on the other.

Since the early 1990s, the foreign music industry had aimed to exploit the pro-Western climate among Chinese youth and eagerly approached the Chinese market. Cui Jian signed the contract for his next album *Solution* (*Jiejue*, 1990) with British EMI in Hong Kong, provocatively including on the recording an altered version of the popular revolutionary song "Nanniwan." Other artists from mainland China followed (Fung 2008, p. 52). In September, 1991, MTV Asia began to broadcast in Hong Kong, opening with Cui Jian's video for his song "Wild in the Snow" ("Kuai rang wo zai xue di shang sa dian ye"). One year later, the Taiwanese company Rock Records & Tapes released the first Beijing-based Chinese rock sampler: *China Fire 1* (*Zhongguo huo 1*, 1992). This was followed by four fairly successful CDs, including a heavy metal album by Tang Dynasty

(*Tang Chao*, 1992) and a rock album by He Yong (*Lajichang*, 1994). The latter was particularly provocative and rebellious; the album's title track "Garbage Dump" ("Lajichang"), offered an especially harsh critique of Chinese society, beginning with the line "The world we live in, is like a garbage dump, people are like insects, fighting and shooting in it." The song, obviously referring to the events of 1989, is celebrated as China's first punk song and the video was banned in the PRC. Less controversial perhaps, Hou Muren released an album of socialist classics entitled *Red Rock* (*Hongse yaogun*, 1992), echoing the success of *The Red Sun*. All in all, these were revolutionary changes, accompanied by the founding of Beijing's International Jazz Festival and the country's first school for alternative music genres, the Beijing Midi School of Music, in 1993. New music channels MTV-Mandarin (1995) and Channel V (1996) also began broadcasting.

Inspired by Cui Jian's success, Chinese rock had become the "newcomer" in the music business, often promoted and discussed with reference to either or both revolution/rebellion and Chinese tradition. For example, Cui Jian's metaphor of the Long March was picked up and discussed in the PRC's largest weekly newspaper, *Southern Weekend* (*Nanfang zhoumo*), published in Guangzhou (Canton). Beijing, moreover, was praised as a joyful space for China's rock musicians, as their spiritual Yan'an. It was seen as the revolutionary base from where to start the Long March and establish "liberated areas" (Yi Zhou, 1993). Furthermore, Chinese rock was presented as the authentic and individual voice of mainland China, providing truly new sounds, and advertised with images of revolution and traditional rightfulness. State-owned companies such as the China Record Corporation did not lag behind and released several samplers of Chinese rock, though with less heroic images, e.g., *Chinese Rock Classics* (*Zhongguo yaogun jingdian*, 1995). Praised in the leaflet as the product of a 10-year struggle—obviously a reference to the Cultural Revolution—the CD offered selected rock songs that had only become "classics" after 10 years. Cui Jian's "Rock on the New Long March" was included. With fortunes changing, Cui Jian had been able to release his latest album, *Balls under the Red Flag* (*Hongqi xia de dan*), the year before. It included a sophisticated set of songs in both jazz and rock styles, combined with Chinese elements and critical lyrics, designed with images of the Cultural Revolution.

By the mid-1990s, various aspects of China's revolutionary past had entered the world of pop and rock music. Even in Hong Kong, in 1994 a record company called Red Star (Hong xing) was founded that started to promote mainland China's rock and pop songs as "Red Star Music" (*Hongxing yinyue*).[4] Localization was necessary in a globalizing music world, yet to regard the incorporation of "Chineseness" as merely an "authentication tactic" used in order to avoid the music being dubbed a copy of Western styles (de Kloet, 2005c) ignores the musicians' biography and national identity. Besides which, the experience of artistic and

---

[4]    To commemorate the tenth anniversary of the label, Beijing's Taihe Rye Music Co. (Taihe Maitian) released a special CD, covering songs of the period 1994-2004. See http://www.trmusic.com.cn/main/89/category-catid-189.html, accessed November 20, 2009.

individual creativity that included exploring and deconstructing China's past for meaningful band names, album cover designs, stage outfits, musical instruments, melodies, lyrics, and poetry was both novel and exciting.

Nevertheless, for many people "the ethos of conscious resistance and rebellion that was embodied in rock lost much of its appeal, as it proved useless" (Baranovitch, 2003, p. 44). Instead, young Chinese concentrated on the advantages of economic reforms and found it more rewarding to engage in education, their careers, and improving their standard of living. After all, rock music was still deemed an imported Western cultural practice; hence, protest, noisy music, and conflictual lyrics were exchanged for listening to popular tunes from Taiwan and Hong Kong and visiting karaoke bars. Moreover, officially rock music was still regarded as a subversive practice, and as it proved to be less commercially successful than expected, some record companies gradually withdrew from the Chinese rock market (de Kloet, 2002, p. 100). Consequently, China's new consumer culture provided the ground for more "popular," non-provoking, and patriotic expressions of Chinese rock. Clearly inspired by the rise of China's new nationalism in the mid-1990s, songs about national unity and strength attained enormous popularity and even Chinese rock musicians expressed "vehemently anti-foreign sentiments" (Huang, 2001, p. 1; see Ho, 2006).

However, the underground remained active throughout this period, and its revitalization is ascribed to the consumption of illegal imports of "cut-CDs" from the West (*dakou* CDs) since the mid-1990s. The so-called *dakou*-culture increased the flow of music from the West and further stimulated the creation of different music styles and scenes in Beijing.[5] Another development that legitimized the mainland's claim as the centre of rock was the arrival of Chinese punk, though it also reflected a delay in communication with the West of about 20 years (the Sex Pistols' "Anarchy in the UK" was released in 1976). More contemporary was the popularity of Nirvana and grunge music in Beijing's underground. Indeed, many musicians and fans experienced Kurt Cobain's death (1994) as a personal crisis, and after Hao Fang published his translated biography of Cobain (*Radiant Nirvana*) in 1997, playing in an underground band became a rather "hip" and popular thing to do (Yan Jun, 2002, p. 151).

### Revolution III: Popular Underground and New Sounds

The year 1997 was crucial, both for China and for Chinese rock. In March, Deng Xiaoping died, and in August, the PRC celebrated the "return of Hong Kong" and the end of British imperialism. Against this rather nationalist background

---

[5]　"Cut-CDs" were rejected music CDs of American and Canadian record companies, which had been made partly useless by a "cut." However, enterprising Chinese middlemen bought them in large quantities and shipped them as "plastic waste" to China. They were sold cheaply at street corners and along the roadside (de Kloet, 2005b).

China's first music magazine, *Audio & Video World* (*Yinxiang shijie*), published in Shanghai, celebrated its tenth anniversary, and young musician Shen Lihui founded China's first independent record company in Beijing: Modernsky (Modeng tiankong). Modernsky grasped the spirit of the times and advertised its products as the "Beijing New Sound Movement" (*Beijing xinsheng yundong*), later also known as "'98 Rock's New Wave" (*'98 Yaogun Xin Lanchao*). With an emphasis on sound and modernity, the movement promoted internationalization and distanced itself from the idealism and heavy ideological debates of the older generation. Making music, no matter the style, was to be regarded as a normal pursuit, based on individual creativity and preference, free from political idealism, for pleasure, enjoyment, contemplation, and to let off steam. Modernsky's innovative approach turned the company into China's biggest independent record company.[6] Including its sub-labels, Modernsky has so far released about 100 CDs of different musicians and styles, ranging from rock, Brit-pop, and heavy metal to punk and folk, experimental and independent, electronic, ambient, and chill-out music. Today it shares the alternative market with the Chinese labels Newbees (Xinfeng), Jingwen, and others, as well as with foreign independent labels.[7]

Modernsky's innovative approach has come from within the music scene and the driving force behind the scene's activities is young Chinese born after the Cultural Revolution. These "little emperors"—so called because of the country's one-child policy—usually belong to the emerging middle class and have matured in the optimistic spirit of reform, surrounded by international consumer culture, equipped with computers and mobile phones, and proud of China's rise as a world power. They respond to the forces of globalization in a variety of ways, many of which are creatively handled in the lyrics of the songs they play and listen to, though these can also be mutually contradictory. "Some may pointedly speak out against commercial forces while others readily accept them or embrace the commodities that are their agents in the popular media of film, music, television, and the Internet" (Moore, 2005, p. 357).

Since the late 1990s, rock musicians from all provinces of China have been marching to Beijing's recording studios and performing a variety of musical styles, both Western and Chinese, including those of national minorities. This musical diversity is accompanied by lyrics which may focus on social criticism, individual introspection and protest, love, sex, irony, humor, ennui, or just plain fun and booze, or they may comprise little stories or abstract wordplays, yet they are rarely offensive in a political sense, at least not directly, and not on CDs and not in the Chinese language. Yang Haisong, lead singer of PK14, explains this attitude: "We haven't been suppressed by the government, and we don't really understand what they are doing. And because it has not yet happened, I'm not really scared" (Liu, 2009). The new generation appears to be insensible to politics, ignorant and

---

[6]  See Steen (2000), and www.modernsky.com.

[7]  For a comprehensive list of record labels, see www.rockinchina.com, accessed June 12, 2009.

self-serving, but international and patriotic. Technically skilled, musicians pursue careers, express thoughts, sentiments, and frustrations. This attitude corresponds with the situation in the West, where protest songs are also difficult to find these days (Weinstein, 2006). Similarities notwithstanding, China's music market is still bound to different rules, and the rock scene revealed its ambivalence toward political protest after Björk's performance in Shanghai in 2008.[8]

Another important development has seen China's alternative music scene dismiss "going pop" in the PRC for "going global." This is grounded in making moves toward internationalization, a strategy to overcome local difficulties and insecurities. The two main problems are well known: censorship and piracy, both of which affect the musician's livelihood in the PRC. Not even famous bands can rely on sales and royalties; usually their income derives from concerts and other jobs. Internationalization, then, started in the late 1990s with the incorporation of English words and phrases, and became professional as band names, CD titles and even song texts were offered in translation on CD sleeves and booklets. Today, bands can be found in Beijing who sing only in English (without retranslating the lyrics into Chinese for local audiences), such as Re-Tros, Hang on the Box, and Joyside, among others, and who incorporate a large portion of English songs, such as the post-punk band Brain Failure (Naozhuo). In order to circumvent local obstacles, musicians and bands may also seek to approach the foreign market directly and cooperate with foreign musicians, producers, and bands, play concerts abroad, and/or sign contracts with foreign independent labels. Seen from their perspective, the local market is considered relatively small and difficult.[9] The problems are manifold and go beyond the scope of this chapter, yet Richard Curt Kraus neatly sums up one of them: "postproduction censorship effectively turns political risk into economic risks" (2004, p. 117). Hence to avoid economic losses, the mass media and the music industry are inclined to self-censorship, but for the same reason and because of its sheer size and fierce competition, they steadily push the boundaries of what is accepted. As a result, censorship is often ineffective or arbitrary, and banned recordings do not ever totally disappear, or alternately find their way onto the internet.

Amid all these activities the "revolutionary spirit" has not disappeared, but has instead taken different forms and continues to be expressed in the rhetoric of

---

[8]    Björk received much criticism from the international music scene after her sudden outcry "Free Tibet" during a performance in Shanghai, March 2, 2008. She was thereafter officially banned from performing in China, the result being that many other Western musicians expressed dismay at her action because they felt it could also jeopardize their concerts in the PRC. See "The Irresponsibility of Björk in China," March 25, 2008.

[9]    Dominic Rushe (2004), writes: "The Chinese [music] market is small. Last year [2003], legitimate sales were $198m (£110m) compared with $3.2 billion in Britain, according to the International Federation of the Phonographic Industry (IFPI). But China's sales grew 22% last year while sales in the developed world were flat at best." On China's music industry, see also de Kloet (2002) and McClure (2008).

Chinese rock. Chinese punk bands, for instance, refer particularly frequently to the Cultural Revolution, its images, spirit, and even songs (de Kloet, 2005c; Steen, 2008). Musicians often perceive themselves as rebels and express this in their lyrics. A recent example, the punk band SMZB from Wuhan, was founded in 1996 and released its sixth album *Ten Years Rebellion* (*Shinian fankang*) in Beijing in 2008. The title song refers to the band's history and experience, and to "individual" rebellion, ending with the line: "Ten years fun, ten years down, ten years chaos and rebellion." Other songs, also in English, deal with daily frustrations, for example "For Friends and Beer," in which "living a true life" without the restrictions of both socialism and democracy becomes the main message. The band Joyside, on *Drunk is Beautiful* (2004), offers similar lyrics of individual discontent. Despite the fact that English lyrics might not be read or understood by audiences in China, "Punk rock in Beijing keeps the flame of revolutionary discourse alive, through the act of performance, while continually struggling against the commodification and dilution of its energy, its signs and its symbols" (Field and Groenewegen, 2008, p. 8).

Today, after the "Mao Fever" of the early 1990s, and at a time when the revolutionary kitsch of that period is available everywhere for tourists, the CD covers and concert flyers illustrated with well-known revolutionary images, especially those of heroic red guards, are likely to carry multiple meanings. References to the PRC's revolutionary period, as already mentioned, fulfill a double purpose: they connect China's youth with a past which in retrospect is imagined as clearly structured and filled with heroic stories, and, equally, they are part of their national identity and function as a marker of distinction, if not Chineseness, patriotism, and anti-Western sentiment. Despite lacking personal experience, this generation refers to a distant past and a revolutionary spirit. This might well be interpreted as the longing for an idealized anti-authoritarian revolution, for frugality and camaraderie, and as a critique of China's present hyper-capitalism (Figures 10.3 and 10.4). From this perspective it is no surprise that the names of the three most famous concert venues in Beijing are related to the PRC's revolutionary history. Nameless Highland (Wuming gaodi) is a military term denoting an unknown mountain area and derives from the period of guerrilla warfare. Mao Live House is self-explanatory and obviously attractive—a "Mao Live House" also opened in Shanghai in late 2009. Yu Gong yi shan takes its name from the title of a famous old parable about a foolish man named Yu who wanted to move two mountains that were blocking his village from the outside world—he succeeded. Mao used the story in his concluding speech at the Seventh National Congress of the Communist Party of China in June, 1945, in order to mobilize forces against the "two mountains" of imperialism and feudalism. During the Cultural Revolution, this speech was included in the *Little Red Book*, the consequence of which is that basically everyone is familiar with the story. Without speculating on whether the venue's name refers to Mr Yu's endurance, or seeks to remove two specific mountains, it reminds people of a certain period and spirit (Figure 10.5). This de- and re-contextualization is part of Chinese rock culture and has become commercially significant because the images truly identify Chinese rock, both at home and in a globalizing music world. Martin Atkins, who runs the label Invisible Records, clearly took this into consideration when he released two CD compilations of the latest Beijing rock in Chicago in 2007: the cover of one features Red Guards with the *Little Red Book*, the other, two steel-workers hitting a drum, painted in the style of socialist realism.[10]

Figure 10.3    Concert flyer for Carsick Cars, Hedgehog, and Snapline at D-22, June 30, 2007. Courtesy of D-22, Beijing

Figure 10.4    Concert flyer for PK 14, Casino Demon, and Candy Monster at D-22, July 14, 2007. Courtesy of D-22, Beijing

---

[10]    *Look Directly into the Sun: China Pop 2007* and *Made in China. Martin Atkins' China Dub Soundsystem*, both produced by Martin Atkins (Invisible Records, Chicago, 2007).

Figure 10.5 *Beyond the Ocean*, concert at Yu Gong yi shan, March 6, 2010.
Courtesy of Maybe Mars Records, Beijing

## Revolution IV: Chinese Rock—Still on the March?

Since the beginning of China's rock revolution with *Rock 'n' Roll on the New Long March*, the country and its people have experienced a radical transformation, economically, culturally, and also politically, as has Chinese rock. Notions of "revolution" and rebellion have accompanied the history of Chinese rock for more than two decades, though with different meanings for different generations. A particular rhetoric and discourse link rock music to the PRC's socialist revolution, its spirit, images, clothing, vocabulary, gestures, music, lyrics, and the use of its names for concert venues. "Revolution," it should be noted, is an official music category in the PRC's music stores today, reserved for the canon of "Red Classics," and for the politically correct music related to "the Revolution."

Like Zhang Shouwang from Carsick Cars, China's new rock generation claims to be interested in neither politics nor "revolution." Also in Hong Kong, after the handover, "there have hardly been any songs with political content" as they have little market value (Ho, 2000, p. 349). In the realm of popular culture, then, it could be argued with Anthony Fung that the "people's desires and the state agenda converge" (2008, p. 157). The music industry concentrates on commercially attractive apolitical pop and rock music, often leaving the niche of alternative music styles for Chinese and foreign independent labels. China's authorities, on the other hand, have long realized that there is more patriotism than political protest in Beijing's underground. The recently growing popularity of China's alternative music, its festivals, various scenes, and styles, can be attributed to new opportunities and a focus on the individual, which corresponds with the rising individualism among Chinese urban youths, who are looking for alternative ways of living (Xi, Sun, and Xiao, 2006). This "revolution" must also be understood as a political statement. Inspired by international music trends, foreign recognition and cooperation, musicians will continue to challenge and comment on aspects of China's society, globalization, etc., thereby keeping the protest potential and a subversive rock spirit alive.

Rock music's struggle with the state is not yet over, but its changing image in China is reflected in the career of Cui Jian, who is seen as the "father of Chinese rock." Today, the rebel has become an accepted artist in the PRC, even a celebrity. In 2005, the state-owned TV channel CCTV 10 featured him in the program *People* (*Renwu*) in a respectful one-and-a-half-hour documentary entitled "Rock 'n' Roll on the New Long March" (prod. Zhao Shujing, 2005). In addition to his musical work, he is engaged in film productions, has published a book (2001), organizes music festivals, and is also initiating a movement against playback singing (*zhenchang yundong*, 2002) to raise the quality of performances. In 2006 he performed with the Rolling Stones in Shanghai and his portrait adorned the front page of the first issue of China's *Rolling Stone* magazine. In the autumn of 2009, he celebrated the twentieth anniversary of his and the PRC's first rock album with a tour of China entitled *Rock 'n' Roll on the New Long March* (Figures 10.6 and 10.7).[11]

---

[11]    See www.cuijian.com, accessed November 24, 2009.

Figure 10.6    Cui Jian, *Rock 'n' Roll on the New Long March* tour 2009. Courtesy of Cui Jian and Beijing East West Music & Art Production Co., Ltd

Figure 10.7    Cui Jian, *Rock 'n' Roll on the New Long March* tour 2009. Courtesy of Cui Jian and Beijing East West Music & Art Production Co., Ltd

On December 31, 2010 and January 1, 2011, Cui Jian played two concerts—entitled the *New Year's Concerts of Rock Symphony*—at the Beijing Workers Stadium. In collaboration with his former working unit, the prestigious Beijing Symphony Orchestra conducted by Tan Lihua, Cui performed songs from the album *Rock 'n' Roll on the New Long March*, demonstrating that in China his songs have clearly become "classics," not only of rock 'n' roll. Three months later the Hollywood Reporter revealed that the concerts, along with several interviews, are to be reworked to create a "3D" film version of the events, tentatively entitled "Stereo Symphony on the New Long March." As Bai Qiang, himself a long-time fan of Cui Jian and the producer of the five-million yuan project said, "We think this film will capture that nothing that's happened in the last 30 years has changed Cui Jian's spirit. ... We can all relate to that."[12]

Indeed, for Cui Jian the March is not over: Chinese rock has been embraced as a means of individual self-expression, but seems to lose itself between commercialization and self-censorship, complacency and self-sufficiency. The young musicians and "revolutionaries" are allowed to ignore him; they may not have heard of Yan'an, or of Cui Jian; but one day they will surely approach Beijing, form a band, perform in the Mao Live House, and establish their own "liberated areas." These could, of course, be either in China or abroad.

---

[12]   http://www.hollywoodreporter.com/news/chinas-top-rocker-cui-jian-170032, accessed March 24, 2011.

Chapter 11

# Fascist Music from the West: Anti-Rock Campaigns, Problems of National Identity, and Human Rights in the "Closed City" of Soviet Ukraine, 1975-84

Sergei I. Zhuk

In 1991 Igor T., a retired KGB officer, who monitored students' activities in Dniepropetrovsk,[1] a large industrial city in eastern Ukraine, recalled how the local KGB triggered special ideological campaigns against Western popular music. These campaigns were related to the major ideological and political crises in the neighboring socialist countries. (The first and most significant campaign in 1968 was triggered by Prague's spring events in Czechoslovakia. Both Soviet ideologists and KGB operatives feared Soviet youth would imitate Czech cultural developments. The final ideological campaign began in 1981 as a direct reaction to events in Poland and youth involvement in the Solidarity movement.)[2]

According to KGB officers, popular music from the West produced four subsequent waves of Western cultural influence among Soviet youth. The first wave began in the early 1960s, "with Beatlemania and the spread of beat music and hippie fashions among high school and college students." The second wave of Western cultural influence was "Deep Purple mania and the cult of rock opera *Jesus Christ Superstar* which led to the mass popularity of hard rock and triggered an interest in religion among not only students, but also young industrial workers" (author interview with Igor T.) by 1976. After this "hard rock mania," an overwhelming majority of the local youth became obsessed with Western mass culture and "accepted disco dances [sic] as their way of life." That obsession was stimulated by tourism and the entertainment business, which involved both Communist and Komsomol *apparatchiks* who made money on the consumption of Western music by Soviet consumers. This period, from 1976 to 1980 (the third

---

[1]   The name of the city is a combination of two words—Dnipro River and Grigorii Petrovskii, a famous Bolshevik and the first President of Soviet Ukraine. After 1991 the spelling became Dnipropetrovs'k.

[2]   Igor T., KGB officer. Personal interview with author, May 15, 1991. Compare with the KGB reports in *DADO* (Derzhavnyi arkhiv Dnipropetrovs'koi oblasti [The State Archive of the Dniepropetrovsk Region]), f. 19, op. 52, d. 72, ll. 1-18.

wave of Western mass culture hysteria) was called "disco madness." According to Igor T., it was a direct result of the politics of détente and the relaxation of international tensions. The fourth and the final wave of Western cultural influence was so-called "fascist punk and heavy metal hysteria" which also affected young Communists and Komsomol activists between 1981 and 1984. Fearing that local heavy metal fans would imitate Polish anti-Soviet sentiments, the KGB and Soviet administration tried to suppress this hysteria. As Igor T. noted, all these efforts to protect young people from "Westernization" eventually failed:

> We lost the entire young generation, instead of the loyal Soviet Ukrainian patriots we had now Westernized imbeciles who had forgotten their national roots and who were ready to exchange their Soviet motherland for Western cultural products. Even more dangerous, this Westernization happened in the most strategically important Soviet city, which became a symbol for the entire Brezhnev rule in the USSR. Dniepropetrovsk, that was closed to foreigners, became ideologically polluted by anti-Soviet bourgeois influences as early as the 1970s. (Personal interview with author)

At the end of his interview, this KGB officer complained about "the ridiculous issue of human rights, which the local rock music fanatics raised all the time after 1975." He explained that during the police raids when they were arrested these "Westernized imbeciles" emphasized that according to the international agreements signed by the Soviet government, they had "human rights" to listen to their "weird fascist" music and "express themselves on the dance floor." Soviet police officers discovered that even rock music fans cared about their "human rights" and were ready to defend their rights in public.

Mass rock music consumption among the youth of Dniepropetrovsk created problems for Soviet ideologists and the KGB because this city had a special strategic importance for the entire Soviet regime. This city was officially closed to foreigners in 1959 because it became the location for one of the biggest missile factories in the Soviet Union. At the same time, the city served as a launching ground for the political careers of many Soviet politicians in Moscow because Dniepropetrovsk was always associated with the Brezhnev clan. This city also played an important role in political life in Ukraine. Before 1985, more than 53 percent of all political leaders in Kyiv came from Dniepropetrovsk. By 1996 80 percent of the post-Soviet Ukrainian politicians had begun their career in the closed city.

In 1975, Soviet ideologists sponsored a special discotheque campaign all over the Soviet Union. Their major goal was to organize ideologically reliable dance parties in order to control Western pop music consumption by Soviet youth. This campaign contributed to the spread of rock music throughout Soviet Ukraine, especially in urban industrial cities such as Dniepropetrovsk. By the beginning of 1982, more than 560 youth clubs with 83 officially registered discotheques existed in the region of Dniepropetrovsk.[3] Komsomol ideologists and their KGB supervisors faced a very serious problem: pop music consumers apparently preferred Western music hits to Soviet ones. A majority of rock music enthusiasts rejected completely what they called Soviet *estrada* (pop music). Therefore Komsomol ideologists promoted discotheques that primarily presented Soviet music, including songs from national republics. *Apparatchiks* responsible for the discotheque movement supported themes by the Ukrainian band Vodograi or Byelorussian band Pesniary because these bands represented Soviet traditions instead of the foreign forms of Western pop culture. To show their ideological loyalty and local patriotism many disc jockeys in Dniepropetrovsk included comments about "glorious Ukrainian history" and criticized "capitalist exploitation in the Western countries."[4] Even in their comments about Ukrainian history, they (as loyal Soviet citizens) always emphasized class struggle. Still, their stories were about Ukrainian Cossacks or melodious Ukrainian poetry, which were not popular subjects among the local KGB operatives. Eventually, the KGB supervisors of the discotheque movement had to accept both the stories being told and the national Ukrainian music being played on the local dance floors. For them it was less evil than capitalist music culture from the West.[5]

Discotheques and rock music became an even more dangerous problem for Komsomol officials after the death of Brezhnev, when Yurii Andropov, the new Soviet leader, began his campaign against corruption in the Communist Party and Komsomol. During 1983-84, he declared war on Western pop music as "a dangerous ideological pollution among Soviet youth" (*Pravda*, July 15, 1983, p. 2). Responding to Andropov's directives, the Komsomol introduced special counter-propagandist measures, which affected the discotheque movement. In the Dniepropetrovsk region the local ideologists used a special Komsomol seminar for disco activists, established between October, 1982 and May, 1983 at the prestigious Palace of Culture in downtown Dniepropetrovsk to control music programs and purge those leaders of disco clubs who resisted collaboration. By 1984, more than a half of the 100 discotheques in the region had been closed by

---

[3]   See *DADO*, f. 22, op. 32, d. 1, l. 44.

[4]   *DADO*, f. 17, op. 10, d. 1, ll. 87, 98; op. 11, d. 25, l. 88; op. 12, d. 18, l. 15; f. 22, op. 36, d. 1, ll. 36-37. See also the local periodicals: Chenous'ko, "Disko-klubu—zelionuiu ulitsu," *Dnepr vechernii*, July 1, 1978; L. Titarenko, "Tsikavi tsentry vidpochynku," *Zoria*, August 15, 1978; I. Rodionov, "Vecher v diskoklube," *Dneprovskaia pravda*, January 14, 1979; A. Belkina, "Vechir u dyskotetsi," *Prapor iunosti*, December 11, 1979.

[5]   They especially liked a Ukrainian song about Ukrainian Cossacks that was a cover in Ukrainian of the old hit "Venus" by the Dutch band Shocking Blue. As one police officer noted in 1976, "it is better to have Soviet young people dance to their national song 'Cossacks' than to the American rock and roll" (Personal interview with Mikhail Suvorov, June 1, 1991). For more detail about this song, see Zhuk (2008a, pp. 25-7).

Dniepropetrovsk ideologists for "ideological unreliability."[6] In December, 1983, all college rock bands and disco clubs in the city participated in a special antiwar and anti-American concert organized by the regional Komsomol organization in the Dniepropetrovsk city circus building. Their participation demonstrated their loyalty and ideological reliability. Dniepropetrovsk Komsomol leaders presented this event both as propagandist action in support of the official policy of the Soviet state, and as proof of their efficient ideological work in the discotheque movement.[7]

In Ukraine, Andropov's campaign against rock music converged with another old ideological campaign which targeted so-called "fascist punks." It began in 1980-81 as a result of confusing reports in the central Soviet periodicals where British punks were presented as neo-fascist skinheads. Consequently, all Western music that was associated with the punk movement and used fascist symbols had to be prohibited for mass consumption in the Soviet Union.[8] For many discotheque activists the new anti-punk campaign was a shock. In Dniepropetrovsk the local disc jockeys played the music of British punk rock bands like the Sex Pistols and The Clash as an obligatory, ideological part of their dance programs during 1979 and 1980. This was in accord with a critique of the "political agenda" of progressive rock and punk musicians offered by *Rovesnik*, a central Komsomol magazine. It praised the anti-capitalist spirit of "young English rock musicians" who followed the traditions of legendary, intellectual rock bands like Pink Floyd. Komsomol journalists from Moscow wrote about the collaboration between The Clash and British Communists in their struggle against racism and neo-fascism, and about the criticism of capitalist reality in Pink Floyd's album *The Wall*.[9] KGB officials and Communist ideologists in Dniepropetrovsk followed conflicting ideological recommendations from their Kyiv supervisors: they interfered in local youth clubs and banned the music of any musician who was associated with the word "punk." According to the KGB's taxonomy from Kyiv, the "punk movement" was considered a part of international neo-fascism. Consequently, music by The Clash or the Sex Pistols was forbidden in the region of Dniepropetrovsk as early as 1980.

The first public scandal of the new anti-punk campaign took place at Club Melodia at a dance party on the eve of 1981. As one organizer of this party

---

[6]   On a seminar for disco activists see M. Sukhomlin, "Shkola zaproshue dysk-zhokeiv," *Prapor iunosti*, November 6, 1982, p. 4. On ideological control see Yu. Lystopad, "Ideologichna borot'ba i molod" "(Notatky z oblasnoi naukovo-praktyuchnoi konferentsii)," *Prapor iunosti*, December 17, 1983, p. 2.

[7]   See in F. Sukhonis, "Pisniu druzhby zaspivuie molod," *Prapor iunosti*, December 13, 1983, p. 1.

[8]   See Troitsky (1987, pp. 42-3). He refers to famous images of Sid Vicious wearing a swastika.

[9]   For The Clash, see *Rovesnik*, 1978, No. 6, pp. 13-15; 1980, No. 10, p. 26; 1982, No. 4, pp. 22-3. *Rovesnik* reprinted sheet music and lyrics of two Clash songs: "The Guns of Brixton" in No. 4 for 1982, and "Know Your Rights" in No. 10 for 1983. For Pink Floyd's *The Wall*, see *Rovesnik*, 1981, No. 11, pp. 24-6.

recalled, the program was officially approved by the city Komsomol committee. The ideological part of the program was devoted to the theme "The World Celebrates New Year." A disc jockey began with a summary of the major political and musical events of the last year. He told the audience that three of the most popular musicians among Soviet youth died in 1980: the Russian bard and guitar poet Vladimir Vysotsky; a popular French singer, Joe Dassin; and ex-Beatle John Lennon. After playing their songs a disc jockey mentioned a *Rovesnik* publication on The Clash, and then noted the strange behavior of the Komsomol *apparatchik* who was in charge of the party. In the middle of "London Calling" by The Clash, this *apparatchik* and two KGB officers approached the disc jockeys and ordered them to stop playing "the fascist music." Then one of the Melodia leaders tried to explain that *Rovesnik* had praised The Clash as an anti-capitalist, "leftist" British band:

> The KGB people interrupted our party for one hour. They checked all our tapes of the dance program. Eventually they confiscated all our music records and tapes with recordings of the Sex Pistols, The Clash, AC/DC, Kiss, and 10cc. They punished our Komsomol supervisors for giving us permission to play the music of "fascist punks." One of these Komsomol supervisors tried again to refer to *Rovesnik* publications in his defense. A KGB officer dismissed this as misinformation. "We know better," he told us. "All this music crap you are playing is a part of the fascist anti-Soviet conspiracy. You call this music punk rock, we call this stuff neo-fascism." When one of our discotheque enthusiasts interfered and told the KGB people that AC/DC and Kiss were not punk rock bands, he was arrested by the police and removed from a dance floor. Two organizers of this dance party argued that it was a violation of human rights, and they were also arrested by the KGB. (Igor T., Mikhail Suvorov, and Andrei Vadimov, personal interviews with author, 1991, 1991, 2003)

This was the beginning of a long ideological campaign waged by both Communist Party ideologists and KGB officers. After 1980 nobody tried to play punk rock at dance parties.

According to Professor Vladimir Demchenko, who worked in the 1980s as a Dniepropetrovsk public lecturer for the Communist Party, local ideologists used a description of a British punk from the secret digest of foreign press for Communist propagandists: the main identifying sign of a fascist punk was his shaven head. Apparently, it was a misunderstanding because the author of the original article dealt with British skinheads, and he compared punks and skinheads as the most fashionable trends in Western popular culture. In a confusing translation from English to Russian, a typical punk had shaved temples or, to put it correctly, according to this description, a punk's hair had to be removed from over his ears. When this interpretation was included in an ideological portrait of "fascist punk," Komsomol ideologists were ready to identify as a punk any young man with long hair and a pony tail. As a result, many heavy metal fans from the Dniepropetrovsk region were arrested during 1983-84 because the ignorant policemen were not able to tell one fashionable hairstyle from another or distinguish between "hard rock" and "punk rock" (Vladimir Demchenko and Serhiy Tihipko, personal interviews with author, 1992, 1993). Police and Komsomol activists thought punk and fascist were the same. All Komsomol propagandists and people in charge of discotheques in the Dniepropetrovsk region received special notices about punk ideology with a Russian translation of British punks' phrases. This information was reprinted in many publications by Dniepropetrovsk journalists who covered this anti-punk campaign (personal interviews with Demchenko and Tihipko).[10] Anti-punk hysteria resulted in the prohibition of bands that were tremendously popular among Soviet high school and vocational school students. AC/DC and Kiss had nothing to do with the punk movement at all, yet after 1980, the local Komsomol *apparatchiks* officially considered them "fascist, anti-Soviet bands." Komsomol ideologists in Kyiv "discovered" elements of insignia from Nazi Germany in the names of these bands. The combination "SS" presented as symbols of lightning in the Kiss logo, for example, was interpreted as an expression of the musicians' fascist ideology. Thus Komsomol leaders in Dniepropetrovsk followed the recommendations of the Kyiv "experts" and tried to ban the music of "fascist rock-n-rollers" (Pozdniakov, 1984, p. 3).

By the end of 1982 two British bands had been added to the list of "pro-fascist, anti-Soviet bands": heavy metal icons Iron Maiden and the "art pop" group 10cc, the latter famous for its ironic, intellectual lyrics and interesting melodic arrangements. Komsomol ideologists explained to KGB officers that these bands were especially dangerous because of their "hellish, anti-human imagery, fascist symbols, and anti-Soviet lyrics" (personal interviews with Demchenko and Tihipko). They cited the name "Iron Maiden," derived from the name of a medieval torture device; the group's artistic symbol, or mascot, a ten-foot tall rotting corpse named Eddie; and their 1982 album *The Number of the Beast*, that allegedly contained images of a "fascist satanic cult." The name of the second group was mistakenly re-interpreted as "Ten SS," referring to Hitler's secret police, the SS (Schutz-Staffel). Given that the English letter "c" is the equivalent of the letter "s" in Russian and Ukrainian, cc (cubic centimeters) was pronounced "ess-ess," and local Komsomol ideologists immediately characterized 10cc as a "fascist name." Moreover, the band's 1978 album *Bloody Tourists* included a musical parody of the

---

[10]     Journalists of youth periodicals quoted the punk slogans: "Live by today's day only! Do not think about tomorrow! Do not give a damn about all these spiritual crutches of religion, utopia and politics! Forget about this. Enjoy your day. You are young, and do not hurry to become a new young corpse" [sic!]. Dniepropetrovsk journalists usually added comments about the anti-human essence of "fascist punk music": "These were slogans of punks, preachers of bestial cynicism and meanness, who were the real spiritual mongrels of the twentieth century." See Gamol'sky et al. (1988, p. 139). Even during *perestroika* local journalists and KGB officials continued to use these materials. Thus, declarations made by British punks were reprinted for the use of Komsomol ideologists.

anti-Soviet hysteria experienced during the Cold War entitled "Reds in My Bed." The refrain of this song shocked the Soviet censors: "I've got Reds in my bed, I'm not easily led to the slaughter, and while the Cold War exists, I'll stay warm with the Commissars daughter ... Let me go home. You're a land full of misery. I don't like your philosophy. You're a cruel and a faceless race." Of course, nobody on a Soviet dance floor cared about these lyrics and nobody understood a word of this song; they just loved the melody. In fact, the major songs from *Bloody Tourists*, including "Reds in My Bed," "Dreadlock Holiday," "For You and I," "Life Line," and "Tokyo," all became hits in discos during 1979-83. Appalled by this "music propaganda" of "anti-Soviet, fascist ideas," Komsomol ideologists asked the police and KGB for help in removing "dangerous" music from the cultural consumption of Soviet youth. In 1981-84 hundreds of the forbidden records were confiscated from young rock fans in the region. An overwhelming majority of these records were albums by AC/DC, Kiss, Iron Maiden, and 10cc.

This anti-punk and anti-fascist hysteria affected even the music of Pink Floyd. This band was traditionally considered by Soviet ideologists an anti-capitalist "progressive" band, and Soviet television and radio occasionally broadcast its music. In the 1970s "One of These Days," from the 1971 album *Meddle*, was constantly heard as the theme song for the political TV show "International Panorama." Moreover, some of the band's more popular songs were included in music compilations produced by the music journal *Krugozor*. "Money" from *Dark Side of the Moon* was praised as "an anti-imperialist anthem" of Western, progressive youth culture. The idealization of Pink Floyd by the Soviet youth media reached a peak with the release of the band's album *The Wall* in 1979, but the official attitude changed in 1983. Its new album, *The Final Cut*, written by Roger Waters, criticized imperialistic aggression all over the world and concentrated mainly on the Falklands War between Argentina and Great Britain. According to Waters's lyrics, three major imperialist powers threatened to destroy the world: the United States, Great Britain, and the Soviet Union. Two tracks, "Get Your Filthy Hands Off My Desert" and "The Fletcher Memorial Home," openly criticized the expansionism of "Mr. Brezhnev and the Party," including the Soviet invasion of Afghanistan. According to KGB officers, the Komsomol experts recognized Brezhnev's name in *The Final Cut* lyrics, and henceforth included Pink Floyd on the list of "forbidden musicians" for discotheques because of their "distortion of Soviet foreign policy." By the end of 1983, all ideological departments of the regional Komsomol organizations in Ukraine had received a complete list of "forbidden music bands" with Pink Floyd at the top.

Soviet cultural consumption of Western products was always very limited and heavily censored. On the one hand, forms of consumption were regulated by various ideological requirements, and, on the other, they were influenced by consumers' demands. The more the ideological experts tried to ban a product, the more desirable it became. Albums by Kiss and AC/DC, for example, became the most profitable items sold on the music market in Dniepropetrovsk.

Both central Komsomol and local periodicals disoriented and confused their readers when they directly connected criminal anti-Soviet and neo-fascist behavior with "forbidden music." The first public scandal, which involved both "fascist music" and the display of "fascist symbols," took place in the closed city during the fall of 1982. The city police arrested two college students, Igor Keivan and Aleksandr Plastun, who had their own collections of Western music records with "fascist symbols" and who demonstrated their "neo-Nazi" behavior in downtown Dniepropetrovsk. These students were dressed in T-shirts bearing images of Kiss and AC/DC which attracted the police who interpreted such images as "fascist." After the arrest of Keivan and Plastun and the confiscation of their "fascist" records, the police sent information about these students' anti-Soviet behavior to their colleges. In December, 1982 the entire city and region of Dniepropetrovsk experienced the beginning of the anti-fascist and anti-punk campaign. The Dniepropetrovsk City Communist Party Committee approached N. Sarana, an old Communist and member of the anti-fascist resistance group during World War II, to write a letter about the dangers of "fascist punks." On December 22, 1982, the Committee staged an open public meeting with participation of all Communist and Komsomol activists in downtown Dniepropetrovsk. During this meeting all activists supported Sarana's letter against punks and "declared war on the punk movement" in the closed city. Later, under KGB pressure, local ideologists organized a special public trial of Keivan, Plastun, and another young punk, Vadim Shmeliov, who were expelled from the Komsomol and their colleges in January, 1983. The KGB officers were especially outraged about an attempt by Keivan and Plastun to "interpret" this punishment as a violation of their human rights. From this time on, all Komsomol organizations of the region began to purge Komsomol members for having unusual enthusiasm for the forbidden music.[11]

Following this scandal, both Communist ideologists and KGB operatives reminded the local Komsomol activists about the ideological danger of Western capitalist culture. They pointed to the case of Polish youth who actively participated in the anti-Soviet movements of the early 1980s. During 1982 and 1983, Dr. Aleksandr Amelchenko, a public lecturer for the regional Communist Party Committee, delivered a series of special lectures about the ideological threat of Western pop music. He visited the major districts and towns of the region and discussed this threat with local activists. In October, 1983, Amelchenko sent some of his material to local periodicals and answered various questions from young rock music fans. In his lectures and publications he emphasized that "the youth was the country's future." For this reason, the ideological enemies of the Soviet

---

[11]　Sarana's letter was titled "We declare war on everybody who interferes in our life and work!" and appeared as "Boi tem, kto meshaet nam stroit' i zhit'!" in *Dnepr vechernii*, December 23, 1982, p. 3. See also A. Liamina and L. Gamol'skii, "Grazhdaninom byt' obiazan," *Dnepr vechernii*, December 23, 1982, about the public trial that took place on December 22, 1982 in Dniepropetrovsk. See also the author's personal interview with Oleksandr Poniezha.

Union tried "to confuse and pollute Soviet youth and undermine the ideological basis of the Soviet Union. Moreover, they tried to distract Soviet audiences with so-called human rights" ("Spetsvypusk 'Politychnogo klubu PIu'," 1983, p. 2). Dniepropetrovsk journalists were so intimidated by the rock music campaign that they rejected any public demonstration of preferences for Western cultural products as an act of betrayal. They even took an active part in a campaign against the Leningrad hard rock band Zemliane during the spring of 1984. The band performed its second concert in the closed city in 1984. Though journalists had lauded the band's first concert in January of that year, the situation changed during the spring. To advertise their concert in Dniepropetrovsk, the Leningrad rock musicians used a photograph of Igor Romanov, their lead guitarist, dressed in a T-shirt bearing a US flag. Moreover, according to the local journalists, during their concert in the closed city, Zemliane played songs by "forbidden fascist and punk bands" (Tishchenko, 1984, p. 4). As a result, the Dniepropetrovsk Komsomol newspaper organized an anti-Zemliane campaign, accusing the Leningrad musicians of "a betrayal of socialist principles of music performance." Despite readers' support for the popular Leningrad band, journalists and local KGB officials insisted on punishing the musicians for their low ideological standards and for promoting "capitalist standards of anti-human mass culture" (Rozumkov and Skoryk, 1984, p. 4). In April, 1984, the administration of "Leningrad Concert," the organization responsible for Zemliane's concert tours, punished the rock musicians by canceling all their concerts and forcing them to rewrite their repertoire. Following this scandal, Dniepropetrovsk officials stopped inviting "suspicious" rock bands from Moscow and Leningrad.

This anti-rock campaign especially affected Dniepropetrovsk heavy metal fans. In 1983, when Dniepropetrovsk police arrested 10 students from a local vocational school for "acts of hooliganism," they discovered that the students had adopted various Nazi and American Ku Klux Klan symbols. As it turned out, Sergei Onushev, Aleksandr Rvachenko, and their friends had made special white robes, put the letters KKK on them, and tried to "imitate acts of this American fascist organization" (Gamol'sky et al., 1988, p. 133). Sergei Onushev, the leader of this "fascist" group, "used to play at home the music tapes of bands which belong to the pro-fascist movement—Kiss, Nazareth, AC/DC, Black Sabbath." Dniepropetrovsk ideologists established direct connections between this music and the fascism of Onushev's group, claiming Kiss provoked the Soviet students to commit inhuman, fascist acts.[12]

Another case that attracted the attention of local journalists concerned Dmitrii Frolin, a student at the Department of Philology at Dniepropetrovsk University.

---

[12]   "What kind of art," a journalist commented, "did the musicians of Kiss represent? They tear apart live chickens and vomit in public during their performances. This band Kiss is a group of four hooligans, who selected the SS Nazi symbol as the symbol of their band. Nevertheless, showbusinessmen transform them into the idols of the contemporary youth and proclaim them 'trendsetters' in popular culture" (Gamol'sky et al., 1988, p. 134).

As a result of the anti-punk and anti-fascist campaign, Frolin was arrested by the police in 1983 and expelled from both the Komsomol and the university in 1985 for "propaganda of fascism." According to the local ideologists, Frolin's activities were the direct result of "intensive listening" to the music of "fascist bands" such as Kiss and AC/DC. As one journalist wrote:

> The musicians of AC/DC, a favorite Frolin band, call themselves the devil's children. Their song "Back in Black" became an anthem of the American Nazi Party. During a Komsomol meeting Dmitrii justified his behavior, "I do not consider my collecting of AC/DC music a crime. As a Soviet citizen and human being, I have my human rights, which are protected by both Soviet and international law. I consider that listening to my favorite music, collecting and listening to music records are part of my private life. And I have a right to protect my privacy according to Soviet and international laws. (Gamol'sky et al., 1988, pp. 135-6)

In December, 1983, a local youth periodical published the results of a sociological analysis of Dniepropetrovsk youth compiled by Komsomol scholars. According to this publication, in many college dorms the special Komsomol raids discovered images of the American band Kiss, "on which any observer could easily find without any difficulty the SS symbols and Nazi signs" (Gamol'sky et al., 1988, pp. 135-6). Indeed, a majority of the student population in Dniepropetrovsk "preferred T-shirts bearing the signs of the US military and insignia of the capitalist countries, the political and military enemies of the Soviet Union." Dniepropetrovsk students bought these T-shirts on the black market and wore them during their college classes.[13]

Komsomol journalists also published translations of the most notorious anti-Soviet songs to become hits in local disco clubs in the late 1970s and early 1980s. As it turned out, the most popular dance songs had obvious or hidden anti-Soviet messages. The journalists drew on publications about various anti-Soviet rock bands issued by Soviet ideologists in Moscow or Kyiv. The range of these bands was wide—from British musicians such as Boy George and Culture Club to West German disco bands such as Genghis Khan. Material about these bands was published under the title: "Beware! Western Poison!" (Dubovyi, 1983, p. 4).

As KGB officers discovered, heavy metal and punk rock music fans also idealized the Ukrainian nationalist leaders of World War II, such as Stepan Bandera. After 1938, Bandera led the radical branch of the Organization of the

---

[13]    Oleksandr Beznosov, a Professor of History at Dniepropetrovsk University, recalled, during a personal interview, how during the same period of time he (an undergraduate history student in 1983) and his roommates were interrogated by the student dorm supervisors because they possessed music records by and posters of Black Sabbath, Iron Maiden, and Kiss. Beznosov was almost expelled from the university. Only interference by his academic mentor saved him.

Ukrainian Nationalists, which became a center of the military resistance to the Soviet Army after 1944 in Western Ukraine. After the suppression of the anti-Soviet activities of the Bandera troops, Bandera became a heroic symbol for many Ukrainian patriots. In 1983 and 1984 the police arrested members of "a fascist Banderite group" who were students of the Dniepropetrovsk agricultural college. These students, Konstantin Shipunov and his five followers, listened to "fascist rock music," organized their own "party," and popularized the ideas of Nazi leaders and the Ukrainian nationalist politicians. They criticized the Russification of cultural life in Ukraine, emphasized the necessity of Ukrainian independence from the Soviet Union, and insisted on protecting the human rights of all Ukrainian patriots. In conversation with a police officer, Shipunov referred to the Final Act of the Conference on Security and Cooperation in Europe signed in Helsinki by the Soviet leaders together with 34 other heads of state on August 1, 1975. According to Shipunov, the Final Act especially emphasized a protection of human rights. By arresting Ukrainian patriots like Shipunov, the local police violated human rights and broke international laws.[14]

Again in December, 1983, the Dniepropetrovsk regional Komsomol committee reported to the Ukrainian Komsomol Central Committee in Kyiv that in February-March, 1983, local ideologists encountered the beginning of a punk movement in the city of Dniepropetrovsk. However, during spring through the fall of that year, they mobilized all activists and "Soviet patriots," organized special counter-propaganda events all over the city and region, and finally stopped this "fascist movement." A secretary of the Dniepropetrovsk regional committee, O. Fedoseiev, concluded this report by saying, "As a result of our anti-punk campaign, there are practically no young people in the region who would imitate 'punks'."[15]

In 1984-85, Dniepropetrovsk police discovered new groups of "fascist-punks" with hundreds of followers. Only a few of them, however, had anything to do with Nazi ideology or fascism. Nonetheless all 10 groups arrested by the police were said to use various fascist symbols and paraphernalia, painted their faces "in punk fashion" and had shaven temples. Because the Komsomol had repeatedly stated that the main sign of punk behavior was "shaven temples of the head," this was enough to be arrested on the streets of Dniepropetrovsk during 1983-85. Hundreds of rock music fans were detained and their music records and audiotapes confiscated in the region of Dniepropetrovsk as a result of the anti-punk and anti-fascist campaign. In addition, a famous discotheque in the cultural center of Dniepropetrovsk University was transformed into a music lecture club called "Dialogue: Music in Ideological Struggle." Instead of dancing, students now listened to lectures about modern music and important issues of

---

[14]   Interviews with Oleksandr Poniezha, Andrei Vadimov, and Mikhail Suvorov. Cf. Gamol'sky et al. (1988, p. 137).

[15]   See his report in *TDAGOU* (Tsentral'nyi derzhavnyi arkhiv vyshchykh organiv vlady ta upravlinnia, Kyiv, Ukraine [Central State Archive of the High Offices of Power and Management]), f. 7, op. 20, d. 3087, l. 43.

international politics. Local ideologists preferred this kind of cultural consumption to the spontaneous dance parties playing bourgeois music, which were difficult to control. As a result, many talented disc jockeys and music engineers left Komsomol discotheques in 1985-86 and moved to the safer ground of ordinary technician's jobs, far away from the dangers surrounding rock music.

In 1983-84 the police also organized special raids on music markets in downtown Dniepropetrovsk. They were not looking for black marketeers, but for anti-Soviet music products, including records and audiotapes of music by Kiss and AC/DC. Thousands of original Western records were confiscated and hundreds of people were arrested during those two years.[16] Although by the beginning of 1985 the police had destroyed a thriving rock music market in the city, they were unable to halt the consumption. Discos, restaurants, and bars continued to thrive because "fresh" Western popular music was part of a very lucrative business. Indeed, the "disco club enterprise" became the first stable source of significant material profit for the local administration, including Komsomol *apparatchiks*. In 1981-83, according to official records, Club Melodia turned a monthly profit of more than 50,000 roubles. In fact, the organizers of this business earned an additional "nonregistered" 20,000 roubles each month (Rodionov, 1979, p. 4).[17]

As a result of the anti-rock music campaign, those in charge of music entertainment had to find nontraditional—and unofficial—sources of products to satisfy the growing demands of Dniepropetrovsk consumers. International tourism became the major source of new material for rock music consumption during 1983-85. In 1972 only 30 percent of all music records and tapes of Western music came directly through the channels of international tourism to the Dniepropetrovsk music market. By the end of 1984 more than 90 percent came from local tourists who traveled abroad, including those who used the services of the Komsomol travel agency.[18] During the anti-rock music campaign the Komsomol *apparatchiks*

---

[16]    The police released those black marketeers who had no "fascist or punk music products." Those who had AC/DC and Kiss records ("fascist products") were detained in police stations for 15 days (Interviews with Igor T. and Mikhail Suvorov).

[17]    Regarding guest numbers, admission fees, and alcohol beverages in 1982 and 1983, see *Prapor iunosti*, June 24, 1982, and January 15, 1983. Regarding the profits of disco club Melodia, see documents in *DADO*, f. 17, op. 11, d. 1, l. 28; f. 22, op. 36, d. 1, ll. 36, 37, 39, 40.

[18]    Many sources for the banned pop music came to Dniepropetrovsk through representatives of the ruling Soviet elite, who visited foreign countries as the members of local tourist groups. According to discotheque activists, in 1979 KGB supervisors of local tourism brought to Dniepropetrovsk the original rock music albums later banned by Communist ideologists. One tourist returning from a trip to Hungary, another from a trip to Poland, brought the albums *Highway to Hell* by AC/DC and *Dynasty* by Kiss for their own children, who were active participants in the music market in the city. Through these children of KGB officials, recordings of AC/DC and Kiss music became available for thousands of rock music consumers in the region. *DADO*, f. 22, op. 19, d. 2, 143, f. 19,

who had an opportunity to go abroad brought new music records and audiotapes. In 1984, 90 percent of all foreign music material in the central disco club of Dniepropetrovsk came directly from the Komsomol tourists who visited European socialist countries. As the active participants in the Dniepropetrovsk music market recalled, approximately nine out of 10 songs played at a central disco club dance party usually came from material that belonged to tourists. According to contemporaries, anti-rock music campaigns in Dniepropetrovsk did not halt the consumption of Western pop music. To the contrary, the campaigns contributed to the immense popularity of forbidden Western cultural products among young consumers and also among their ideological supervisors who already greatly appreciated and enjoyed these products. The most unpleasant discovery for local KGB officers who supervised student activities in the city was the involvement of political elements in the discussion of forbidden Western cultural products such as rock music. Dniepropetrovsk rock music fans referred to international documents, signed by the Soviet leaders, regarding the protection of human rights and, after 1975, they frequently raised the issue of human rights when police harassed them.

A search for the authentic West became part of the process of identity formation for millions of young Soviet consumers of Western cultural products. These consumers tried to identify themselves only with the West, which as an ideal lost any connections with Soviet Ukrainian culture by the end of the 1970s. In the imagination of these consumers, the official Soviet Ukrainian culture represented all the most conservative, backward, and anti-Western elements in their life. By accepting the real West as a part of their identity, they rejected the official Soviet version of their own ethnic identity. Through consumption of Western pop music, both rock music enthusiasts and young Komsomol activists involved in the disco club business tried to form their own notion of human rights, which became an important part of their self-identity. Eventually, the new cultural activities and tastes resulted in new values and demands for cultural consumption, which gradually replaced and transformed the traditional Soviet values and Communist ideological practices among both ordinary Komsomol members and the young Komsomol elite of the 1980s.

op. 60, d. 85, ll. 9-11. See interviews with Oleksandr Beznosov, Oleksandr Poniezha, and Serhiy Tihipko.

# Bibliography

Aboriginal and Torres Strait Islander Commission, "Everybody's Talking: Treaty," *ATSIC News* (February, 2001): 37.

Aboriginal and Torres Strait Islander Commission, *ATSIC Home* (Canberra: National Library of Australia, 2005) <http://pandora.nla.gov.au/pan/41033/20060106-0000/ATSIC/default.html>, accessed September 7, 2009.

Acevedo, Claudio, et al., *Víctor Jara: Obra Musical Completa*. Textos Partes I y II, Rodrigo Torres (Santiago: Fundación Víctor Jara, 1996).

Ādamsons, G., "Cienīgi līdztautieši!," *Padomju Ceļš*, 29, 5409 (March 9, 1982).

Adorno, Theodor, *Prisms*, Trans. Samuel and Sherry Weber (Cambridge, Mass.: MIT Press, 1983a).

Adorno, Thoedor, *Negative Dialectics* (New York: Continuum, 1983b).

Adorno, Thoedor, *Aesthetic Theory* [1970], Trans. R. Hullot-Kentor (Minneapolis: University of Minnesota Press, 1997).

Adorno, Thoedor, *Essays on Music*, Trans. Susan Gillespie (Berkeley: University of California Press, 2002).

Adorno, Theodor, and Max Horkheimer, *Dialectic of Enlightenment*, Trans. Edmund Jephcott (Stanford: Stanford University Press, 2002).

Adorno, Theodor, and Rolf Tiedemann (eds.), *Can One Live after Auschwitz? A Philosophical Reader* (Palo Alto: Stanford University Press, 2003).

Ahern, Daniel, *Nietzsche as Cultural Physician* (University Park, Pa.: Penn State Press, 1995).

Allen, Lara, "Commerce, Politics, and Musical Hybridity: Vocalizing Urban Black South African Identity during the 1950s," *Ethnomusicology*, 47, 2 (2003): 228-49.

Alvarez, R.R., "The Mexican-US Border: The Making of an Anthropology of Borderlands," *Annual Review of Anthropology*, 24 (1995): 447-70.

Anaya, James, "Indigenous Intervention Discriminatory: UN," *ABC News* (August 27, 2009) <http://www.abc.net.au/news/stories/2009/08/27/2668915.htm>, accessed September 8, 2009.

Andree Zaimović, Vesna, "Muzička politika na javnom radijskom servisu Bosne i Hercegovine—muzikološki izazov u specifičnoj poslijeratnoj stvarnosti" [Music Policy in the Public Radio Service of Bosnia and Herzegovina—Musicolocigal Challenge in Specific PostWar Reality], in Ivan Čavlović (ed.), *Zbornik radova 3. međunarodnog simpozija "Muzika u društvu"* [Proceedings from the 3rd International Symposium "Music in Society"] (Sarajevo: Muzikološko društvo, 2002): 125-31.

Andree Zaimović, Vesna, "O medijskom pristupu popularnoj muzici zemalja bivše SFRJ" [On the Media Approach to Popular Music in the Countries of the Former Socialist Federative Republic of Yugoslavia], in Tamara Karača and Senad Kanić (eds.), *Zbornik radova 4. međunarodnog simpozija "Muzika u društvu"* [Proceedings from the 4th International Symposium "Music in Society"] (Sarajevo: Muzikološko društvo, 2004): 161-5.

Androutsopoulos, Jannis, and Arno Scholz, "Spaghetti Funk: Appropriations of Hip-hop Culture and Rap Music in Europe," *Popular Music and Society*, 26, 4 (2003): 463-79.

Ansell, Gwen, *Soweto Blues: Jazz, Popular Music and Politics in South Africa* (Johannesburg: Continuum International, 2004).

Ascherson, Neal, "From Multiculturalism to Where?" (August 19, 2004) <opendemocracy.net>, accessed November 9, 2009.

Australia, Northern Territory Supreme Court, no. 341, *Milirrpum [Marika] and Others* v. *Nabalco Pty Ltd and the Commonwealth of Australia* (*Milirrpum* v. *Nabalco*), Statement of Claim (Darwin: Australia, 1968).

Australia, *Milirrpum* v. *Nabalco*, Judgment of Justice Blackburn, *Federal Law Reports*, 17 (1971): 141-294.

Australia, High Court of no. 23, *Mabo and Others* v. *Queensland* (*Mabo* v. *Queensland*) (no. 2), Judgment of Chief Justice Mason and Justice McHugh, *Commonwealth Law Reports*, 175 (1992): 1-216.

Australia Council, *Resolutions Carried in the Plenary Meetings of the National Seminar on Aboriginal Arts Held in Canberra from 21-25 May, 1975* (Canberra: Australia Council, 1973).

Australian Human Rights Commission, *Bringing Them Home: Report of the National Inquiry into the Separation of Aboriginal and Torres Strait Islander Children from Their Families* (April, 1997) <http://www.humanrights.gov.au/social_justice/bth_report/report/index.html> (Canberra: Australia, 1997), accessed September 4, 2009.

Australian Human Rights Commission, *Submission of the Human Rights and Equal Opportunity Commission (HREOC) to the Senate Legal and Constitutional Committee on the Northern Territory National Emergency Response Legislation, 10 August 2007* (Canberra: Australia, 2007) <http://www.hreoc.gov.au/legal/submissions/2007/NTNER_Measures20070810.htm>, accessed September 8, 2009.

Baines, Gary, "The Rainbow Nation? Identity and Nation Building in Post-Apartheid South-Africa," *Mots Pluriels*, 7 (1998) <http://www.arts.uwa.edu.au/MotsPluriels/MP798gb.html>, accessed October 25, 2009.

Baines, Gary, "The Politics of Public History in Post-Apartheid South Africa," in Hans Eric Stolten (ed.), *History Making and Present Day Politics: The Meaning of Collective Memory in South Africa* (Uppsala: Nordic Africa Institute, 2006): 167-82.

Ballantine, Christopher, *Marabi Nights: Early South African Jazz and Vaudeville* (Johannesburg: Raven Press, 1993).

Baranowitch, Nimrod, *China's New Voices: Popular Music, Ethnicity, Gender and Politics, 1978-1997* (Berkeley: University of California Press, 2003).

Barber-Keršovan, Alenka, "Na sledi kulturni identiteti. Kaj je 'slovenskega' v slovenski rock glasbi?," *Glasnik Slovenskega etnološkega društva*, 39, 1 (1999): 4-9.

Barmé, Geremie (ed.), *Shades of Mao: The Posthumous Cult of the Great Leader* (London: East Gate Books, 1996).

Barmé, Geremie, "CCPTM & ADCULT PRC," *The China Journal*, 41 (1999): 1-23.

Beinhart, William, *The Rise of Conservation in South Africa: Settlers, Livestock, and the Environment 1770-1950* (Oxford: Oxford University Press, 2008).

Benjamin, Walter, "The Work of Art in the Age of Mechanical Reproduction" (1936) <http://www.marxists.org/reference/subject/philosophy/works/ge/benjamin. htm>, accessed July 25, 2009.

Bhabha, Homi, *The Location of Culture* (New York: Routledge, 1994).

Bird Rose, Deborah, *Hidden Histories: Black Stories from Victoria River Downs, Humbert River and Wave Hill Stations* (Canberra: Aboriginal Studies Press, 1991).

Bizjak, Anja, et al. (eds.), *Petrovardinsko pleme: Raziskovanje fenomena Festivala EXIT/Petrovaradinsko pleme: Istraživanje fenomena Festivala EXIT /Petrovaradin Tribe: Reflections of the Phenomenon of Music Festival EXIT* (Ljubljana: KUD Pozitiv, 2005) <http://www.pozitiv.si/petrovaradintribe/>, accessed July 25, 2009.

Blacking, John, *How Musical is Man?* (Seattle: University of Washington Press, 1973).

Bowdler, Sandra, "A Study of Indigenous Ceremonial (*Bora*) Sites in Eastern Australia" (Perth: University of Western Australia, 1999) <http://www. archaeology.arts.uwa.edu.au/about/research/bowdler/a_study_of_indigenous_ ceremonial_(bora)_sites_in_eastern_australia>, accessed September 7, 2009.

Brauns, Joahims, "10. Zur Hermeneutik der sowjetisch-baltischen Musik: ein Versuch der Deutung von Sinn und Stil," in Mārtiņš Boiko (ed.), *Joahims Brauns. Raksti. Studies. Schriften: Mūzika Latvijā. Music in Latvia. Musik in Lettland* (Rīga: Musica Baltica, 2002): 204-26.

Brooks, Shirley, "Re-reading the Hluhluwe-Umfolozi Game Reserve: Constructions of 'Natural' Space," *Transformations*, 44 (2000): 63-79.

Bruton, Michael N., and Keith H. Cooper (eds.), *Studies on the Ecology of Maputaland* (Grahamstown: Rhodes University Press; Durban: Natal Branch of the Wildlife Society of Southern Africa, 1980).

Burgmeistere, M., "Koklē savas zelta kokles," *Dzimtenes Balss*, 30 (1982).

Carrasco Pirard, Eduardo, "The *nueva canción* in Latin America." *International Social Science Journal*, 94, 34, 4 (1982): 599-623.

Central Land Council, *Central Land Council: The Land is Always Alive* (Alice Springs: Central Land Council, 2008) <http://www.clc.org.au>, accessed September 7, 2009.

Clarke, Gary, "Defending Ski-Jumpers: A Critique of Theories of Youth Subcultures," in Ken Gelder and Sara Thornton (eds.), *The Subcultures Reader* (London: Routledge, 1997): 175-80.

Cloonan, Martin, *Banned! Censorship of Popular Music in Britain, 1967-92* (Aldershot: Arena, 1996).

Cohen, Ronald D., *Rainbow Quest: The Folk Music Revival and American Society, 1940-1970* (Amherst: University of Massachusetts Press, 2002).

Conrad, Joseph, *Heart of Darkness* [1902] (New York: Penguin, 1950).

Corn, Aaron, "Burr-gi wargugu ngu-ninya rrawa: The Letterstick Band and Hereditary Ties to Estate through Song," *Musicology Australia*, 25 (2002): 76-101.

Corn, Aaron, with Neparrŋa Gumbula, "Djiliwirri ganha dhärranhana, wäŋa limurruŋgu," *Australian Music Research*, 7 (2003): 55-66.

Corn, Aaron, and Neparrŋa Gumbula, "Now Balanda Say We Lost Our Land in 1788: Challenges to the Recognition of Yolŋu Law in Contemporary Australia," in Marcia Langton et al. (eds.), *Honour among Nations? Treaties and Agreements with Indigenous Peoples* (Melbourne: Melbourne University Publishing, 2004): 101-14.

Corn, Aaron, with Neparrŋa Gumbula, "Ancestral Precedent as Creative Inspiration: The Influence of Soft Sands on Popular Song Composition in Arnhem Land," in Graeme Ward and Adrian Muckle (eds.), *The Power of Knowledge, the Resonance of Tradition: Electronic Publication of Papers from the AIATSIS Conference 2001* (Canberra: AIATSIS, 2005): 31-68.

Corn, Aaron, and Neparrŋa Gumbula, "*Buḏutthun ratja wiyinymirri*," *Australian Aboriginal Studies*, 2 (2007): 116-27.

Corn, Aaron, *Reflections and Voices: Exploring the Music of Yothu Yindi with Mandawuy Yunupiŋu* (Sydney: Sydney University Press, 2009).

Coulter, Carol, *The Hidden Tradition: Feminism, Women and Nationalism in Ireland* (Cork: Cork University Press, 1993).

Council for Aboriginal Reconciliation, "Royal Commission into Aboriginal Deaths in Custody" (Sydney: Australian Legal Information Institute, 1998) <http://www.austlii.edu.au/au/other/IndigLRes/rciadic>, accessed September 4, 2009.

Council for Aboriginal Reconciliation, *Reconciliation, Australia's Challenge: Final Report of the Council for Aboriginal Reconciliation to the Prime Minister and the Commonwealth Parliament* (Sydney: Australian Legal Information Institute, 2000) <http://www.austlii.edu.au/au/other/IndigLRes/car/2000/16>, accessed September 4, 2009.

Cui, Jian, and Guowei Zhou, *Ziyou fengge* [Free Style] (Guilin: Guangxi Pedagogical University Publishing House, 2001).

Dahal, Semanta, "Post Conflict Constitution Making in Nepal: Towards 'Inclusiveness' in Democracy," Social Science Research Network (2008) <http://ssrn.com/abstract=1300132>, accessed July 26, 2009.

Daly, Mary E., *Women and Work in Ireland* (Dublin: Economic and Social History Society of Ireland, 1997).

Dambrāns, B., "Par avotu tīrību," *Cīņa* (December 15, 1984).

Damm, Jens, and Andreas Steen (eds.), *Postmodern China*, Berliner China-Hefte/ Chinese History and Society 34 (Berlin/Zürich: Lit-Verlag, 2008).

Debord, Guy, *La société du spectacle* (Paris: Buchet-Chastel, 1967).

Debord, Guy, *Commentaires sur la société du spectacle* (Paris: Editions Gérard Lebovici, 1988).

de Kloet, Jeroen, "Rock in the Hard Place: Commercial Fantasies in China's Music Industry," in Stephanie Hemelryk Donald, Michael Keane, and Yin Hong (eds.), *Media in China: Consumption, Content and Crisis* (London: Routledge, 2002): 93-104.

de Kloet, Jeroen, "Sonic Sturdiness: The Globalization of 'Chinese' Rock and Pop," *Critical Studies in Media Communication*, 22, 4 (2005a): 321-38.

de Kloet, Jeroen, "Popular Music and Youth in Urban China: The *Dakou* Generation," *The China Quarterly* (2005b): 609-26.

de Kloet, Jeroen, "Authenticating Geographies and Temporalities: Representations of Chinese Rock in China," *Visual Anthropology*, 18 (2005c): 229-55.

*Derzhavnyi arkhiv Dnipropetrovs'koi oblasti* [The State Archive of the Dnipropetrovs'k Region].

Dirlik, Arif, and Xudong Zhang (eds.), "Introduction: Postmodernism and China," *boundary 2*, 24, 3 (Autumn, 1997): 1-18.

Dragičević-Šešić, Milena, *Neofolk kultura: Publika i njene zvezde* [Neofolk Culture: Audience and Its Stars] (Sremski Karlovci and Novi Sad: Izdavačka knjižarnica Zorana Stojadinovića, 1994).

Dubovyi, G., "Oberezhno! Zakhidna otruta!," *Prapor iunosti* (November 24, 1983): 4.

Erlmann, Veit, *African Stars: Studies in Black South African Performance* (Chicago: University of Chicago Press, 1991).

Eyerman, Ron, and Andrew Jamison, *Music and Social Movements: Mobilizing Traditions in the Twentieth Century* (Cambridge: Cambridge University Press, 1998).

Fairley, Jan, "La nueva canción Latinoamericana," *Bulletin of Latin American Research*, 3, 2 (1984): 107-15.

Feld, Steven, "From Schizophonia to Schismogenesis: On the Discourse and Commodification Practices of 'World Music' and 'World Beat'," in Charles Keil and Steven Feld (eds.), *Music Grooves* (Chicago: University of Chicago Press, 1994): 257-89.

Field, Andrew, and Jeroen Groenewegen, "Explosive Acts: Beijing's Punk Rock Scene in the Postmodern World of 2007," in Jens Damm and Andreas Steen (eds.), *Postmodern China*, Berliner China-Hefte 34 (Berlin/Zürich: Lit-Verlag, 2008): 8-26.

Finnegan, Ruth, "Music, Experience, and the Anthropology of the Emotions," in Martin Clayton, Trevor Herbert, and Richard Middleton (eds.), *The Cultural Study of Music: A Critical Introduction* (New York: Routledge, 2003): 181-92.

Finnegan, Ruth, *The Oral and Beyond: Doing Things with Words in Africa* (Scottsville: University of KwaZulu-Natal Press, 2007).

Flynn, Leo, "The Missing Body of Mary McGhee: The Constitution of Women in Irish Constitutional Adjudication," *Journal of Gender Studies*, 2, 2 (November, 1993): 238-52.

Fond 17, Dnepropetrovskii Gorkom LKSMU (Komsomola Ukrainy).

Fond 18, Dnepropetrovskii Gorkom KPU (Kommunisticheskoi partii Ukrainy).

Fond 19, Dnepropetrovskii Obkom KPU (Kommunisticheskoi partii Ukrainy).

Fond 22, Dnepropetrovskii Obkom LKSMU (Komsomola Ukrainy).

Fornäs, Johan, and Göran Bolin (eds.), *Youth Culture in Late Modernity* (London: Sage, 1995).

Foster, Roy Fitzroy, *Luck and the Irish: A Brief History of Change 1970-2000* (London: Allen Lane, 2007).

Foo, Janis, "Rocking Beijing: China's Underground Music Scene," *The Wall Street Journal* (July 24, 2009) <http://online.wsj.com/article/ SB124831869681774897.html>, accessed September 12, 2009.

Frank, Thomas, *The Conquest of Cool* (Chicago: University of Chicago Press, 1998).

Freemuse, "What is Music Censorship?" (2001) <http://www.freemuse.org/ sw2338.asp>, accessed June, 2009.

Freemuse, "Conference on Freedom of Expression and Music in the Middle East, Beirut, October 2005" (November 25, 2005) <http://www.freemuse.org/ sw9757.asp>, accessed June, 2009.

Friedman, Susan Stanford, *Mappings: Feminism and the Cultural Geographies of Encounter* (Princeton: Princeton University Press, 1998).

Frith, Simon, "The Discourse of World Music," in Georgina Born and David Hesmondhalgh (eds.), *Western Music and Its Others: Difference, Representation, and Appropriation in Music* (Berkeley: University of California Press, 2000): 305-22.

Frith, Simon, *Popular Music: Critical Concepts in Media and Cultural Studies* (London: Routledge, 2004).

Fung, Anthony, *Global Capital, Local Culture: Transnational Media Corporations in China* (New York: Peter Lang, 2008).

Gajić, Branka, "Neće Oliver, neće ni Ceca" [Oliver Does Not Want, and Ceca Does Not Want], *Ilustrovana politika*, 2279 (September 21, 2002), <http:// ilustrovana.com/2002/2279/7.htm>, accessed July 5, 2009.

Gamol'sky, Leonid, Nikolai Efremenko, and Vladimir Inshakov, *Na barrikadakh sovesti: Ocherki, razmyshlenia, interviu* (Dniepropetrovsk, 1988).

Gelder, Ken, and Sarah Thornton (eds.), *The Subcultures Reader* (London: Routledge, 1997).

Gellner, David, "Introduction," in David Gellner, J. Pfaff-Czarnecka, and J. Whelpton (eds.), *Nationalism and Ethnicity in a Hindu Kingdom: The Politics of Culture in Contemporary Nepal* (Amsterdam: Harwood Academic, 1997): 3-32.

Gilbert, Shirli, "Singing against Apartheid: ANC Cultural Groups and the International Anti-Apartheid Struggle," in Grant Olwage (ed.), *Composing Apartheid: Music for and against Apartheid* (Johannesburg: Witwatersrand University Press, 2008): 155-84.

Giri, Saroj, "Taking the Bait: Maoists and the Democratic Lure in Nepal," *Journal of Contemporary Asia*, 38, 2 (2008): 277-99.

Gobyn, Winne, "From War to Peace: The Nepalese Maoist's Strategic and Ideological Thinking," *Studies in Conflict and Terrorism*, 32 (2009): 420-38.

González, Juan Pablo, "Jara, Víctor," <http://www.oxfordmusiconline.com/ subscriber/article/grove/music/49866?q=victor+jara&search=quick&pos=1& _start=1#firsthit>, accessed February 12, 2009.

Gordy, Eric D., *The Culture of Power in Serbia: Nationalism and the Destruction of Alternatives* (University Park, Pa.: Penn State University Press, 1999).

Gould, Peter, "'Mi Pueblo Creador': Remembering Víctor Jara" (Ph.D. dissertation: Brandeis University, 2002).

Grebe, Maria Ester, *The Chilean Verso: A Study in Musical Archaism*, Trans. Bette Jo Hileman (Los Angeles: UCLA Latin American Center, 1967).

Greene, Paul, Personal interviews at a concert of Rubber Soul, Kathmandu, December 31, 2002.

Greene, Paul, Email interview with Prateek Nyoupane, member of Ugra Karma, July 5, 2009.

Greene, Paul, "Electronic and Affective Overdrive: Tropes of Transgression in Nepali Heavy Metal," in Jeremy Wallach, Harris M. Berger, and Paul Greene (eds.), *Metal Rules the Globe: Heavy Metal Music and Globalization* (Durham, NC: Duke University Press, forthcoming, 2012).

Grlja, Dušan, "(De)generation in 'Protest' or the Defense and the Last Days of 'Other Serbia'," *Break*, 2, 2-3 (2002): 34-44.

Grujičić, Nebojša, "R'n'r i protesti: Kamenje na system" [R'n'r and Protests: Stones to the System], *Vreme*, 464 (November 27, 1999).

Guo Facai, *Jiasuo yu benpao: 1980-2005 Zhongguo yaogunyue duli wenhua shengtai guancha* [Chained and Running: An Investigation of the Independent Cultural Attitude of Chinese Rock Music, 1980-2005] (Wuhan: Hubei People's Publishing House, 2006).

Guy, Jeff, "Battling with Banality," *Journal of Natal and Zulu History*, 18 (1998): 156-93.

Hardy, Frank, *The Unlucky Australians* (Melbourne: Nelson, 1968).

Harries, Patrick, *Work, Culture, and Identity: Migrant Labourers in Mozambique and South Africa, c.1860—1910* (Johannesburg: Witwatersrand University Press, 1994).

Hausmanis, Viktor, "Svētki beigušies, darbs turpinās," *Cīṇa* (December 24, 1985).

Heath, Joseph, and Andrew Potter, *Nation of Rebels: Why Counterculture Became Consumer Culture* (New York: HarperCollins, 2004).

Hebdidge, Dick, *Subculture: The Meaning of Style* (London: Routledge, 1979).

Hecker, Pierre, "Contesting Islamic Concepts of Morality: Heavy Metal in Istanbul," in Karin van Nieuwkerk (ed.), *Muslim Rap, Halal Soaps, and Revolutionary Theatre: Artistic Developments in the Muslim World* (Austin: University of Texas Press, 2011).

Hegel, G.W.F., *Phenomenology Of Sprit* [1807] (Oxford: Oxford University Press, 1977).

Helmling, Steven, "'Immanent Critique' and 'Dialectical Mimesis' in Adorno and Horkheimer's *Dialectic of Enlightenment*," *boundary 2*, 32, 3 (2005): 97-117.

Hesketh, Tom, *The Second Partitioning of Ireland: The Abortion Referendum of 1983* (Dublin: Brandsma Books, 1990).

Ho, Wai-chung, "The Political Meaning of Hong Kong Popular Music: A Review of Sociopolitical Relations between Hong Kong and the People's Republic of China since the 1980s," *Popular Music*, 19, 3 (October, 2000): 341-53.

Ho, Wai-chung, "Social Change and Nationalism in China's Popular Songs," *Social History*, 31, 4 (2006): 435-53.

Hribar, Tine, "Pankrti, tovariši in drugi" [Pankrti, Comrades, and Others], in Peter Lovšin, Peter Mlakar, and Igor Vidmar (eds.), *Punk je bil prej: 25 let punka pod Slovenci* [Punk Happened Before: 25 Years of Punk under the Slovenes] (Ljubljana: Cankarjeva založba and Ropot, 2002): 5-7.

Huang, Hao, "Yaogun yinyue: Rethinking Mainland Chinese Rock 'n' Roll," *Popular Music*, 20, 1 (2001): 1-11.

Huang, Hao, "Voices from Chinese Rock, Past and Present Tense: Social Commentary and the Construction of Identity in *Yaogun Yinyue*, from Tiananmen to the Present," *Popular Music and Society*, 26, 2 (June, 2003): 183-202.

Husband, William B., "Review of Timothy Ryback's *Rock around the Bloc: A History of Rock Music in Eastern Europe and the Soviet Union*," *Russian Review*, 49, 4 (October, 1990): 521-2.

Hutnyk, John, "Adorno at Womad: South Asian Crossovers and the Limits of Hybridity Talk," *Postcolonial Studies*, 1, 3 (1998): 401-26.

Impey, Angela, Interview with Women's Group, Usuthu Gorge, August 27 and 28, 2003.

Impey, Angela, Interview with Women's Group, Eziphosheni, August 31, September 3, 2003.

Impey, Angela, Interview with Siphiwe Mzila, Eziphosheni, August 31, 2003.

Impey, Angela, Interview with Siphiwe Cele and Fambile Khumalo, Eziphosheni, August 31, 2003.

Impey, Angela, Interview with Fambile Khumalo, Eziphosheni, September 1, 2003.

Impey, Angela, Interview with Makete Nkomonde, Usuthu, November 18, 2003.

Impey, Angela, Interview with MaNonyi Ndabeni, Usuthu, November 18, 2003.

Impey, Angela, Interview with Makete Nkomonde, Usuthu, April 24, 2004.

Impey, Angela, "Sounding Place in the Western Maputaland Borderlands," *Journal of the Musical Arts in Africa*, 3 (2006): 55-79.

Impey, Angela, "Sound, Memory and Dis/Placement: Exploring Sound, Song and Performance as Oral History in the Southern African Borderlands," *Oral History* (Spring 2008): 44-55.

"The Irresponsibility of Björk in China," *Music 2.0: Exploring Chaos in Digital Music* (March 25, 2008) <www.music2dot0.com/archives/104>, accessed July 12, 2009.

Isaac, Graeme, and Ned Lander (prod.), *Wrong Side of the Road* (Adelaide: Aboriginal Advancement League of South Australia, 1981).

Ivanović, Goran, "Mesić oštel hrvaško diplomacijo zaradi Thompsona" [Mesić Blamed Croatian Diplomacy for Thompson], *Dnevnik* (October 6, 2009): 6.

Janjatović, Petar, "Global Music Pulse: Slovenia/Serbia," *Billboard*, 108, 25 (1996): 61.

Janjatović, Petar, "Global Music Pulse: Bosnia," *Billboard*, 109, 5 (1997): 49.

Janjatović, Petar, "A Retrospect: Yugoslav Pop and Rock," *Novi zvuk*, 13 (1999): 30-35.

Janjatović, Petar, "Global Music Pulse: The Latest Music News from around the Planet. Belgrade," *Billboard*, 112, 9 (2000): 53.

Jara, Joan, *An Unfinished Song: The Life of Victor Jara* (New York: Ticknor & Fields, 1984).

Jara, Joan, and Adrian Mitchell, *Victor Jara: His Life and Songs* (London: Elm Tree Books, 1976).

Jaušovec, Matjaž, "CD-teka: Let 3—Bombardiranje Srbije i Čačka" [Review of Let 3's Bombing of Serbia and Čačak], *RockOnNet* (August 23, 2007) <http://www.rockonnet.com/>, accessed December 9, 2008.

Jeffs, Nikolai, "Some People in This Town Don't Want to Die Like a Hero: Multiculturalism and the Alternative Music Scene in Sarajevo, 1992-1996," in Mark Yoffe and Andrea Collins (eds.), *Rock 'n' Roll and Nationalism: A Multinational Perspective* (Newcastle: Cambridge Scholars Press, 2005): 1-19.

Johnson, Bruce, and Martin Cloonan, *Dark Side of the Tune: Popular Music and Violence* (Aldershot: Ashgate, 2008).

Johnston, Vivien, *Copyrites: Aboriginal Art in the Age of Reproductive Technologies* (Sydney: National Indigenous Arts Advocacy Association, 1996).

Jones, Andrew F., *Like a Knife: Ideology and Genre in Contemporary Chinese Popular Music* (New York/Ithaca: Cornell University Press, 1992).

Kahn-Harris, Keith, *Extreme Metal: Music and Culture on the Edge* (Oxford: Berg, 2007).

Kahn-Harris, Keith, Interview "Treehouse of Death" (August 8, 2008) <http://www.treehouseofdeath.com/?p=715>, accessed December, 2009.

Keating, Paul, "Redfern Park Speech," *Aboriginal Law Bulletin*, 3 (1992) <http://www.austlii.edu.au/au/journals/ILB/2001/57.html>, accessed September 7, 2009.

Kidd, Rosalind, *The Way We Civilise: Aboriginal Affairs, The Untold Story* (Brisbane: University of Queensland Press, 1997).

Kloppers, Roelie, "'We Are Only Here for the Pension; Tonight We Will Go Back to Mozambique': State Welfare and Development Projects that Transcend Borders," *Africanus Journal of Development Studies*, 36, 2 (2006): 154-65.

Klotiņš, Arnolds, "The Latvian Neo-folklore Movement and the Political Changes of the Late 20th Century," *The World of Music*, 44, 3 (2002): 107-30.

Knopoff, Steven, "Yolŋu," in Warren Bebbington (ed.), *The Oxford Companion to Australian Music* (Melbourne: Oxford University Press, 1997): 602-3.

Kommunisiticheskaia partiia Sovetskogo Soiuza, Ob ideologicheskoi rabote KPSS: Sbornik dokumentov (Moscow: Izdatel'stvo politicheskoi literatury, 1983).

Kraus, Richard Curt, *The Party and the Arty in China: The New Politics of Culture* (Lanham, Md.: Rowman and Littlefield, 2004).

Kronja, Ivana, "Politics, Nationalism, Music, and Popular Culture in 1990s Serbia," *Slovo*, 16, 1 (2004): 5-15.

Lanning, Greg, *Zhongguo Yaogun: China Rocks*, Film Documentary, "Rhythms of the World" (BBC TV, 1990).

Lee, Joanna Ching-Yun, "All for Freedom: The Rise of Patriotic/Pro-Democratic Popular Music in Hong Kong in Response to the Chinese Student Movement," in Reebee Garofalo (ed.), *Rockin' the Boat: Mass Music and Mass Movements* (Boston: South End Press, 1992): 129-48.

LeVine, Mark, *Why They Don't Hate Us: Lifting the Veil on the Axis of Evil* (Oxford: Oneworld, 2005).

LeVine, Mark, Personal interview with Salman Ahmad, Los Angeles, August, 2007.

LeVine, Mark, "Media Reform in Six Arab States," SAIC Research Report (December 31, 2007).

LeVine, Mark, Personal interview with Bruce Dickinson, Irvine, May, 2008.

LeVine, Mark, *Heavy Metal Islam: Rock, Resistance and the Struggle for the Soul of Islam* (New York: Random House, 2008).

LeVine, Mark, Personal interview with Layla al-Zubaidi, Beirut, 2006.

LeVine, Mark, Personal interview with Layla al-Zubaidi, Beirut, April 2009.

Li Hongjie, *Zhongguo yaogun shouce* [Encyclopedia of Chinese Rock 'n' Roll] (Chongqing: Chongqing Publishing House, 2006).

Liu, Alice, "China's Rockers too Pampered for Politics," *Asia Times Online* (October 14, 2009) <http://www.atimes.com/atimes/China/KJ14Ad02.html>, accessed October 30, 2009.

Lu Lingtao/Li Yang, *Nahan wei le Zhongguo cengjing de yaogun* [Scream for China's Rock 'n' Roll] (Guilin: Guangxi Pedagogical University Publishing House, 2003).

Lu, Sheldon H., *China, Transnational Visuality, Global Postmodernity* (California: Stanford University Press, 2001).

Luković, Petar, *Bolja prošlost: Prizori iz muzičkog života Jugoslavije 1940-1989* [Better Past: Scenes from the Musical Life in Yugoslavia, 1940-1989] (Beograd: Mladost, 1989).

Malečkar, Nela, and Tomaž Mastnak (eds.), *Punk pod Slovenci* [Punk under the Slovenes] (Ljubljana: UK ZSMS, 1985).

Maluleke, Justinus, "*Toyi-toyi* Freedom Dance of the 90s: Where Did It Originate?," *Drum Magazin'* (August, 1993): 32-3.

*Man vienai māsiŋai*, dir. Roze Stiebra (Latvijas Televīzija, 1984).

Marcuse, Herbert, "Repressive Tolerance" (1965), <http://www.marcuse.org/herbert/pubs/60spubs/65repressivetolerance.htm>, accessed July, 2009.

Marika, Mawalan, et al., "Yirrkala Petition to the House of Representatives" (Yirrkala: Yirrkala Community, 1963).

Marika, Wandjuk, *Life Story as Told to Jennifer Isaacs* (Brisbane: University of Queensland Press, 1995).

Marika, Wandjuk, et al., "Yirrkala Church Panels" (Yirrkala: Waruki Cooperative, 1962-63).

Marx, Karl, *A Contribution to the Critique of Hegel's Philosophy of Right* (1844a) <http://www.marxists.org/archive/marx/works/1843/critique-hpr/intro.htm>, accessed September, 2009.

Marx, Karl, with Frederick Engels, *The Holy Family, or Critique of Critical Criticism* (1844b) <http://www.marxists.org/archive/marx/works/1845/holy-family/index.htm>, accessed September, 2009.

Marx, Karl, *Communist Manifesto* (1848) <http://www.marxists.org/archive/marx/works/1848/communist-manifesto/>, accessed September, 2009.

Marx, Karl, *Capital* (1867) <http://www.marxists.org/archive/marx/works/1867-c1/ch01.htm>, accessed September, 2009.

Marx, Karl, *The German Ideology* (1932) <http://www.marxists.org/archive/marx/works/1845/german-ideology/>, accessed September, 2009.

Masekela, Barbara, Interview with Wolfie Kodesh. MA, Oral History and Sound, MCA6-312 in Grant Olwage (ed.), *Composing Apartheid: Music for and against Apartheid* (Johannesburg: Witwatersrand University Press, 2008): 177.

McClure, Steve, "Powerful Promise: Turning Expectations into Results in China Demands Patience and Partnerships," *Billboard*, 120, 4 (January 26, 2008): 49, 50, 54.

McEwan, Cheryl, "Building a Postcolonial Archive? Gender, Collective Memory and Citizenship in Post-apartheid South Africa," *Journal of Southern African Studies*, 29, 3 (September 2003): 739-54.

McGrath, Ann (ed.), *Contested Ground: Australian Aborigines under the British Crown* (Sydney: Allen, 1995).

Melhuish, Martin, *Celtic Tides: Traditional Music in a New Age* (Kingston, Ontario: Quarry Music, 1998).

Mercantini, Luigi, "La spigolatrice di Sapri" <http://it.wikisource.org/wiki/La_spigo latrice_di_Sapri>, accessed January 16, 2010.

Merriam, Alan P., *The Anthropology of Music* (Chicago: Northwestern University Press, 1964).

Mijatović, Brana, "'Throwing Stones at the System': Rock Music in Serbia during the 1990s," *Music and Politics*, 2, 2 (2008) <http://www.music.ucsb.edu/

projects/musicandpolitics/archive/2008-2/mijatovic.html>, accessed July 19, 2009.

Milojević, Jasmina, "Novo guslarstvo: Ogled o tradicionalnom muzičkom obliku u popularnoj kulturi" [New Gusle Music: A Study of Traditional Musical Form in Popular Culture], *Kultura*, 116-17 (2007): 123-40.

Mirković, Igor, *Sretno dijete* [The Lucky Kid] (Zaprešič: Fraktura, 2004).

Mitchell, Adrian, *The Apeman Cometh: Poems by Adrian Mitchell* (London: Jonathan Cape, 1975).

Mitchell, Gillian, *The North American Folk Music Revival: Nation and Identity in the United States and Canada, 1945-1980* (Aldershot: Ashgate, 2007).

Monroe, Alexei, "Balkan Hardcore: Pop Culture and Paramilitarism," *Central Europe Review*, 2, 24 (July 19, 2000), <http://www.ce-review.org/00/24/monroe 24.html>, accessed April 15, 2005.

Moore, Robert, "Generation Ku: Individualism and China's Millennial Youth," *Ethnology*, 44, 4 (2005): 357-67.

Moreno Chá, Ercilia, "Chapter Six: Music in the Southern Cone: Chile, Argentina, and Uruguay," in John M. Schechter (gen. ed.), *Music in Latin American Culture: Regional Traditions* (Belmont, Calif.: Schirmer/Wadsworth/Thomson Learning, 1999): 236-301.

Muktupāvels, Valdis, "On Some Relations between Kokles Styles and Contexts in the Twentieth Century," *Journal of Baltic Studies*, 31, 4 (Winter 2000): 388-405.

Muktupāvels, Valdis, Personal interview with Ilga Reizniece, February 5, 2006.

Mundine, Djon, "Saltwater," in Buku-Larrŋgay Mulka Centre, *Saltwater: Yirrkala Bark Paintings of Sea Country* (Sydney: Isaacs, 1999).

Muršič, Rajko, *Neubesedljive zvočne igre: Od filozofije k antropologiji glasbe* [Non-verbal Sound Games: From Philosophy to the Anthropology of Music] (Maribor: Akademska založba Katedra, 1993).

Muršič, Rajko, "Popularna glasba v krempljih represije in cenzure" [Popular Music in the Clutches of Repression and Censorship], *Časopis za kritiko znanosti, domišljijo in novo antropologijo (ČKZ)*, 27, 195-6 (1999): 179-99.

Muršič, Rajko, "Provocation and Repression after Socialism: The Strelnikoff Case," in Tony Mitchell, Peter Doyle, and Bruce Johnson (eds.), *Changing Sounds: New Directions and Configurations in Popular Music. IASPM 1999 International Conference Proceedings* (Sydney: University of Technology, 2000): 309-18.

Nandorfy, Martha, "The Right to Live in Peace: Freedom and Social Justice in the Songs of Violeta Parra and Víctor Jara," in Daniel Fischlin and Ajay Heble (eds.), *Rebel Musics: Human Rights, Resistant Sounds, and the Politics of Music Making* (Montreal: Black Rose Books, 2003): 172-209.

Nash, Catherine, "Reclaiming Vision: Looking at Landscape and the Body," *Gender, Place and Culture*, 3, 2 (1996): 149-69.

Nash, Catherine, "Embodied Irishness: Gender, Sexuality and Irish Identities," in Brian Graham (ed.), *In Search of Ireland: A Cultural Geography* (London: Routledge, 1997): 108-27.

Negus, Keith, "Sinéad O'Connor: Miniature Portrait of the Artist as an Angry Young Woman," in Will Straw et al. (eds.), *Popular Music: Style and Identity* (Montreal: Centre for Research on Canadian Cultural Industries and Institutions, 1995): 221-3.

Neuenfeldt, Karl, "Yothu Yindi and *ga*n*ma*," *Journal of Australian Studies*, 38 (1993): 1-11.

Nieves, Diana, "Breve muestra de la nueva canción" (M.A. Thesis: University of California, Santa Cruz, 1991).

Northern Land Council, *NLC: Northern Land Council* (Darwin: Northern Land Council, 2002) <www.nlc.org.au>, accessed September 7, 2009.

Northern Territory Emergency Response Review Board, *Report of the Northern Territory Emergency Response Review Board, October 2008* <http://www.nterreview.gov.au/docs/report_nter_review/execsumm.htm>, accessed September 8, 2009.

Nuttall, Sarah, and Carli Coetzee (eds.), *Negotiating the Past: The Making of Memory in South Africa* (Cape Town: Oxford University Press, 1998).

O'Boyle, Sean, *The Irish Song Tradition* (Dublin: Dalton, 1976).

Olwage, Grant, "Apartheid's Musical Signs: Reflections on Black Choralism, Modernity and Race-Ethnicity in the Segregated Era," in Grant Olwage (ed.), *Composing Apartheid: Music for and against Apartheid* (Johannesburg: Witwatersrand University Press, 2008a): 35-54.

Olwage, Grant (ed.), *Composing Apartheid: Music for and against Apartheid* (Johannesburg: Witwatersrand University Press, 2008b).

Ostertag, Bob, *Creative Life: Music, Politics, People, and Machines* (Urbana: University of Illinois Press, 2009).

"Otchet Dnepropetrovskogo OK LKSMU ot 23 dekabria 1983 g," in Tsentral'nyi Derzhavnyi Arkhiv Gromads'kykh Ob'ednan' Ukrainy, f. 7, op. 20, d. 3087, l. 43.

Pančić, Teofil, "Muzika i rat: imate li srca?" [Music and War: Are You Human?], *Vreme*, 9 (May 8, 1999) <http://www.vreme.com/arhiva_html/vb9/8.html#Muzika>, accessed July 5, 2009.

Parra, Violeta, *Décima: Autobiografía en Versos Chilenos* (Santiago de Chile: Ediciones Nueva Universidad, Universidad Católica de Chile, Editorial Pomaire, 1970).

Pasolini, Pier Paolo, *Le ceneri di Gramsci* (Milano: Garzanti, 1957).

Paterson, Mike, "Latvians Rekindle a Piping Heritage: Republic of Latvia," *Piping Today*, 18 (2005): 35-41.

Pelše, Roberts, Jānis Niedre, and Arturs Ozols (eds.), *Latviešu padomju folklora*, Reprinted from 1950 edition (Stokholma: Memento, 1986).

Perkins, Rachel, and Marcia Langton (eds.), *First Australians: An Illustrated History* (Melbourne: Melbourne University Publishing, 2008).

Perks, Robert, and Alistair Thomson (eds.), *The Oral History Reader*, 2nd edition (London: Routledge, 2006).

Pettan, Svanibor, "'Lambada' in Kosovo: A Profile of Gypsy Creativity," *Journal of the Gypsy Lore Society*, 5, 2 (1992): 117-30.

Pettan, Svanibor (ed.), *Music, Politics, and War: Views from Croatia* (Zagreb: Institute of Ethnology and Folklore Research, 1998).

Pieterse, Jan Nederveen, *Globalization and Culture: Global Melange* (Chicago: Rowman and Littlefield, 2009).

Pikhovshek, Vyacheslav, et al. (eds.), *Dnipropetrovsk vs. Security Service* (Kyiv: Lybed, 1996).

Port, Mattijs van de, "The Articulation of Soul: Gypsy Musicians and the Serbian Other," *Popular Music*, 18, 3 (1999): 291-308.

Pozdniakov, M., "Piraty vid muzyky (v tumani antymystetstva)," *Prapor iunosti* (June 14, 1984): 3.

Ramet, Sabrina Petra (ed.), *Rocking the State: Rock Music and Politics in Eastern Europe and Russia* (Boulder: Westview Press, 1994).

Redmond, Dennis, "ND Keywords" <http://www.efn.org/~dredmond/ND_Keywords.html>, accessed October, 2009.

Reuss, Rihard A., *American Folk Music and Left-Wing Politics, 1927-1957* (Lanham, Md.: Scarecrow Press, 2000).

Riaz, Ali, and Subho Basu, "The State-Society Relationship in Political Conflicts in Nepal (1768-2005)," *Journal of Asian and African Studies*, 42, 2 (2007): 123-42.

Rice, Timothy, "The Dialectic of Economics and Aesthetics in Bulgarian Music," in Mark Slobin (ed.), *Returning Culture: Musical Changes in Central and Eastern Europe* (Durham, NC: Duke University Press, 1996): 176-99.

Rodionov, I., "Vecher v diskoklube," *Dneprovskaia pravda* (January 14, 1979): 4.

Rossinow, Doug, *The Politics of Authenticity: Liberalism, Christianity and the New Left in America* (New York: Columbia University Press, 1998).

Roszak, Theodore, *The Making of a Counter Culture: Reflections on the Technocratic Society and Its Youthful Opposition* (Berkeley: University of California Press, 1995).

Rothwell, Nicolas, "Sorry State of Affairs," *The Australian* (February 13, 2009) <www.theaustralian.news.com.au/story/0,25197,25046025-5018771,00.html>, accessed September 8, 2009.

Rozumkov, O., and M. Skoryk, "Komu zemliaky "Zemliane"? (Rozdumy pislia kontsertu)," *Prapor iunosti* (March 15, 1984): 4.

Rush, Alfred C., *Death and Burial in Christian Antiquity* (Doctor of Sacred Theology dissertation: Catholic University of America Studies in Christian Antiquity, no. 1, J. Quasten (ed.) Washington, D.C.: Catholic University of American Press, 1941).

Rushe, Dominic, "China Could Top the Music Industry Charts," *The Sunday Times* (Business) (October 17, 2004) <http://business.timesonline.co.uk/tol/business/article1069308.ece>, accessed January 4, 2010.

Ryback, Timothy W., *Rock around the Bloc: A History of Rock Music in Eastern Europe and the Soviet Union* (New York: Oxford University Press, 1990).

Salvatore, Armando and Mark LeVine (eds.), *Religion, Social Practices and Contested Hegemonies: Reconstructing the Public Sphere in Muslim Majority Societies* (New York: Palgrave, 2005).

Šavija, Nebojša, "Ambrosia Souvenir: Department for Text Pathology," Performance/presentation in the event *On Divided Society*, IUC Dubrovnik, April 1-11, 1998 (unpublished manuscript, 1998).

Schechter, John M., "*Corona y baile*: Music in the Child's Wake of Ecuador and Hispanic South America, Past and Present," *Revista de Música Latinoamericana/Latin American Music Review*, 4, 1 (Spring/Summer 1983): 1-80.

Schechter, John M., "Latin America/Ecuador," in Jeff Todd Titon (gen. ed.), *Worlds of Music: An Introduction to the Music of the World's Peoples*, 2nd edition (New York: Schirmer, 1992a): 376-428.

Schechter, John M., *The Indispensable Harp: Historical Development, Modern Roles, Configurations, and Performance Practices in Ecuador and Latin America* (Kent: Kent State University Press, 1992b).

Schechter, John M., "Divergent Perspectives on the *velorio del angelito*: Ritual Imagery, Artistic Condemnation, and Ethnographic Value," *Journal of Ritual Studies*, 8, 2 (Summer 1994): 43-84.

Schechter, John M., "Themes in Latin American Music Culture," in John M. Schechter (gen. ed.), *Music in Latin American Culture: Regional Traditions* (Belmont, Calif.: Schirmer/Wadsworth/Thomson Learning, 1999a): 1-33.

Schechter, John M., "Beyond Region: Transnational and Transcultural Traditions," in John M. Schechter (gen. ed.), *Music in Latin American Culture: Regional Traditions* (Belmont, Calif.: Schirmer/Wadsworth/Thomson Learning, 1999b): 424-57.

Schechter, John M., "Latin America/Ecuador," in Jeff Todd Titon (gen. ed.), *Worlds of Music: An Introduction to the Music of the World's Peoples*, 4th edition (Belmont, Calif.: Schirmer/Thomson Learning/Wadsworth Group, 2002): 385-446.

Schechter, John M., "Latin America/Chile, Bolivia, Ecuador, Peru," in Jeff Todd Titon (gen. ed.), *Worlds of Music: An Introduction to the Music of the World's Peoples*, 5th edition (Belmont, Calif.: Schirmer Cengage Learning, 2009): 415-71.

Scott, James C., *Domination and the Arts of Resistance: Hidden Transcripts* (New Haven: Yale University Press, 1990).

Sharp, Nonie, *No Ordinary Judgment: Mabo, the Murray Islanders' Land Case* (Canberra: Aboriginal Studies Press, 1996).

Silverman, Carol, "Music and Marginality: Roma (Gypsies) of Bulgaria and Macedonia," in Mark Slobin (ed.), *Returning Culture: Musical Changes in Central and Eastern Europe* (Durham, NC: Duke University Press, 1996): 231-53.

Sinclair, David, and Petar Janjatović, "Music Acts as Healing Force in the Balkans: A Special Report on the Music and Musicians of the Balkans since the Breakup of Yugoslavia and the War of 1991-95," *Billboard*, 109, 23 (1997): 1-4.

Skinner Sawyers, June, *The Complete Guide to Celtic Music: From the Highland Bagpipe and Riverdance to U2 and Enya* (London: Aurum Press, 2000).

Smilga, J., Personal letter to Valdis Muktupāvels, January 14, 1985.

Smith, Nick, "Adorno vs. Levinas: Evaluating Points of Contention," *Continental Philosophy Review* (Spring 2006) <http://papers.ssrn.com/sol3/papers.cfm?abstract_id=1213275>, accessed October, 2009.

Smyth, Gerry, "'The Natural Course of Things': Matthew Arnold, Celticism, and the English Poetic Tradition," *Journal of Victorian Culture*, 1, 1 (March, 1996): 35-53.

Smyth, Gerry, *Noisy Island: A Short History of Irish Popular Music* (Cork: Cork University Press, 2005).

Song, Berwin, "Just Say No: Call Cui Jian a Troublemaker; Just Don't Call Him the Godfather," *That's Beijing* (December, 2006): 22-4.

"Spetsvypusk 'Politychnogo klubu Plu'," *Prapor iunosti* (October 20, 1983): 2.

Steen, Andreas, *Der Lange Marsch des Rock 'n' Roll: Pop- und Rockmusik in der Volksrepublik China* (Hamburg/Münster: Lit-Verlag, 1996).

Steen, Andreas, "Sound, Protest and Business: Modernsky Co. and the New Ideology of Chinese Rock," Berliner China-Hefte 18 (Berlin/Zürich: Lit-Verlag, 2000): 40-64.

Steen, Andreas, "Postsocialist Creativity and Confusion: CD-Covers and the Visual Presentation of Chinese Popular Music," in Jens Damm and Andreas Steen (eds.), *Postmodern China* (Berliner China-Hefte 34; Berlin/Zürich: Lit-Verlag, 2008): 27-52.

Stokes, Martin, and Philip V. Bohlman (eds.), *Celtic Modern: Music at the Global Fringe* (Lanham, Md.: Scarecrow Press, 2003).

Stubington, Jill, and Peter Dunbar-Hall, "Yothu Yindi's 'Treaty'," *Popular Music*, 13 (1994): 243-59.

Tarlač, Goran, "Turbo Folk Politics," *Transitions Online* (April 14, 2003) <http://www.tol.cz/>, accessed July 19, 2009.

Tishchenko, Igor, "Poiot VIA 'Zemliane'," *Dnepr vechernii* (January 21, 1984): 4.

Troitsky, Artemy, *Back in the USSR: The True Story of Rock in Russia* (London: Omnibus Press, 1987).

*Tsentral'nyi Derzhavnyi Arkhiv Gromads'kykh Ob'ednan' Ukrainy (TDAGOU)* [The Central State Archive of Ukrainian Public Organizations], Fond 7, Tsentral'nyi Komitet LKSMU.

Tumás-Serna, Jane, "The 'Nueva Canción' Movement and Its Mass-Mediated Performance Context," *Revista de Música Latinoamericana/Latin American Music Review*, 13, 2 (Autumn/Winter 1992): 139-57.

Vallely, Fintan (ed.), *The Companion to Irish Traditional Music* (Cork: Cork University Press, 1999).

van Zyl, Paul, Seminar No. 8, "Female Circumcision: Cultural Right or Human Wrong?" Center for the Study of Violence and Reconciliation, October 26, 1994, Johannesburg <http://www.csvr.org.za/wits/papers/papfemc.htm>, accessed October, 2009.

Vansina, Jan, *Oral Tradition: A Study in Historical Methodology* (New Brunswick, NJ: Transaction, 2006).

Vaughan, Megan, *Story of an African Famine: Gender and Famine in Twentieth-Century Malawi* (Cambridge: Cambridge University Press, 1987).

Vertkov, Konstantin, Georgij Blagodatov, and Èl'za Jazovickaja, *Atlas muzykal'nyh instrumentov narodov SSSR*, 2nd edition (Moskva: Muzyka, 1975).

Vilches, Patricia, "De Violeta Parra a Víctor Jara y Los Prisioneros: Recuperación de la memoria colectiva e identidad cultural a través de la música comprometida," *Revista de Música Latinoamericana/Latin American Music Review*, 25, 2 (Fall/Winter 2004): 195-215.

Vojnović, Goran, *Čefurji raus!* (Ljubljana: Študentska založba, 2008).

Vrdoljak, Dražen, *Moje brazde: Bilješke o hrvatskoj zabavnoj, pop i jazz glazbi* [My Grooves: Notes on Croatian Entertainment, Pop and Jazz Music] (Zagreb: V.B.Z, 2008).

Wang, Jing, "Culture as Leisure and Culture as Capital," *positions*, 9, 1 (2001): 69-104.

Ward, Margaret, *The Missing Sex: Putting Women into Irish History* (Dublin: Attic Press, 1991).

Weinstein, Deena, "Rock Protest Songs: So Many and So Few," in Ian Peddie (ed.), *The Resisting Muse: Popular Music and Social Protest* (Aldershot: Ashgate, 2006): 3-16.

Witkin, Robert, *Adorno on Music* (London: Routledge, 1998).

White, Harry, *The Keeper's Recital: Music and Cultural History in Ireland, 1770-1970* (Cork: Cork University Press, 1998).

Xi, Jieying, Junxiao Sun, and Jingjian Xiao (eds.), *Chinese Youth in Transition* (Aldershot: Ashgate, 2006).

Yan Jun, *Didixia: Xin yinyue qianxingji* [Underground: New Music's Secret Records] (Beijing: Culture and Art Publishing House, 2002).

Yang, Changzheng, "Popular Culture among Chinese Youth," in Jieying Xi, Junxiao Sun, and Jingjian Xiao (eds.), *Chinese Youth in Transition* (Aldershot: Ashgate, 2006): 171-92.

Yeats, W.B., "Sailing to Byzantium" (1928), *The Collected Poems of W.B. Yeats* (London: Macmillan, 1981): 217-18.

Yi Zhou, "Yaogunyue chongchu haimian" [The Spread of Rock Music], *Nanfang Zhoumo* [Southern Weekend] (March 13, 1993): 4.

Yothu Yindi, "Treaty," Yothu Yindi, *Diṱi Murru* [sic *Diṯimurru*]: *The Videos* (Mushroom, 1992).

Yugambeh Museum, *Yugambeh Museum Language and Heritage Research Centre* (Beenleigh: Yugambeh Museum, 2006) <http://www.yugambeh.com>, accessed September 7, 2009.

Yunupiŋu, Galarrwuy, "Tradition, Truth and Tomorrow," *The Monthly*, 41 (2009): 32-40.

Yunupiŋu, Galarrwuy, et al., "Barunga Statement" (Barunga: Northern Land Council and Central Land Council, 1988).

Yunupiŋu, Mandawuy, "Yothu Yindi," *Race and Class*, 35, 4 (1994): 114-20.

Yurchak, Alexei, *Everything Was Forever, Until It Was No More: The Last Soviet Generation* (Princeton: Princeton University Press, 2005).

al-Zubaidi, Layla, "Shouting for Change: Moroccan Youth between Rock and Gnawa"(2006)<http://www.qantara.de/webcom/show_article.php/_c-587/_nr-24/i.html>, accessed December, 2005.

Zhang, Xudong, *Postsocialism and Cultural Politics: China in the Last Decade of the Twentieth Century* (Durham, NC: Duke University Press, 2008).

Zhao Shuling, dir., *Cui Jian: Xin Changzheng lushang de yaogun* [Cui Jian: Rock 'n' Roll on the New Long March], Film Documentary, China Central TV (CCTV), broadcast October, 2005.

Zhuk, Sergei I., Personal interview with Aleksandr Gusar, Dnipropetrovs'k, May 4, 1990.

Zhuk, Sergei I., Personal interview with Igor T., retired KGB officer, Dnipropetrovs'k, May 15, 1991.

Zhuk, Sergei I., Personal interview with Mikhail Suvorov, Dnipropetrovs'k, June 1, 1991.

Zhuk, Sergei I., Personal interview with Vladimir Demchenko, Dnipropetrovs'k University, January 12, 1992.

Zhuk, Sergei I., Personal interview with Serhiy Tihipko, director of "Privatbank," Dnipropetrovs'k, October 12, 1993.

Zhuk, Sergei I., Personal interview with Andrei Vadimov, Dnipropetrovs'k, July 20-21, 2003.

Zhuk, Sergei I., Personal interview with Oleksandr Beznosov, Department of History, Dnipropetrovs'k University, July 19, 2008.

Zhuk, Sergei I., "Popular Culture, Identity and Soviet Youth in Dniepropetrovsk, 1959-84," in *The Carl Beck Papers in Russian and East European Studies*, no. 1906 (Pittsburgh: University of Pittsburgh Press, 2008a): 1-68.

Zhuk, Sergei I., Personal interview with Oleksandr Poniezha, Dnipropetrovs'k, July 22, 2008b.

Zhuk, Sergei I., "Religion, 'Westernization,' and Youth in the 'Closed City' of Soviet Ukraine, 1964-84," *The Russian Review*, 67, 4 (October, 2008): 661-79.

Žolt, Lazar, Aleksandra Višnjevac, and Anđelija Vučurević, "Aktuelno stanje omladinskih potkultura i publika Exit-a" [Current State of Youth Subcultures and Audience of the Exit Festival], *Teme*, 28, 4 (2004): 361-80.

Zorc, R. David, *Yolŋu-Matha Dictionary* (Batchelor, Northern Territory: Batchelor College, 1996).

# Discography

10cc, "Dreadlock Holiday," *Bloody Tourists* (Polygram, 1978).

10cc, "For You and I," *Bloody Tourists* (Polygram, 1978).

10cc, "Life Line," *Bloody Tourists* (Polygram, 1978).

10cc, "Reds in My Bed," *Bloody Tourists* (Polygram, 1978).

10cc, "Tokyo," *Bloody Tourists* (Polygram, 1978).

72 Hours, "Jaya Bandh," *72 Hours* (self-released, 2008).

72 Hours, "Kunni Ke," *72 Hours* (self-released, 2008).

AC/DC, *Highway to Hell* (Atlantic, 1979).

AC/DC, "Back in Black," *Back in Black* (Sony, 1980).

Arthimoth, "Baptize," *Flowers in the Desert* (EMI, 2010).

Atkins, Martin, *Look Directly into the Sun: China Pop 2007* (Invisible Records, 2007).

Atkins, Martin, *Made in China. Martin Atkins' China Dub Soundsystem* (Invisible Records, 2007).

Baja Mali Kninđa, "Srbi se nikog ne boje" ["Serbs Aren't Afraid of Anyone"], *Još se ništa ne zna* [It is Not Yet Known] (Serbia Music, 1994).

Baja Mali Kninđa, "Nisu suze za Srbina" ["Tears Aren't for Serbs"], *Još se ništa ne zna* [It is Not Yet Known] (Serbia Music, 1994).

Baja Mali Kninđa, "Kosovo je naša duša" ["Kosovo is Our Soul"], *Biti il ne biti* [To Be or Not To Be] (Renome, 1999).

Bajaga i Instruktori, *Zmaj od Noćaja* (PGP RTS, 2001).

The Beach Boys, "Surfin' USA" b/w "Shut Down" (Capitol, 1963).

The Beatles, "Roll over Beethoven," *With The Beatles* (Parlophone 1963).

Berry, Chuck, "Roll over Beethoven," *Roll over Beethoven* (Membran, 2007).

*The Best of "Rock za Hrvatsku"* (Croatia Records, 1992).

Beyond East, "Beyond the East," *Flowers in the Desert* (EMI, 2010).

Carsick Cars, *Carsick Cars* (Maybe Mars Records, 2008).

Carsick Cars, *You Can Listen, You Can Talk* (Maybe Mars Records, 2009).

Clannad, "Theme from 'Harry's Game'," *Magical Ring* (RCA, 1983).

The Clash, "London Calling," *London Calling* (Sony, 1979).

Coloured Stone, *Koonibba Rock* (RCA, 1985).

Coloured Stone, *Island of Greed* (RCA, 1985).

Coloured Stone, *Human Love* (RCA, 1986).

Coloured Stone, *Black Rock from the Red Centre* (RCA, 1986).

Coloured Stone, "Black Boy," *Black Rock from the Red Centre* (RCA, 1986).

Creative Waste, "War Machine," *Flowers in the Desert* (EMI, 2010).

Cui Jian, "Yiwu suoyou" ["Nothing to My Name"] (EMI Music Publishing, S.E. Asia, 1989).

Cui Jian, *Xin changzheng lushang de yaogun* [Rock 'n' Roll on the New Long March] (Zhongguo lüyou shengxiang chubanshe/China Tourism Sound and Video Publishing, 1989).

Cui Jian, *Jiejue* [Solution] (EMI Music Publishing, S.E. Asia, 1990).

Cui Jian, *Hongqi xia de dan* [Balls under the Red Flag] (EMI Music Publishing, S.E. Asia, 1994).

De Gregori, Francesco, *Scacchi e tarocchi* (RCA italiana, 1985).

Enya, "Orinoco Flow," *Watermark* (WEA, 1988).

Goanna, "Solid Rock, Sacred Ground," *Spirit of Place* (WEA, 1982).

González, Jorge, "La voz de los '80," *Los Prisioneros: la voz de los '80* (EMI, 1984).

Grupa 220, *Naši dani* (Jugoton, 1968).

Guthrie, Arlo, "Víctor Jara," *The Best of Broadside 1962-1988: Anthems of the American Underground from the Pages of Broadside Magazine* (Smithsonian Folkways Recordings, 2000).

He Yong, *Lajichang* [Garbage Dump] (Rock Records & Tapes, 1994).

*Hong taiyang: Mao Zedong songge xin jiezou lianchang* [The Red Sun: Odes to Mao Zedong, Uninterrupted Songs in New Rhythm] (China Record Corporation, 1992).

Hoola Bandoola Band, *Hoola Bandoola Band, 1971-76* (MNW, 1980).

Hou Muren and Xiandairen, *Hongse yaogun* [Red Rock] (Shenzhen jiguang jiemu chuban/Shenzhen Laser Program Publishing, 1992).

Iļģi, *Zemgales dziesmas* (Latvijas Radio, 1986), unpublished recording on magnetic tape.

Iļģi, *Pieśni łotewskie, Vedību dziesmas. Bāriņu dziesmas* (Poljazz, 1989).

Iron Maiden, "Number of the Beast," *Number of the Beast* (Harvest, 1982).

Ivčić, Tomislav, *Stop the War in Croatia* (Croatia Records, 1991).

Jara, Víctor, "'Movil' Oil Special," *Víctor Jara: Pongo en tus manos abiertas* (unknown publisher, 1969).

Jara, Víctor, "El pimiento," *Vientos del Pueblo/Víctor Jara* (Monitor, 1974).

Jara, Víctor, "Plegaria a un labrador," *Vientos del Pueblo/Víctor Jara* (Monitor, 1974).

Jara, Víctor, "Preguntas por Puerto Montt," *Vientos del Pueblo/Víctor Jara* (Monitor, 1974).

Jara, Víctor, "Despedimiento del angelito," *Víctor Jara: Desde Lonquén Hasta Siempre* [vol. 4] (Monitor, 1981).

Jara, Víctor, "El aparecido," *Víctor Jara: Desde Lonquén Hasta Siempre* [vol. 4] (Monitor, 1981).

Jara, Víctor, "El lazo," *Víctor Jara: Desde Lonquén Hasta Siempre* [vol. 4] (Monitor, 1981).

Jara, Víctor, "Angelita Huenumán," *Canto Libre* (Monitor, 1993).

Jara, Víctor, "¿Qué sacó rogar al cielo?," *Víctor Jara* (WEA, 2003).

Joyside, *Drunk is Beautiful* (Modernsky Records, 2004).

Kelly, Paul, "Special Treatment," Paul Kelly et al., *Building Bridges* (CBS, 1989).

Kelly, Paul, and the Messengers, "From Little Things, Big Things Grow," *Comedy* (Mushroom, 1991).

Kiss, *Dynasty* (Island/Mercury, 1979).

*Korak napred 2 koraka nazad* [Step Further, Two Steps Beyond] (B92, 1999).

Kumsārs, Artis, "Tādi vīri kungam tika," from a performance with the Madonas Skandenieki ensemble in the early 1980s.

*Latvian Folklore: Ceļatiesi, bāleliņi!* (KGB, 1986).

Lolli, Claudio, *Ho visto anche degli zingari felici* (EMI, 1976).

Lolli, Claudio, *Disoccupate le strade dai sogni* (Ultima spiaggia, 1977).

Magnifico, *Kdo je čefur* [Who is čefur] (Magnifico, 1996).

Midnight Oil, "Beds Are Burning," *Diesel and Dust* (CBS, 1987).

Moore, Christy, *Paddy on the Road* (Mercury, 1969).

Moore, Christy, *Prosperous* (1970; Tara (CD), 2000).

Moore, Christy, *Ride On* (1984; Platinum, 1999).

Moore, Christy, *Ordinary Man* (1985; Warner Platinum, 2007).

Moore, Christy, *Voyage* (WEA, 1989).

Nabarlek Band, *Munwurrk "Bushfire"* (Skinnyfish Music, 1999).

Nabarlek Band, *Bininj Manborlh "Blackfella Road"* (Skinnyfish Music, 2001).

Nabarlek Band, *Live* (Skinnyfish Music, 2005).

Nabarlek Band, *Manmoyi Radio* (Manmoyi Music, 2007).

*Nas slušaju svi, mi ne slušamo nikoga!* [Everybody Listens to Us, We Don't Listen to Anybody] (Radio Index, 1997).

Near, Holly, "It Could Have Been Me," *Holly Near: A Live Album* (Redwood Records, 1974).

No Fixed Address, "We Have Survived," No Fixed Address and Us Mob, *Wrong Side of the Road* (Black Australia Records, 1981).

No Fixed Address, "Genocide," No Fixed Address and Us Mob, *Wrong Side of the Road* (Black Australia Records, 1981).

No Fixed Address, *From My Eyes* (Mushroom, 1982).

No Fixed Address and Us Mob, *Wrong Side of the Road* (Black Australia Records, 1981).

O'Connor, Sinéad, "Nothing Compares 2 U," *I Do Not Want What I Haven't Got* (Ensign 1990).

Orphaned Land, "Ocean Land," *Flowers in the Desert* (EMI, 2010).

*Ovo je zemlja za nas?!? Radio Boom 93 (1992-1997)* [Is This Country for Us?] (B92 and Radio BOOM 93, 1997).

Paoli, Gino, *Senza fine* (Dischi Ricordi, 1961).

Pietrangeli, Paolo, *Mio caro padrone domani ti sparo* (Edizioni del gallo, 1969).

Pink Floyd, "One of These Days," *Meddle* (Capitol, 1971).

Pink Floyd, "Money," *The Dark Side of the Moon* (Capitol, 1973).

Pink Floyd, *The Wall* (Capitol, 1979).

Pink Floyd, "Get Your Filthy Hands Off My Desert," *The Final Cut* (CBS, 1983).

Pink Floyd, "The Fletcher Memorial Home," *The Final Cut* (CBS, 1983).

Rimtutituki, "Slušaj 'vamo" b/w "Slušaj 'vamo (voljno mix)" (B92, 1992).

Roach, Archie, "Took the Children Away," *Charcoal Lane* (Hightone, 1992).

*Rock under the Siege* A (Radio Zid, 1995).

*Rock under the Siege* B (Radio Zid, 1996).

Saltwater Band, *Gapu Damurruŋ'* (Skinnyfish Music, 1998).

Saltwater Band, *Djarridjarri* [sic *Djärritjarri*] (Skinnyfish Music, 2004).

Shocking Blue, "Venus," *At Home* (Pink Elephant, 1969).

Simon, Paul, *Graceland* (Warner, 1986).

SMZB, *Shinian fankang* [Ten Years Rebellion] (Maybe Mars Records, 2008).

Stublić, Jura, "E, moj druže beogradski" ["Hey, My Belgrade Comrade"], Stublić, Jura and Film, *Hrana za golubove* [Food for Pigeons] (Croatia Records, 1992).

Tang Chao [Tang Dynasty], *Tang Chao* (Rock Records & Tapes/Magic Stone Co., 1992).

Thompson, "Jer, Hrvati smo" ["Because We Are Croats"], *Moli mala* [Prey, My Baby] (Croatia Records, 1992).

Thompson (Marko Perković), "Pukni, puško" ["Shut the Gun"], *Vjetar s Dinare* [Winds from Dinara] (Croatia Recorts, 1998).

Thompson, "Duh ratnika" ["The Spirit of the Warrior"], *Bilo jednom u Hrvatskoj* [It Was Once in Croatia] (Croatia Records, 2006).

Tiddas, "Malcolm Smith," *Sing about Life* (Polygram, 1994).

U2, "One Tree Hill," *The Joshua Tree* (Island, 1987).

Warumpi Band, *Big Name, No Blankets* (Festival, 1985).

Warumpi Band, *Go Bush!* (Festival, 1987).

Warumpi Band, "Blackfella, Whitefella," *Go Bush!* (Festival, 1987).

Yilila, *Manilamanila* (Yilila, 2005).

Yilila, *Aeroplane* (Yilila, 2006).

Yothu Yindi, "Mainstream," *Homeland Movement* (Mushroom, 1989).

Yothu Yindi, "Homeland Movement," *Homeland Movement* (Mushroom, 1989).

Yothu Yindi, "Ḻuku-Wäŋawuy Manikay 1788," *Homeland Movement* (Mushroom, 1989).

Yothu Yindi, "Treaty," *Tribal Voice* (Mushroom, 1991).

Yothu Yindi, "Baywara," *Freedom* (Mushroom, 1993).

Yothu Yindi, "Gunitjpirr Man," *Freedom* (Mushroom, 1993).

Yothu Yindi, "Our Generation," *Freedom* (Mushroom, 1993).

Yothu Yindi, "Mabo," Yothu Yindi et al., *Our Home, Our Land ... Something to Sing About* (CAAMA, 1995).

Yothu Yindi, "Written on a Bark," *One Blood* (Mushroom, 1999).

Yothu Yindi, "Lonely Tree," *Garma* (Mushroom, 2000).

Yothu Yindi et al., *Our Home, Our Land ... Something to Sing About* (CAAMA, 1995).

Yunupiŋu, Gurrumul, *Gurrumul* (Skinnyfish Music, 2008).

X-Mantra, "Shaheed," *Crying for Peace* (Tik and Tok Records, 2003).

X-Mantra, "Sinoo," *Crying for Peace* (Tik and Tok Records, 2003).

X-Mantra, "Chidiyaghar," *Crying for Peace* (Tik and Tok Records, 2003).

X-Mantra, "Ek," *Crying for Peace* (Tik and Tok Records, 2003).

*Zhongguo huo 1* [China Fire 1] (Rock Records & Tapes, 1992).
*Zhongguo yaogun jingdian* [Chinese Rock Classics] (China Record Corporation, 1995).

# Index

References to illustrations are in **bold**

Garrett, Peter 23, 25
gay rights 100
gender 4, 43, 58
Genghis Khan 156
Gladio 12
globalization 11
    and heavy metal 4, 53-4, 55-6, 63-7
*Glorija* 96
Goanna
    WORKS
        "Solid Rock, Sacred Ground" 19
Goblins 101
González, Jorge 112
goth 56
Gramsci, Antonio 9, 10, 31, 71
Grandmaster Flash
    WORKS
        "The Message" 57
grind metal 56
grindcore 56
grunge 138
Grupa 220
    WORKS
        *Naši dani* 97
Guccini, Francesco 14
Guevara, Che 113
Gurindji 19
Gurungs 28
*gusle* singing 103
Guthrie, Arlo 106, 117
    WORKS
        "Víctor Jara of Chile" 113, 114-16
Guthrie, Woody 15, 122
Gyanendra, King 29-30, 33
*gyanmalabhajans* 30

Habermas, Jürgen 27
hair metal 55
Haisong, Yang 139
Hang on the Box 140
hard rock 56
hardcore 56, 57, 64
Hasni, Cheb 54
Hate Suffocation 63, 68
Hawke, Bob 19, 22-3, 24
heavy metal
    and culture 54, 60-71
    and globalization 4, 53-4, 55-6, 63-7

and identity 63-9
    in Middle East 3-4, 53-60, 61-71
    in Nepal 3, 27-8, 30-37
    in North Africa 53-60, 61-71
    and political rights 27-8, 30-37, 53-60,
        62-3, 68, 70-71
    and politics 3-4, 27-8, 30-37, 53-60,
        62-3, 68, 70-71, 151-8
    and religion 32-3, 53-60, 61-71
    and social rights 3-4, 27, 36-7, 53-60,
        62-3, 68, 70-71
    in Southeast Asia 53
    in Ukraine 148, 151-8
    and war 56
    as world music 4, 53-4, 55-6, 63-7, 71
Hedgehog **142**
Hegel, G.W.F. 63
hegemony 28, 29, 31, 37, 68
Heping, Liang 133
Hezb al-Rock 70-71
Hezbollah 70-71
Hinduism 28-30, 32-3, 86
hip-hop 14, 57, 61, 93
hippies 8, 61, 62-3, 147
Hong Kong 132, 133, 136, 137, 138, 144
Hoola Bandoola Band 106, 113-14, 117
    WORKS
        "Vem kan man lita på?" (Who Can
            You Depend On?) 113
        "Víctor Jara" 113-14, 117
Horkheimer, Max 63
Howard, John 24
human rights 1-4
    and popular music 2, 91, 92, 102, 104
    and Ukrainian music fans 148, 151,
        154-6, 157, 159
    universal 2, 54, 91, 102, 104
    *see also* civil rights/liberties; economic
        and social rights; ethnic rights; gay
        rights; political rights; women's
        rights
hybridity 66-7, 69

identity
    border 3, 40-42, 43, 44
    Celtic 123-4
    cultural 3, 5, 40-42, 43, 63-9, 120-24,
        129